# BETWEEN TWO HORIZONS

# BETWEEN TWO HORIZONS

*Spanning New Testament Studies
and Systematic Theology*

*Edited by*

Joel B. Green *and* Max Turner

WILLIAM B. EERDMANS PUBLISHING COMPANY
GRAND RAPIDS, MICHIGAN / CAMBRIDGE, U.K.

© 2000 Wm. B. Eerdmans Publishing Co.
255 Jefferson Ave. S.E., Grand Rapids, Michigan 49503 /
P.O. Box 163, Cambridge CB3 9PU U.K.

Printed in the United States of America

05 04 03 02 01 00      7 6 5 4 3 2 1

ISBN 0-8028-4541-X

# Contents

v

# CONTENTS

# Contributors

**Stephen E. Fowl**, Associate Professor of Theology, Loyola College in Maryland.

**John Goldingay**, David Allan Hubbard Professor of Old Testament, Fuller Theological Seminary.

**Joel B. Green**, Dean of the School of Theology and Professor of New Testament, Asbury Theological Seminary.

**Trevor Hart**, Professor of Divinity, University of St. Andrews.

**Steve Motyer**, Lecturer in New Testament and Hermeneutics, London Bible College.

**John Christopher Thomas**, Professor of New Testament, Church of God School of Theology.

**Max Turner**, Professor of New Testament Studies and Vice-Principal for Academic Affairs, London Bible College.

**Robert W. Wall**, Professor of Biblical Studies, Seattle Pacific University.

**N. T. Wright**, Canon Theologian of Westminster Abbey.

# *Abbreviations*

## 1. General Abbreviations

| | |
|---|---|
| ca. | *circa,* about (with dates) |
| C.E. | Common Era (A.D.) |
| cf. | *confer,* compare |
| chap(s). | chapter(s) |
| ed. | edition; editor, edited by |
| e.g. | *exempli gratia,* for example |
| esp. | especially |
| ET | English Translation |
| GNB | Good News Bible |
| i.e. | *id est,* that is |
| IT | Intertestamental |
| LXX | Septuagint |
| mg | marginal notation |
| MT | Masoretic text |
| n. | note |
| NEB | New English Bible |
| NIV | New International Version |
| NRSV | New Revised Standard Version |
| NT | New Testament |
| OT | Old Testament |
| p(p). | page(s) |

| | |
|---|---|
| pt(s). | part(s) |
| trans. | translated by |
| v(v). | verse(s) |
| vol(s). | volume(s) |

## 2. Ancient Literature

Eusebius
   *Hist. eccl.*    *Historia ecclesiastica*
Irenaeus
   *Adv. haer.*    *Adversus haereses*
Tertullian
   *Adv. Marc.*    *Adversus Marcionem*
   *De praesc.*    *De praescriptione haereticorum*

## 3. Modern Literature

| | |
|---|---|
| A1CS | The Book of Acts in Its First Century Setting |
| AB | Anchor Bible |
| AS | Advances in Semiotics |
| *Bib* | *Biblica* |
| *BibInt* | *Biblical Interpretation* |
| CBET | Contributions to Biblical Exegesis and Theology |
| *CBQ* | *Catholic Biblical Quarterly* |
| *CSR* | *Christian Scholar's Review* |
| CSS | Cistercian Studies Series |
| CTL | Cambridge Textbooks in Linguistics |
| *EvQ* | *Evangelical Quarterly* |
| *HBT* | *Horizons in Biblical Theology* |
| IBRB | Institute for Biblical Research Bibliographies |
| *IDB* | *The Interpreter's Dictionary of the Bible: An Illustrated Encyclopedia.* 4 vols. Edited by George Arthur Buttrick |
| *JETS* | *Journal of the Evangelical Theological Society* |
| *JPT* | *Journal of Pentecostal Theology* |
| JPTSup | Journal of Pentecostal Theology Supplement Series |
| *JR* | *Journal of Religion* |

| | |
|---|---|
| JSNTSup | Journal for the Study of the New Testament Supplement Series |
| *JSOT* | *Journal for the Study of the Old Testament* |
| JSOTSup | Journal for the Study of the Old Testament Supplement Series |
| *JTS* | *Journal of Theological Studies* |
| *LT* | *Literature and Theology* |
| NICNT | New International Commentary on the New Testament |
| NTT | New Testament Theology |
| PTMS | Pittsburgh Theological Monograph Series |
| RR | Ressourcement: Retrieval and Renewal in Catholic Thought |
| SBLDS | Society of Biblical Literature Dissertation Series |
| *SBLSP* | *Society of Biblical Literature Seminar Papers* |
| SBT | Studies in Biblical Theology |
| *SJT* | *Scottish Journal of Theology* |
| SNTSMS | Society for New Testament Studies Monograph Series |
| THC | Two Horizons Commentary |
| *TLZ* | *Theologische Literaturzeitung* |
| VTSup | Vetus Testamentum Supplements |
| WBC | Word Biblical Commentary |
| *WTJ* | *Wesleyan Theological Journal* |

CHAPTER 1

# New Testament Commentary and
# Systematic Theology: Strangers or Friends?

MAX TURNER AND JOEL B. GREEN

I n their recent study, *The Bible for Theology*, Gerald O'Collins and Daniel
Kendall ask, "What effects should biblical texts produce in theology?
What does it mean for theologians to read, understand, interpret, and apply the Scriptures?"[1] We believe this is a good question, an important one,
well predicated on the observation that, in the last century or two, biblical
exegetes have had little traffic with systematic theologians. When dialogue
has ensued, different aims and interests, sometimes even difficult vocabulary, have inhibited its usefulness. O'Collins and Kendall are especially
helpful on this score, since they work toward finding a common ground
for relating the results of biblical exegesis to the theological enterprise.
Nevertheless, it is interesting that, in posing and addressing their questions, these two theologians do not grapple with a related question of at
least equal if not more importance: What effects should theology produce
in biblical interpretation? In terms of the concerns of this book, *Between
Two Horizons*, this issue might be recast slightly: What effects should an interest in theology produce in the reading of Scripture?

Our general concern is with the relationship of biblical studies to the
theological enterprise of the Christian church. Although we could attempt

1. Gerald O'Collins and Daniel Kendall, *The Bible for Theology: Ten Principles for
the Theological Use of Scripture* (New York and Mahwah, N.J.: Paulist, 1997), p. 2.

to span these disciplines from the side of the chasm occupied by systematic and practical theologians,[2] our interest here is more focused toward the nature of a biblical hermeneutics appropriate to doing theology. Our deliberations are part of a much larger project, the Two Horizons Commentary (THC) series, which seeks to reintegrate biblical exegesis with contemporary theology in the service of the church. Such an enterprise requires both some explanation and a measure of justification.

## 1. Why Another Commentary Series?

The latter part of this century has seen a burgeoning growth of commentaries. Not only are the old series such as the International Critical Commentary, Black's New Testament Commentary, New International Commentary on the New Testament, and others being repristinated, but formidable new enterprises such as the Word Biblical Commentary and the Baker Exegetical Commentary on the New Testament, not to mention a host of less detailed initiatives, are jostling for a place on our bookshelves. So why launch another? Several important reasons present themselves to us.[3] One reason is that the great commentary series have become increasingly detailed and methodologically complex, and many individual volumes are now so exhaustive that they are virtually inaccessible to all but the most well trained. The reader often finds it difficult to see the theological wood for the exegetical trees. Another, more important reason is that nearly all the major commentaries leave the reader firmly within the horizon of the ancient author's world, and offer little or no academically disciplined guidance concerning the contemporary theological significance of the work in question. Those who write and use such commentaries almost

---

2. Among recent discussions, see Charles J. Scalise, *From Scripture to Theology: A Canonical Journey into Hermeneutics* (Downers Grove, Ill.: InterVarsity, 1996); Trevor Hart, *Faith Thinking: The Dynamics of Christian Theology* (London: SPCK; Downers Grove, Ill.: InterVarsity, 1995), pp. 107-62. Cf. the older collection of essays edited by Robert K. Johnston, *The Use of the Bible in Theology: Evangelical Options* (Atlanta: John Knox, 1985).

3. See the challenges the genre "commentary" now faces in Leslie Houlden's article, "Commentary (New Testament)," in *A Dictionary of Biblical Interpretation*, ed. R. J. Coggins and J. L. Houlden (London: SCM, 1990), esp. pp. 131-32. Cf. Richard Coggins, "A Future for the Commentary?" in *The Open Text: New Directions for Biblical Studies?* ed. Francis Watson (London: SCM, 1993), pp. 163-75.

inevitably tend to be more rigorous in their understanding of exegetical issues than in their acumen vis-à-vis theological appropriation today. While there have been some notable attempts to correct this,[4] they have not until recently really gotten off the ground (for reasons we shall see).

The purpose of the THC series is to help the reader (1) understand individual books theologically in their ancient context and (2) be able to interpret them competently into the theological contexts of the turn of the twenty-first century. Hence the title of the series, Two Horizons Commentary. It differs markedly in conception and method, however, from what might at first glance be considered similar ventures, such as Zondervan's NIV Application Commentary. The latter seeks to explore the ancient text, passage by passage, to distinguish what is timely from what is timeless, what is culture-bound from what is transcultural, and to suggest modern applications of these "timeless truths" in each case. Guidance on the latter is usually immediately pastoral, and only rarely engages with the literature of modern theological discussion. The difference between this and the Two Horizons Commentary is immediately clear from the latter's format. The first third of each commentary provides introduction and theological exegesis of the writing. The middle third elucidates the key theological themes of the book, their relationship to each other, and their contribution to and place in a broader biblical theology. The final section attempts to articulate the significance of the book and its themes for theology and praxis today, and to do this *in conscious dialogue with serious contributions to modern systematic, constructive, and practical theology.* In that sense, the Two Horizons Commentary will represent an attempt to bring biblical exegesis back into vital relationship with theology, but in a dialogical and critical way that will not suppress either.[5]

The church, of course, has always maintained that Bible and theol-

---

4. See, e.g., Christopher Rowland and Mark Corner, *Liberating Exegesis: The Challenge of Liberation Theology to Biblical Studies* (London: SPCK; Louisville: Westminster/John Knox, 1989), and the survey and comprehensive *programme* offered by Brevard S. Childs, *Biblical Theology of the Old and New Testaments* (London: SCM; Philadelphia: Fortress, 1992), pp. 1-106.

5. The seriousness with which the interaction with modern theology is taken is shown in the appointment of three experts in systematic theology as consulting editors (Professor Trevor Hart of the University of St. Andrews, Dr. Graham McFarlane of London Bible College, and Professor Kevin Vanhoozer of Trinity University). Some contributions to the series will be made by "teams" consisting of an NT expert and a systematician.

ogy belong together. But driven by developments within the academy, following Gabler's programmatic distinction between the tasks of biblical theology and those of dogmatics, the two became separated, if not divorced. The sharp compartmentalization of university disciplines (Hebrew Bible, New Testament, systematic theology, practical theology, etc.) has until recently kept the two at a distance. But changes are taking place in the academy and the broader intellectual world that presage new approaches to commentary writing.

## 2. The Intellectual Setting for the Two Horizons Commentary

A number of interconnected trends and shifts together provide the setting for THC. First, predominantly under the influence of literary studies, there has been a shift of focus from so-called "behind the text" issues to "in the text" and "in front of the text" issues. Second, there has been an associated shift from historical criticism to methodological pluralism in biblical studies. Third, there has been a partial recovery of interest in the relationship between biblical studies and contemporary theology. Each of these requires some further explanation.

### 2.1. The Focus of Biblical Interpretation

It is now customary to distinguish three different dimensions (or "foci") of approach to a written text. We may first think about the author and the historical "world" he was addressing, the reason(s) why he wrote, the situation to which he wrote, and his purposes in doing so. These are not usually issues directly spoken of "in the text," but rather lie on the other side of the text from ourselves, so (as Ricoeur put it) "behind the text." Such issues are the classical property of the subdiscipline of "NT introduction." Second, our attention may shift from looking *through* the window of the text (to what lies "behind" it) to looking *at* the window. Now we are examining matters "in the text" itself. How is it structured? What does it say about the characters? How does it develop themes, plot, and argument? Third, we may change our focus and look at *ourselves* as readers. How do we, who stand "in front" of the text (examining it as it lies before us in our hands), come to understand it and relate to it?

Until the 1940s, "traditional" literary criticism tended to focus pri-

4

marily on "behind the text" issues — e.g., on the personal history and circumstances of the writer. As Gordon J. Thomas put it, "In its extreme forms the unspoken assumption underlying the traditional approach seems to be that if we discover that Anne Hathaway had an obsessive predilection for washing her hands and that Shakespeare felt hag-ridden by her in the early 1600's we have somehow 'explained' the character of Lady Macbeth."[6] Still working within a modernist framework, the "New Criticism" of the 1940s onward decisively shifted the focus of literary interpretation from the author to the text. The whole attempt to locate textual meaning "behind the text," in the author's thought and will, was seen as a confusion of intent with achievement (and dubbed the "intentional fallacy").[7] The "text-as-it-stands" — set adrift from its mooring to authorial intent by the very act of publication, and by distance in time and space from the author — became the focus of attention.

The New Criticism was still essentially a brand of hermeneutical realism. New critics thus believed that a stable "meaning" could be teased out of the text, even if it was not necessarily the author's meaning, and even if it could only be discovered through the most meticulous and attentive reading. The approach was "formalist" in that it located "meaning" in the text's evocation of the structures of linguistic convention. But with Iser's 1974 work, *The Implied Reader,*[8] it became obvious that "the text" neither makes all its meaning(s) explicit nor even "contains" all that it means, and that the penetrating interpreter has also to read between the lines in order to understand the lines.

Traditional criticism located this "unstated" meaning in the intention of the author. With the author now hustled away, it was natural for attention to fall on the role of the reader in interpretation (whether the "ideal reader," flagged up by the text, or the more distant, "empirical" one); she was the one who "filled in the gaps" and "united" the disparate textual themes into a harmonious whole. With the advent of reader-response criticism, we move more or less decisively to issues "in front of the text." Conservative reader-response critics might give more place to the author or

6. Gordon J. Thomas, "Telling a Hawk from a Handsaw? An Evangelical Response to the New Literary Criticism," *EvQ* 71 (1999): 37-50 (38).

7. See the landmark essay, "The Intentional Fallacy," by William K. Wimsatt and Monroe C. Beardsley, first published in 1946 but now available in *Twentieth Century Literary Criticism,* ed. David Lodge (London: Longman, 1972), pp. 334-44.

8. Wolfgang Iser, *The Implied Reader: Patterns of Communication in Prose Fiction from Bunyan to Beckett* (Baltimore: Johns Hopkins University Press, 1974).

text as "prompting" or "constraining" the reader's interpretive steps (e.g., Iser and Eco),[9] but more radical reader-response advocates, like Stanley Fish, simply deny outright that there is any meaning in the texts themselves.[10] For Fish, "meaning" is nothing more than an attribute of reading.[11] In that sense readers "write" the very "text" itself; they are the ones who invest marks on a page with "meaning." On the whole, they do not do so arbitrarily and individualistically, but read through the culturally conditioned reading conventions of the communities in which they live.

Here we meet, on the plains of literary criticism, Kant's insistence that the subjective mind does not merely "perceive," but actually shapes and organizes the world it encounters. But it now has some of the radical edge — the suspicion of any claim to objectivity — that is the hallmark of postmodernity. That radical edge would finally cleave through both text and reader too. Within structuralism, what looks like meaning is little more than a mirage of universal binary oppositions; in deconstruction, following Derrida, all meaning is unstable, for all texts are polyvalent, and none can authentically "refer" to entities outside language. The loss of the author's communicative act leads to the death of determinate meaning. What effect did these discussions have within biblical studies?

## 2.2. The Shift from Historical-Critical Hegemony

The Enlightenment, especially from the late eighteenth century onward, tended "towards a single preoccupation with historical method."[12] In ef-

---

9. Umberto Eco provides the most comprehensive theoretical treatment, setting the act of reading within a general semiotic system of signification and sign-production; see esp. *The Role of the Reader: Explorations in the Semiotics of Texts,* AS (Bloomington: Indiana University Press, 1979; London: Hutchinson, 1981); cf. Iser, *The Implied Reader.*

10. Stanley Porter refuses to accept what he regards as the halfway house of Eco and Iser ("Why Hasn't Reader-Response Criticism Caught on in New Testament Studies?" *LT* 4 [1990]: 278-92); for response see Anthony C. Thiselton, *New Horizons in Hermeneutics: The Theory and Practice of Transforming Biblical Reading* (London: Collins, 1992), pp. 548-49.

11. See esp. Stanley Fish, *Is There a Text in This Class? The Authority of Interpretive Communities* (Cambridge: Harvard University Press, 1980).

12. Anthony C. Thiselton, "New Testament Interpretation in Historical Perspective," in *Hearing the New Testament: Strategies for Interpretation,* ed. Joel B. Green (Grand Rapids: Eerdmans; Carlisle: Paternoster, 1995), p. 10.

fect, as Morgan perceives, scholarship largely confused historical *method* with the *aims* of biblical interpretation, allowing the former to swallow up the latter.[13] Historical-critical method, liberated from the shackles of dogma by Gabler and Wrede, expended enormous energy on "behind the text" issues. These included the attempt at "critical history" (especially in relation to the Gospels' picture of Jesus), source criticism, form criticism, redaction criticism, authorship analysis, provenance, history-of-religion issues, and so forth. There was also advance in the understanding of "in the text" issues, in the form of detailed critical exegesis. All this led to a few notable attempts at the "theology" or "religion" of Jesus, John, and Paul, but to little serious reflection on how the "behind the text" and "in the text" issues might relate to theological interpretation on *our* side of the text (Schlatter, Bultmann, Fuchs, Ebeling, Stuhlmacher, and a few others honorably excepted). In the Enlightenment/modernist view, critical historical inquiry dealt with "objective facts" (and so was worth pursuing), while "theology" belonged to the more subjective realm of "values" and "beliefs" (and so could be ignored by the academy). Ironically, the bid for the freedom of biblical studies from its perceived slavery to dogmatic theology only led to a prison in the biblical past, filled with the clamor of discordant voices.

In the final decades of the twentieth century, biblical studies has at last been caught up in the turbulent maelstroms of late- and post-modernity. Curiously, the New Criticism only really became widely disseminated in biblical studies in the 1980s, through such (reader-response-orientated) narrative-critical works as those of Rhoads and Michie (on Mark) and Culpepper (on John).[14] By that time it was of course no longer "new" criticism, for fashion had already moved on, in literary circles, to structuralism, to more radical brands of reader-response theory, deconstruction, new historicism, postcolonialism, and more.[15] These all thus

13. Robert Morgan with John Barton, *Biblical Interpretation* (Oxford: Oxford University Press, 1988), chap. 6 (esp. p. 171).

14. David Rhoads and Donald Michie, *Mark as Story: An Introduction to the Narrative of a Gospel* (Philadelphia: Fortress, 1982); R. Alan Culpepper, *Anatomy of the Fourth Gospel: A Study in Literary Design* (Philadelphia: Fortress, 1983). For antecedents, see Morgan with Barton, chap. 7; Stephen D. Moore, *Literary Criticism and the Gospels: The Theoretical Challenge* (New Haven: Yale University Press, 1989).

15. These and other innovations are chronicled in Stephen Greenblatt and Giles Gunn, eds., *Redrawing the Boundaries: The Transformation of English and American Literary Studies* (New York: Modern Language Association, 1992).

came more-or-less together as a tidal wave to flood biblical studies. Scholars have also plunged into a pool of other approaches such as canon criticism, linguistics and discourse analysis, rhetorical criticism and speech-act theory, and those of a variety of socio-scientific disciplines. The period from the eighties to the present can thus be seen as the "great escape" from the oppressive clutches of the all-dominating "historical critical" method into the freedom of methodological eclecticism and pluralism.[16] The current interpretive situation in the academy is pluralistic in a double sense: (1) it advocates a wide variety of "in the text" and "in front of text" approaches, in addition to historical criticism, and (2) it resists the claims of any approach to arrive at objective/absolute meaning.

### 2.3. Biblical Studies and Contemporary Theology

Although the sheer diversity of the biblical writings seemed to threaten the very possibility of a "biblical theology" — and Wrede and Räisänen have claimed that the very terms "*biblical* theology" and "*NT* theology" presume a confessional stance that was inappropriate in the academy — several factors have provoked a renewed interest in such theological approaches, and in the relation of biblical theologies to contemporary theology.[17] These include (1) the substantial collapse of modernity's dream of "objectivity," with its allied dichotomy of discoverable "facts" from merely subjective "beliefs"/"values" (i.e., "theology"); (2) critical-realist recognition that overtly theological study need not compromise academic integrity, and can maintain its place in the public domain; (3) the growing recognition that the sheer amount of effort expended on studying the short and otherwise rather unexceptional NT writings is incongruous and unjustifiable, unless its findings relate significantly to broader and contemporary concerns and truth claims; (4) the recognition that the subject matter and implied readership of the NT are overtly theological and religious, and so invite nuanced theological reflection; (5) the understanding that from the outset the NT writings were read

16. See Thiselton, "New Testament Interpretation," pp. 17-20. For a sampling of the methodological smorgasbord in NT studies today, see Green, ed., *Hearing the New Testament*.

17. See especially the collection of essays in *JR* 76 (1996): 167-327, which originated as papers presented at a conference entitled "The Bible and Christian Theology," held at the University of Chicago, 1995.

"canonically," and thus that the unity of the Testaments was and remains a substantial and significant issue; (6) the perception that the reading of the Bible throughout the ages has been in constantly shifting dialogue with theology; and (7) that renewed emphasis on the role of the reader (in history and today) has blurred the distinction between exegesis and interpretation and has opened up the (postmodern) way to a plethora of ideological and theological readings, rooted in the readers' contexts.[18] Indeed, one astute observer has recently suggested that unless "NT studies" considers the history of the effects of the text *(Wirkungsgeschichte)* and develops criteria for appropriate theological engagement with the text — of the kind that would be expected of the "implied [i.e., ecclesial] reader" — the degenerating discipline of NT studies is bound to collapse into "a number of entirely separate enterprises" and wither away.[19] In short, the "purely descriptive" task (whether conceived in historical-critical or in literary terms) is a means to an end, not a suitable end in itself.

If biblical scholars are becoming aware of the need for more theological analysis and reflection, it must also be said that systematic theology is enjoying both new life and more positive engagement with biblical studies.[20] The term "systematic theology," of course, is itself used in a variety of ways. It is regularly used as a title for works that offer comprehensive discussions of Christian doctrines, and of their logical relations and order. But it is used in broader senses as well. One can write a "systematic theology" of such subjects as Christology, atonement, creation, and the nature

---

18. On these points, see, *inter alios*, A. K. M. Adams, *Making Sense of New Testament Theology: "Modern" Problems and Prospects* (Macon, Ga.: Mercer University Press, 1995); Markus Bockmuehl, "'To Be or Not to Be': The Possible Futures of New Testament Scholarship," *SJT* 51 (1998): 271-306; Childs, pts. 1-2; Max Turner, *The Holy Spirit and Spiritual Gifts: Then and Now* (Carlisle: Paternoster, 1996), chap. 9; Robert W. Wall and Eugene E. Lemcio, *The New Testament as Canon: A Reader in Canonical Criticism*, JSNTSup 76 (Sheffield: Sheffield Academic Press, 1992); Francis Watson, *Text, Church, and World: Biblical Interpretation in Theological Perspective* (Edinburgh: T. & T. Clark; Grand Rapids: Eerdmans, 1994); Francis Watson, "Bible, Theology and the University: A Response to Philip Davies," *JSOT* 71 (1996): 3-16; N. T. Wright, *Christian Origins and the Question of God*, vol. 1, *The New Testament and the People of God* (London: SPCK; Minneapolis: Fortress 1992), pts. I-II.

19. Bockmuehl, esp. pp. 294-302.

20. See, e.g., Colin E. Gunton, ed., *The Cambridge Companion to Christian Doctrine*, Cambridge Companions to Religion (Cambridge: Cambridge University Press, 1997).

of personhood. What is it that makes the adjective "systematic" applicable to such works? Gunton identifies three major "requirements":[21]

1. *The writing will be concerned to elucidate in coherent fashion the internal relations of one aspect of belief to other potentially related beliefs.* So, for example, when Pinnock writes a "systematics" of the Holy Spirit, his starting point is an exploration of the Spirit as the personal uniting bond of love within the triune God. The Spirit's role in creation then suggests that the latter should be understood primarily as an expression of God's intertrinitarian love, and so a manifestation of grace. Within such a conceptualization, anthropology, culture, and work all come to be seen in a potentially most positive and relational light. Similarly, viewing the Spirit as the bond of love between the Father and the Son suggests a relevant Christology and makes atonement a more fully united and triune work than is possible in some other models — and the consequences of such a view of the Spirit for ecclesiology, eschatology, and mission may also be reevaluated.[22] Pinnock's is a case of examining the effects of one theological model on related areas of theology, and this is what makes it "systematic," though clearly there are other ways of being so. Gunton includes not only Aquinas, Schleiermacher, and Barth but also Irenaeus, Origen, and Anselm among "systematic" theologians of different stripes.
2. *The writing will show an understanding of the relation between the content of theology and "the sources specific to the faith"* (among which Gunton specifies especially the Bible, but also the related church tradition).
3. *Similarly, but in a more distanced way, systematics will show an awareness of the relation between the content of theology and "claims for truth in human culture in general, especially perhaps philosophy and science."*[23]

Systematic theology is thus essentially Christian doctrine that is epistemologically self-aware.[24] Such a description evidently covers not

21. See Colin E. Gunton, "Historical and Systematic Theology," in *The Cambridge Companion to Christian Doctrine*, pp. 3-20 (esp. pp. 11-18).
22. Clark H. Pinnock, *Flame of Love: A Theology of the Holy Spirit* (Downers Grove, Ill.: InterVarsity, 1996).
23. Gunton, "Historical and Systematic Theology," p. 12.
24. Gunton, "Historical and Systematic Theology," p. 18.

merely works like Wolfhart Pannenberg's comprehensive three-volume *Systematic Theology,*[25] but also detailed studies of individual aspects of theology, and of their relationship to more widely held scientific, philosophical, and/or ideological views. An example would be Alistair McFadyen's *The Call to Personhood.*[26] As the subtitle of this work indicates, this is a Christian theory of the individual in social relationships. It explores a relational model of personhood, theologically and empirically derived, and the consequences for community, culture, politics, education, marriage, sexual relationships, and so on. And it conducts this study in active and engaging critique with more generally held individualist and collectivist interpretations of human personhood.[27] Sometimes people prefer to use the label "constructive theology" for such works, instead of "systematic theology," and we have no quarrel with this. The former term is more sharply nuanced. But that said, like the terms "practical theology" and "pastoral theology," it applies to a subgenre of more generally "systematic" theological writings. We shall usually use the term "systematic" theology in the latter, broader sense.

The Two Horizons Commentary is designed to address this intellectual setting, providing theological exposition of the text, analysis of its main contribution to biblical theology, and broader contemporary theological reflection.

## 3. Introducing *Between Two Horizons*

How does one engage in biblical exegesis oriented toward a constructive theological enterprise? Three years of meetings designed to address this question among those assigned volumes in the THC repeatedly brought to the surface a number of important issues. Theological interpretation of

25. Wolfhart Pannenberg, *Systematic Theology,* 3 vols. (Edinburgh: T. & T. Clark; Grand Rapids: Eerdmans, 1991, 1994, 1998).

26. Alistair I. McFadyen, *The Call to Personhood: A Christian Theory of the Individual in Social Relationships* (Cambridge: Cambridge University Press, 1990).

27. Compare also the essays in Christoph Schwöbel and Colin E. Gunton, eds., *Persons, Divine and Human: King's College Essays in Theological Anthropology* (Edinburgh: T. & T. Clark, 1991). See also Gunton's own impressive critique of post-Enlightenment trends either to monism (from deism onward) or to (at times almost anarchic) pluralism, in Colin E. Gunton, *The One, the Three, and the Many: God, Creation, and the Culture of Modernity* (Cambridge: Cambridge University Press, 1993).

Scripture, we quickly observed, does not come naturally to those of us weaned on the interests and approaches to exegesis sponsored by the history-oriented paradigm that has monopolized biblical studies since the Enlightenment. Many biblical interpreters today are possessed by habits of mind and by hermeneutical practices that either disallow the need for building a bridge from biblical to theological studies or undermine (unself-consciously?) the necessary engineering. Clearly, a new set of dispositions and habits needs to be cultivated.

Our ongoing contemplation of a specifically theological reading of Scripture brought to the surface two additional sets of related issues. The first, understandable given the current diversity (some would say chaos) within the broad discipline of biblical studies, is a lack of commonality with regard to important hermeneutical questions. What is meaning? Is there a meaning in this text? In the interpretive process, do authors "count"? Given diversity within the biblical texts, can one speak of a biblical theology at all? And so on. The second was more surprising. This was a disagreement concerning what constituted "systematic theology." Our disagreement on this score, we came to realize, had to do both with ongoing controversies among systematicians regarding definitions of their task as theologians and with some of our own caricatures of "theology" as attempts merely to organize the core, historic doctrines of Christian faith. Again and again in our deliberations, it became clear that this interdisciplinary project needed sharper focus.

The present book arose therefore out of the need for THC contributors to address in more sustained and focused ways some of the questions that stand prior to actual engagement in a new form of commentary writing. The essays that follow were originally presented and discussed among the editors of and contributors to the THC during the Annual Meeting of the Society of Biblical Literature held in Orlando in November 1998. In light of those conversations, those essays now appear here in revised form.

Given the contemporary state of biblical studies, the project before us is inherently interdisciplinary in character. To work on "the Bible and theology" or "the Bible and ethics," or even "the Bible and preaching," is to work somehow at the interface of disciplines not only with their own discrete interests, but now with their own histories and literature. In **chapter 2**, "Scripture and Theology: Uniting the Two So Long Divided," Joel Green briefly documents how we achieved this state of affairs and discusses the most prominent of modern attempts to bring Scripture and theology into conversation. This approach, popularized in the rigid distinction often drawn between "meaning" (i.e., what this biblical text meant originally) and "significance" (i.e., the message of this text for me or us today), is in some arenas taken for granted, now broadcast even more widely in approaches to Scripture that champion three discrete steps: observation, interpretation, and application. Critical engagement with this perspective allows Green to bring to the surface a catalog of issues that any serious engagement of Scripture and theology must take into account. Finally, drawing on recent literature in interdisciplinarity, Green sketches a way forward in the discussion, a "theological hermeneutics" that refuses to posit "historical distance" as the primary gulf separating contemporary Christians and biblical texts, and which invites readers into the transformative discourse of Scripture itself.

As Steve Motyer will demonstrate in chapter 8, those interested today in engagement in "biblical theology" must first come to terms with the historical character of the biblical texts. This is because biblical studies has only recently begun to wake up from a two-centuries-old spell of historical preoccupation. In "Historical Criticism and Theological Hermeneutics of the New Testament" (**chapter 3**), Max Turner shows that the problem here is not so much that historical issues have been imported into the study of the NT as foreign and unwelcome goods. In fact, these texts themselves invite, even demand this form of probing. The problem, rather, is that biblical scholarship has tended to reduce the meaning of those texts to their historical referents and/or to their historical witness, without remainder. Drawing on important insights from the cognate disciplines of sociolinguistics and pragmatics, Turner insists that writers and their texts always communicate more than can be signified by markings on a page, that writers and texts always assume various levels of common understanding with their audiences — understanding that is necessarily historical, whether grounded in the taken-for-granted norms of a particular culture or drawn from shared experiences that help to shape and give meaning to any discourse situation. Because, for Turner, theological hermeneutics stipulates a conference table where the biblical writers are allowed fully to be present, speaking with their own voices, just as we also are to be present fully with ours, historical inquiry cannot be abandoned or marginalized. Only through historical inquiry can we begin to approximate hearing Luke, for example, on his own terms — without transforming him (and his NT writings) into a puppet whose movements and utterances are actually our own.

One of the important points of dialogue within biblical scholarship today, and thus within these pages, is the role and significance of "authors" in interpretation. There were days, not so long ago, when questions of meaning were presumed to be regulated by "authorial intent": What did the author intend to say? Quite apart from the sometimes romantic and psychoanalytical ways in which such questions were often put, biblical texts like Genesis or 1 Kings or the Gospels — "published" without identification of or reference to their "authors" — complicate such concerns since we have little or no access to authorial identity, much less (internal) authorial aspirations. Accordingly, in his exploration of the importance of historical questions, Turner nuances the concept of "authorial intent" in two ways. First, when he writes of "authorial intent" he is concerned with "authorial discourse meaning": What intentional acts has the author performed in and through the words of this text, understood within the linguistic and cultural world within which that text was inscribed? Second, he allows that different modes of expression in the NT are capable of different levels of interest in authorial meaning. Thus, we are able to grapple more clearly with the authorial discourse meaning of 1 Corinthians (and other letters) than of a narrative book like the Acts of the Apostles. As has been argued from many perspectives, including discourse analysis, literary theory, and philosophical hermeneutics, when literature is reckoned fundamentally as a communicative activity, then central roles must be allocated not only to readers and texts but also to authors.[28]

In **chapter 4**, "The Role of Authorial Intention in the Theological Interpretation of Scripture," Stephen Fowl approaches similar questions somewhat differently. Although he at first engages in efforts to resuscitate authors (following two decades of pronouncements in some quarters that "the author is dead") so as to speak (like Turner) of an author's communicative intention, he is unwilling to identify "meaning" with "authorial intent" in any sense of this latter phrase. A student of Scripture might legitimately seek to discover, say, Paul's intent in writing 1 Thessalonians, but one's claims to have discovered that intent ought not to be confused with

---

28. Cf. Richard Freadman and Seumas Miller, *Re-Thinking Theory: A Critique of Contemporary Literary Theory and an Alternative Account* (Cambridge: Cambridge University Press, 1992), p. 210: "A central task of literary theory is to give an account of the text and its relations to the author and reader. . . . A literary text must be conceived as a communicative entity, with the author as communicator and the reader as communicant"; Gillian Brown and George Yule, *Discourse Analysis*, CTL (Cambridge: Cambridge University Press, 1983), e.g., p. ix: "[I]t is people who communicate and people who interpret."

claims that one has discovered "the meaning" of 1 Thessalonians. Neither, Fowl argues, would a return to the classic interest in a text's "literal sense" mitigate plurality of interpretations. Texts can be examined in different ways reflecting the different interpretive interests of their readers, but none of the results of these diverse interpretive strategies may be equated with "the (one, correct) meaning" of a text. What typifies a peculiarly Christian reading of Scripture, then, is not the adoption of a particular method of interpretation or one's allegiance to authorial intent; pivotal, instead, is that Christians nurture the sort of communal life that will sponsor wise and accountable readings of Scripture that lead one into ever deeper faithfulness before God and with others.

Robert Wall has contributed two essays to this collection, both related to issues of the canon. The burden of the first, **chapter 5**, "Reading the Bible from within Our Traditions: The 'Rule of Faith' in Theological Hermeneutics," rests on a historical observation with profound theological ramifications. This is the reality that, before there was a collection of books known as "the NT," there existed already criteria by which to adjudicate between competing claims to the substance of the Christian message and, indeed, between competing lists of what would come to be regarded as the church's "Scripture." Though Wall is not first concerned with the process of canonization, we might be helped to appreciate his argument were we to observe that one of the pivotal (if not the central) criteria for granting canonical status to a document had to do with its consonance with "the kerygma." Thus, e.g., when Bishop Serapion was asked in the late second century C.E. regarding the place of the *Gospel of Peter* within congregational life, he did not engage in a historical, linguistic, or philological analysis in order to certify whether this text was penned by Peter the apostle. He inquired, rather, whether the *Gospel of Peter* was consonant with the kerygma of the church. That is, prior to the canon (as "list of books") stands the canon ("Christian message"). Hence, even in the presence of the Scriptures of Israel (which would come to be joined with the NT to form the Christian Bible), documents such as Pauline letters emanating from the apostolic period which were being used as if they were Scripture, and other oral and written traditions of all sorts (liturgical, hymnic, catechetical, and so on), narrative and confessional constructions of the Christian message were qualifying the substance of what could stand as "Christian." These constructions, or "rules of faith," provided what Wall terms "the normative grammar" by which Christian faith and life might be construed. If this is true, he argues, then (1) theological readings of Scrip-

15

ture must be evaluated not in terms of how well they follow accredited methods, but by their coherence with classical faith; and (2) Christians concerned with the theological interpretation of Scripture must first work to overcome the church's theological illiteracy. It is not enough to know the content of the Bible; we must learn how to read biblical texts Christianly — i.e., in light of and in ways consonant with Scripture's aim to monitor and enrich our relationships with God and God's people.

Read in tandem with chapter 6, Wall's essay also suggests why well-intentioned Christians might justifiably differ on matters of emphasis and theological content in their readings of Scripture. Wall's presentation embraces not only the grand theological matrix, the Rule of Faith, which helps to determine the outer boundaries of all Christian readings of Scripture and, thus, all Christian faith and life. He also observes the presence of a variety of particularizations of that Rule in the "rules" of relatively distinctive Christian communities and Christian faith traditions. John Christopher Thomas, who writes **chapter 6**, "Reading the Bible from within Our Traditions: A Pentecostal Hermeneutic as Test Case," illustrates Wall's point with reference to Pentecostalism.

Observing that the heart of Pentecostalism's message is a fivefold christological message (Jesus is Savior, Sanctifier, Holy Spirit Baptizer, Healer, and Coming King), Thomas moves on to document how the roots of Pentecostalism, especially its social roots, have led to particular attitudes toward the Bible. Pentecostals have a high view of Scripture's authority, Thomas avers, and are ambivalent about the role of rationalism in biblical interpretation, preferring instead to accentuate the roles of the Holy Spirit and the community of believers in the interpretive process. The heart of Thomas's essay is his attempt to show how Scripture itself authorizes the approach to Scripture practiced among Pentecostals. Thomas's examination of the biblical hermeneutics on display at the Jerusalem Council of Acts 15 is interesting not only for the important points of contact between the Acts narrative and Pentecostalism, but also for how it illustrates the negotiation of different and competing biblical traditions by those who take seriously Scripture's authority and relevance.

One of the obstacles to a mutually informing conversation among biblical scholars and systematic theologians has to do with how truth claims are conceived and represented in theological discourse. For this reason, Robert Wall's discussion of the importance of the Rule of Faith in theological hermeneutics finds an interesting counterpoint in John Goldingay's **chapter 7**, "Biblical Narrative and Systematic Theology."

Goldingay, an OT professor, is the only contributor to the present book who is not also involved directly in the THC; we invited his involvement on the basis of the stimulating and significant work he has already done in the theology and interpretation of Scripture.[29] (In addition, we hope to stimulate similar interest in a THC series devoted to the OT!)

"Narrative" for Goldingay refers primarily to a mode of discourse (over against, say, the discursive writing of the NT letters or psalmic literature) — with plot, character development, and theme. Although the biblical narratives (as well as other accounts, in film or novels or songs, for example) are profoundly theological, because they embody a manifestly nondiscursive mode of writing, biblical texts like 1-2 Samuel or the Gospel of Mark do not give themselves easily to distillation in confessional summaries. Narrative has a capacity for embodying complexity within God-human relations, for holding in tension competing ideas about God or humanity or the cosmos, and for transformation within characters (including God himself) that defies the sorts of categories typically associated with systematic theology. Goldingay is concerned, therefore, that systematic theology often does violence to biblical narrative — either by neglecting it altogether or by condensing its message into theological affirmations that denude narrative of its dynamic in favor of modes of thought more devoted to coherence and analytical reflection. It is not for nothing that, when NT scholars have turned to the task of NT "theology," they have tended to focus on John and Paul, whose writings are most at home in the world of traditional systematic theology.

In the end, Goldingay is not sanguine about the relationship of Scripture, which is overwhelmingly narrative (or grounded in narrative), and systematic theology as traditionally practiced. This is because of systematic theology's tendency to bring to Scripture its concerns and categories (i.e., its "systems" and systematizing impulses), while turning a deaf ear to the invitation of scriptural narrative to inhabit its sometimes chaotic and quixotic world and to be transformed accordingly. Even when balanced by his own constructive proposals for conversation between Scripture and systematic theology, Goldingay's skepticism is an important reminder of the ease with which the way of thinking that gives rise to theological "confessions" and

---

29. Among his many relevant publications, see most recently, John Goldingay, *Models for Scripture* (Carlisle: Paternoster; Grand Rapids: Eerdmans, 1994); Goldingay, *Models for Interpretation of Scripture* (Carlisle: Paternoster; Grand Rapids: Eerdmans, 1995).

"creeds" is already a step or two removed from the mystery, vitality, and sometimes disheveled appearance of biblical narrative.

As a number of these essays acknowledge, historical criticism has more brought to the surface the diversity within and among the biblical texts than it has clarified or featured the unity or harmony of Scripture's many voices. In fact, not least among Christians concerned with constructive ethics, the problem of finding a common voice within Scripture has been a major stumbling block.[30] Steve Motyer takes up this concern in **chapter 8**, "Two Testaments, One Biblical Theology." On the one hand, the Bible comprises a series of texts grounded in particular historical moments; on the other, as "the Christian Bible," it presents a claim to theological coherence. How can these two competing claims be resolved? Motyer first surveys a century of attempts to adumbrate the history-theology dilemma — some of which simply reject the historical-critical project, and others that undertake various forms of recasting how we understand "history" or "theology" in order to span the two. Having canvassed the primary, representative options, Motyer defines biblical theology as "that creative theological discipline whereby the church seeks to hear the integrated voice of the whole Bible addressing us today," and insists that the earliest Christians were already involved in this kind of theological task, even when their "Bible" consisted of only the Scriptures of Israel. Motyer explores the implications of this definition in a series of theses before taking up the account of the sacrifice of Isaac (Gen. 22:1-19) in order to provide an example of exegesis performed with (1) an integrated, whole-Scripture awareness of diversity and development and (2) a keen eye turned to our theological questions of this troublesome text.

The problem of the diversity of Scripture is also the subject of Robert Wall's second contribution. In **chapter 9**, Wall discusses these and related concerns under the heading "Canonical Context and Canonical Conversations." The first half of his chapter is devoted to the importance of taking seriously the canonical "address" of biblical texts. Clearly, this emphasis stands in opposition to those points of view for which (say) the first-cen-

30. The contours of and various responses to this problem are explored in a helpful way in William C. Spohn, *What Are They Saying about Scripture and Ethics?* rev. ed. (New York and Mahwah, N.J.: Paulist, 1995); cf. Sondra Ely Wheeler, *Wealth as Peril and Obligation: The New Testament on Possessions* (Grand Rapids: Eerdmans, 1995); Richard B. Hays, *The Moral Vision of the New Testament: Community, Cross, New Creation: A Contemporary Introduction to New Testament Ethics* (San Francisco: Harper San Francisco, 1996).

tury Roman world, or the moods and exigencies of today's reader, provide the primary (or sole) horizon of interpretive interest. For Wall, a biblical text no longer "belongs" to its author, nor to its original audience, but to the global church through time that embraces these texts as Scripture and desires to hear its message as a challenge and exhortation to maturity in Christ. In the second half of his essay, Wall turns more explicitly to the task of a canon-based hermeneutic with three discrete but integral parts: (1) locating texts within their canonical context, which takes seriously both the relation of Old to New Testament and the location of a text within the design of the canon itself; (2) an exegesis of the "plain meaning" of the biblical text; and (3) "canonical conversations," in which the various voices within Scripture are portrayed as an intramural debate regarding the meaning of things generally agreed to be true and substantial. These "conversations," Wall insists, are not adversarial but complementary and mutually corrective. Here one may hear the reverberation of echoes of language associated with the "conference table" image, borrowed from George Caird by other contributors to this volume.[31]

Anyone engaged in biblical studies at the turn of the twenty-first century will be aware that people turn to Scripture for any number of reasons. In his survey of biblical interpretation and biblical scholarship, Robert Morgan narrows these down to two — positing a basic dichotomy of interpretive aims between those of the scholarly community, concerned with historical reconstruction, literary appreciation, or both; and those of religious communities, for whom the Bible is read as Scripture.[32] As if to accentuate further this dichotomy, Morgan states bluntly that, today, few biblical scholars also wear the hat of the theologian. Broadly speaking, this characterization rings true, though we can be grateful that there are many persons (and many communities of interpretation as well) engaged in serious biblical study within and for the church who must be regarded as standing with feet firmly planted in both realities. Morgan's recognition that different persons and communities have different interpretive interests is an important one — one that suggests the necessity of declaring our own interests (whoever we are and for whatever reason we engage in the study of Scripture). In fact, readers of Stephen Fowl's essay will realize that this coming-clean with one's own aims in engaging Scripture is one of his

31. G. B. Caird, *New Testament Theology*, ed. L. D. Hurst (Oxford: Clarendon, 1994).

32. Morgan and Barton, pp. 1-43.

primary concerns. It is also the central concern of **chapter 10**, though in this case Trevor Hart is occupied not with cataloging the various ways in which the biblical texts might be read or used, but rather with delineating a properly *Christian* approach to Scripture.

In "Tradition, Authority, and a Christian Approach to the Bible as Scripture," Hart stakes a claim in territory not often allowed persons of his ilk. As he is himself aware, professional societies devoted to biblical studies have reputations for holding at bay interpretive interests other than those raised by the text itself: social settings, literary artistry, historical faithfulness, and the like fall in this latter category of acceptable issues. On the one hand, one might reply that the biases of historical criticism are no less prejudicial than the biases of faith, so that to rule only one of these out of court seems strange, even arbitrary. On the other, it is worth asking whether questions of faith and the formation of Christian identity are not themselves endemic to these texts and are therefore not alien influences on interpretation after all.[33] Rather than mounting an apology for faith-full readings of Scripture, however, Hart takes this as a given necessity, and along with it the authority of Scripture for the church. His essay focuses on other matters, particularly on how theological voices, in the guise of "tradition" broadly defined, shape our reading.

Hart argues, first, that a Christian reading of Scripture has always been a "regulated" reading, that there are and always have been limits on what might count as a properly *Christian* reading of the Bible. For persons interested in the theological interpretation of Scripture within the church in a time like ours — where words like "constraints" and "limitations" and even "authority" are often regarded as unbecoming, even repellent — this is a crucial reminder. What rules "regulate" a Christian reading of the Bible as Scripture? Hart expands upon three. (1) A properly Christian approach to Scripture is one that seeks to submit to the text, presuming on the presence of communicative intent mediated through the text, seeking to be constrained in its initial approaches and subsequent responses to the text by the discipline of hearing what the text is saying, and recognizing the provisional character of all readings and thus maintaining an openness to continued, disciplined hearing. (2) A properly Christian approach to Scripture attends to the whole of Scripture — it is not deaf to the distinctive voices within Scripture but is always keen to hear each voice for what it adds to the whole and the whole for how it brings particular voices into harmony with the rest.

33. This is highlighted in Bockmuehl, "'To Be or Not to Be.'"

In this respect, it is especially true today that the voice of the OT needs more clearly to be heard so as to restore vitality to our claim that the God revealed in Scripture is the Father of Jesus Christ. (3) Finally, a properly Christian approach to Scripture is characterized by a reading that occurs "in the Spirit." Here the Holy Spirit is not cast in the role of yet one more interpretive tool or agenda, but as the divine presence who finally renders the text authoritative for faith and life as God speaks to us in and through these texts to fashion our identity, understanding, and practices.

N. T. Wright illustrates the task of bringing theological and exegetical concerns into conversation in **chapter 11**, "The Letter to the Galatians: Exegesis and Theology." Wright is writing the THC on Galatians. This means that, in the end, he will have far more space, a book rather than an essay, to work out the details both of his exegesis and of his theological reflection. This also means that here we are given a foretaste of the kind of thing we can expect from his completed project. Thus, Wright begins with a discussion of interpretive issues central to the study of Galatians today. He serves as a kind of tour guide, inviting us at once into the text and into exegetical debates — which, of course, feature his own spin on how best to make sense of Paul's letter. Following this we see Wright the theologian, exploring ways in which this short letter might contribute to the church's overall understanding of God, Jesus, the Spirit, humanity, salvation, and so on. Interestingly, Wright argues that, were we to take Galatians seriously, our theological reflections would be far more oriented toward Israel than they have been, while at the same time suggestively indicating how, in Galatians, one finds a proto-trinitarian understanding of God. In a brief discussion like this, we have only the barest glimpses of how the theology of Galatians might interface with that of other biblical books, but some interesting conversations are nonetheless broached. Wright then devotes a lengthy section to a programmatic discussion of how the voice of Galatians might address itself to such contemporary issues as the challenges of postmodernity, global security and tribalism, and encroaching secularity. A concluding section attempts to draw together reflections on the whole enterprise of spanning theological studies and NT exegesis in the case of Paul's letter to the Galatians.

## 4. Joining the Conversation

In an important sense, the historical genesis of *Between Two Horizons* was discourse, a series of conversations among contributors to the Two Horizons Commentary. The questions motivating our exchanges are hardly peculiar to us, however. In many quarters throughout the world, whether among professional biblical scholars or theological students, whether in local church or campus or neighborhood Bible studies, many persons are engaged, some knowingly and others not, in theological hermeneutics. How are these words the Word of God for us, the church of Jesus Christ in this place? What is the Spirit saying to the churches? These are our questions, but not only ours, and they are pressing.

Given our own historical moment, at the intersection of the ages, with an era dominated by historical questions waning and a new era characterized at least for now by methodological anarchy, our conversations on such matters are necessarily involved. We can take so little for granted. The foundations on which to build hermeneutical constructs are no longer shared. This is good news in a way, since it allows for new questions and requires reexamination of tried-but-not-necessarily-true answers. Fresh engagement is needed on a whole host of questions related to how Christians read the Bible as Scripture in the service of the church's faith and life. Given the collapse of older paradigms, fresh engagement is today possible in ways that were unthinkable even a half-century ago. If this is hardly a moment for the fainthearted, it is nonetheless true that the current disorder in biblical studies has produced an environment in which exactly these sorts of questions — questions about the practice of biblical studies within and for faith communities — can again be raised and receive reflection. In offering these essays to a wider public, we do not imagine that we have grasped the answers in any final sense — or, indeed, that we have surfaced all of the necessary questions. We are engaged, however, in what we believe is the right conversation.

# CHAPTER 2

# Scripture and Theology: Uniting the Two So Long Divided

## JOEL B. GREEN

Not long ago, Brevard Childs wrote of the "iron curtain" separating the two disciplines, biblical studies and systematic theology.[1] Evidence of this seemingly impregnable wall is difficult to overlook — whether one is the theological student searching for ways to connect one part of the seminary curriculum with the other or the scholar trained according to accredited standards that guard the one discipline from what are typically regarded as the naive or imperialistic efforts of the other.

The title of this chapter notwithstanding, in the grand scheme of things the segregation of theological studies and biblical studies is a relatively new innovation in the life of the people of God, and it represents a significant if (at least arguably) unfortunate shift of emphasis. Karl Barth is often remembered for his programmatic expression of the task of theology: "dogmatics does not ask what the apostles and prophets said but what we must say on the basis of the apostles and prophets."[2] What is haunting about Barth's formulation is that the past two centuries of biblical studies have left both the church and those engaged in constructive theology with little access to "what the apostles and prophets said." The "apostles and

---

1. Brevard Childs, *Biblical Theology of the Old and New Testaments* (Minneapolis: Fortress, 1992), p. xvi.
2. Karl Barth, *Church Dogmatics*, 1.1 (Edinburgh: T. & T. Clark, 1975), p. 16.

prophets" have instead become the almost exclusive property of professional biblical studies, which alone (so it is supposed) possess the methodological and hermeneutical keys to unlock their riches. In spite of the variety of its incarnations, the twentieth-century branch of study known as "biblical theology" has typically been so enamored with its own disciplinary integrity — generally as a discrete, intermediary step between exegesis and systematics — that it has been little oriented toward a more constructive theological enterprise. It is surely to Barth's credit, then, that his own *Church Dogmatics* seeks as fully as it does to weave together serious engagement with Scripture and the larger theological enterprise. At the close of the twentieth century, however, "biblical scholars" and "theologians" are rarely seen as "two of a kind."

In this essay we will not assume that this "iron curtain" is a necessary one, nor that it cannot be breached or even razed. First, we will explore its foundations in the modern period, suggesting both the importance of the historical consciousness of modernity for understanding the segregation of theological and biblical studies as well as some areas in which this aspect of the Enlightenment project invites critique and revision. Second, we will briefly sketch one of the most pervasive twentieth-century attempts to overcome the separation of Scripture and theology. These first two steps will allow us to show why fresh models are now needed, and to provide an inventory of the sorts of issues for which these models must account. Third, we will explore the nature of the interdisciplinarity now necessary to unite the two so long divided, Scripture and theology.

## 1. History, Theology, Interpretation, and Modernity

The fissure separating Scripture and theology is not a new phenomenon, but is the consequence of tectonic shifts and their aftershocks over the last three centuries. Alister McGrath conveniently refers to the epicenter of this movement as the sense of "being condemned to history": "The confident and restless culture of the Enlightenment experienced the past as a burden, an intellectual manacle which inhibited freedom and stifled creativity."[3]

3. Alister E. McGrath, *The Genesis of Doctrine: A Study in the Foundation of Doctrinal Criticism* (Grand Rapids: Eerdmans, 1990), p. 81. See Carl E. Schorske, *Thinking with History: Explorations in the Passage to Modernism* (Princeton: Princeton University Press, 1998), pp. 3-4: "In most fields of intellectual and artistic culture, twentieth-century Europe and America learned to think without history. The very word 'modernism'

Interest in a theology without tradition has resulted in perennial questions about the place of the study of Scripture in the curriculum, just as the increasingly historical definition of the meaning of Scripture has led to the segregation of "serious" biblical studies from issues of biblical authority and biblical relevance. While conservatives in the USA found themselves embattled over more and more particular ways of depicting the authority of Scripture, those outside of conservative Christian circles, who were nonetheless willing to embrace some sense of authority for Scripture in their theological prolegomena, found it less and less easy to articulate or demonstrate any particular role for an authoritative Bible.[4]

Put sharply, the massive shift of which we speak has to do with the problematizing of "history." If all knowledge is historically grounded, as has been increasingly recognized, then we moderns should not be governed in our knowing by someone else's history (e.g., by the Christian tradition). What is more, the only viable history within which to construe the meaning of biblical texts is the history within which those texts were generated — or the history to which those texts point.

Painting with the broadest of strokes, the relation of Scripture to theology can thus be portrayed with regard to the relationship between biblical text and historical context. *Premodern perspectives* on text and history worked with the unreflective assumption that text and history were coterminous — or, at least, that the history behind the text was not the sole or determinative factor in meaning making. Writing in the early 700s, the Venerable Bede can recognize that Acts 1:12 ("which is near Jerusalem, a sabbath day's journey" [NRSV]), from a historical reading, locates the Mount of Olives "a thousand paces distant from the city of Jerusalem," but this does not deter his further reflection on this detail of the Lukan account: "[A]nyone who becomes worthy of an interior vision of the glory of the Lord as he ascends to the Father, and of enrichment by the promise of the Holy Spirit, here enters the city of everlasting peace by a Sabbath jour-

---

has come to distinguish our lives and times from what had gone before, from history as a whole, as such. Modern architecture, modern music, modern science — all these have defined themselves not so much *out* of the past, indeed scarcely *against* the past, but detached from it in a new, autonomous cultural space."

4. E.g., John Macquarrie (*Principles of Christian Theology*, 2nd ed. [New York: Scribner, 1977], pp. 9-11) refers to Scripture as a "norm in the theology of the community," a "formative factor in theology," a means by which "the primordial revelation" is mediated to us, but reference to Scripture is scarce in his study of theology, and engagement with Scripture is practically nonexistent.

ney. There will be for him [*sic*], in Isaiah's words, *Sabbath after Sabbath*, because he will be at rest there in heavenly recompense."[5] Theology, after all, is not separated from exegesis.[6]

Since the second century C.E., contradictions alleged, say, among the Gospels regarding particular historical events, were resolved via allegorical interpretation or simple harmonization. When it comes to Luke's recounting of the election of Matthias to complete the number of the apostles following Judas's betrayal, for example, Bede — who had immediate access to the significant library at Wearmouth-Jarrow in the northeast of England, as well as access to manuscripts in such centers of learning as the nearby Lindisfarne and, in the south, Canterbury — does not worry with the basic historicity of the account, wrestle with the relation of this account to the somewhat disparate material in Matthew 27, or wonder why Matthias is never again mentioned in the narrative of Acts. He writes, instead, "He [Peter] restored the number of apostles to twelve, so that through two parts of six each (for three times four is twelve) they might preserve by an eternal number the grace which they were preaching by word, and so that those who were to preach the faith of the holy Trinity to the four parts of the world . . . might already certify the perfection of the work by the sacramental sign of [their] number as well."[7] If exegesis of this sort sounds alien to us, as though it derives from an altogether different era from our own and from a person whose formation as a Christian and reader of Scripture must likewise have been different from our own, this is exactly the point. As those of the modern period came to appreciate, readings of Scripture arise in particular historical contexts, just as, indeed, the "original" meaning of a scriptural text is historically occasioned.

This means that, according to the *modern perspective* (again, painting with broad strokes), we find a purposeful segregation of "history" and "text" — or, to put it in a slightly different way, of "history" and "textual interpretation." Here we learn that the history to which the biblical text gives witness and the biblical text that provides such a witness are not coterminous. Since interpretive privilege is accorded to "history" in this perspective, the biblical text is to be regarded with critical suspicion, and historical inquiry is the or-

5. The Venerable Bede, *Commentary on the Acts of the Apostles*, translated, with an introduction and notes, by Lawrence T. Martin, CSS 117 (Kalamazoo: Cistercian, 1989), p. 14.

6. See Henri de Lubac, *Medieval Exegesis*, vol. 1, *The Four Senses of Scripture*, RR (Grand Rapids: Eerdmans, 1998), esp. chap. 2.

7. Bede, p. 17.

der of the day. Biblical interpretation, then, is construed as a discipline of "validation" (when the biblical text is judged to represent historical events with accuracy) or of "reconstruction" (when it is not). Lest it be imagined that, in thus characterizing the modern period, we have fabricated a straw dog, consider the recent book by Maurice Casey, *Is John's Gospel True?*[8] Apparently, Casey does not think that, in posing this question, he has begged the question, In what sense "true"? for he quickly answers his own question in the negative, and proceeds to document what he regards as the serious inaccuracies of the Fourth Gospel with reference to its chronology, Christology, portrait of the Baptist, and the passion and resurrection of Jesus. If Casey goes on to argue that John's Gospel is "false" in another sense — namely, in its alleged anti-Jewishness — this is only after he has pulled the rug from under its claims to historical veracity.

In the modern era, the importance of the Bible for theology or the authority of Scripture in theology is marginalized by casting off the perceived shackles of the theological tradition. With the ascendancy of the historical, (1) the meaning of Scripture is first and foremost the meaning of the history to which it gives witness (source, historical, and tradition criticism), (2) the meaning of Scripture can then also be located within its own historical moment (redaction criticism), and (3) however important a role a biblical text might have had in its own history, it is not a part of ours. As Gordon Fee observes, these issues are all the more acute for persons in the evangelical Christian community. He cannot reject exegesis, which he defines in historical terms: "what it meant then"; but neither can he neglect the question, What does this biblical text say today?[9] As this statement of Fee's dilemma evidences, even in the modern period we have seen attempts to rehabilitate the meaning of Scripture for our own day, and we will turn to what we take to be the most prominent effort momentarily.

First, however, it is worth reflecting a moment further on the interpretive situation in which the modern period has left us. On the one hand, we may refer to the course of Jesus studies in this century, which has fashioned and sharpened "precision tools" for slicing through the layers of theology and interpretive agenda in the Gospels in order to grasp the "historical core" of the life of Jesus of Nazareth. Because we cannot ignore what we have learned in the modern period about the historical conditioning of all knowl-

---

8. Maurice Casey, *Is John's Gospel True?* (New York: Routledge, 1996).
9. Gordon D. Fee, *Gospel and Spirit: Issues in New Testament Hermeneutics* (Peabody, Mass.: Hendrickson, 1991), p. 4.

edge, we do not have the luxury of giving up altogether the quest of the historical Jesus, as though it were unimportant or irrelevant to our understanding of our faith. At the same time, the particular way in which this discussion is often cast — by those in and outside of the church, and across the theological spectrum — is of grave concern. Must we, as children of the Enlightenment, accord privilege, even authoritative status, to the Jesus our historians, even our most able ones, are able to reconstruct; or do we accord authoritative status to the Gospels that give witness to his life in its significance, to the Old Testament that points to his coming, and to the New Testament that takes as its fundamental point of departure the advent of the Messiah? To what do we accord the status of "Scripture" — these texts or this (reconstructed) historical figure? At the same time that the modern era has emphasized the historical conditioning of our knowing, it has also effected a kind of eclipse of the reality that, for us, the good news is textually mediated.

Our recognition of the historical roots of our knowledge has further implications, and some of these have been developed by such progenitors of suspicion in the modern world as Karl Marx, Sigmund Freud, and Michel Foucault. In his own way, each has drawn attention to the ways in which our "knowing" is shaped by influences that we scarcely recognize — our unconsciousness, for example, or our relationship to the means of production. Indeed, for Foucault, all discourse is to some degree imperialistic or colonizing; discourse is a mode of power by which inequality is enacted, promulgated, and sanctioned. "Truth" itself is a social construct, and whoever has power can and does determine its content.[10] Little wonder, then, that the late-modern period has been characterized in part by a hermeneutics of suspicion, whether directed against other readers of Scripture and the tradition of biblical interpretation or against the interpretation of events written into the Scriptures.

In spite of its important insights, one of the areas in which the modern period has miscarried is in its failure to regard itself as a historical moment. In its attempt to free the Bible from the stranglehold of the dogmatic theology that determined in advance exegetical outcomes, it failed to understand how it had located the legitimate interpretation of Scripture in its own modern ideology. Reading the stories of healing in the Gospels or Pauline accounts of visionary experiences within a naturalistic, deistic framework predetermined a reading of those narrative and epistolary texts that disallowed the possibility of the phenomena they presupposed. The

10. See Paul Rabinow, ed., *The Foucault Reader* (New York: Pantheon, 1984).

cultural horizons against which Scripture was to be read were now "modern." That is, even if Scripture must be allowed to speak within its own social environment, the allowable content of that social environment was determined by the predispositions of modernity.

A second failure of the Enlightenment project has to do with its failure to account for the possibility that cultural products, like biblical texts, do indeed grow out of particular sociohistorical exigencies but are not of necessity entirely bound to those exigencies. Thus has biblical scholarship in the modern period been plagued by the troublesome tendency to assume that meaning belongs, without remainder, to the point of a text's formation. With regard to Christian self-understanding, to embrace this accounting is to deny a foundational element of our identity as the people of God — namely, the continuity of Israel, the first followers of Jesus, and all subsequent communities of his disciples, including the eschatological community. How can Ruth and Esther be Scripture *for us* if their meaning is solely the property of these biblical texts at the historical moment of their origin? In sociological terms, Robert Wuthnow has taught us to grapple with how cultural products sometimes relate in an enigmatic fashion to their social environments: "They draw resources, insights, and inspiration from the environment: they reflect it, speak to it, and make themselves relevant to it. And yet they also remain autonomous enough from their social environment to acquire a broader, even universal and timeless appeal."[11] From this perspective, such cultural products as texts have the capacity to speak to but also beyond the situations within which they were formed. Even products of cultures distinct from our own may speak to us in our own encultured situations, by means of the juxtaposition of those cultural structures, alien and familiar, that lend certainty to everyday life, with the result that we find ourselves disoriented, our perceptions altered, our imaginations transformed.[12] Indeed, at least

---

11. Robert Wuthnow, *Communities of Discourse: Ideology and Social Structure in the Reformation, the Enlightenment, and European Socialism* (Cambridge: Harvard University Press, 1989), p. 3.

12. "Juxtaposition" is discussed in George E. Marcus and Michael M. J. Fischer, *Anthropology as Cultural Critique: An Experimental Moment in the Human Sciences* (Chicago: University of Chicago Press, 1986). The importance of the reformation of the moral imagination has entered into biblical study via various avenues — cf., e.g., Wayne A. Meeks, *The Origins of Christian Morality: The First Two Centuries* (New Haven: Yale University Press, 1993), pp. 1-36; Richard B. Hays, *The Moral Vision of the New Testament: Community, Cross, New Creation: A Contemporary Introduction to New Testament Ethics* (San Francisco: Harper San Francisco, 1996).

part of what we mean when we speak of "the inspiration of Scripture," assuming that we take our cues from the representation of "inspiration" in the Old Testament prophets, is that these words have significance for people beyond their effectiveness for those to whom they were first uttered; "these words are meaningful, indeed make special demands, in a later context than the one in which they were originally uttered."[13] The interpretation of the Scriptures of Israel by Jesus and Paul, and the inclusion of those Scriptures in the Christian Bible, is profound testimony to our claim that the meaning of Scripture cannot be relegated or reduced to its historical moment. The modern period has, on various grounds, therefore, erred in its failure to appreciate the phenomenological reality and theological necessity that biblical texts speak in contexts in addition to those of their original generation.

Finally, the modern era has misconstrued the role of texts and the role of interpreters. Our canons of interpretation have tended toward an account of meaning with one or another primary focus — the definition of "meaning" as a property of the historical events one might view through the text-as-window, or the definition of "meaning" as a property of the text itself. The first minimizes or obliterates the text as an instrument of meaning, while the latter (which developed historically in reaction to the former) regards the text as a self-contained, hermetically sealed, meaning-making machine. In either case, meaning is objectified and the text is regarded as an object to be explored, interrogated, even manipulated so that it might divulge its deposits of "meaning." Clearly, in this regard we have traveled far from medieval affirmations of Scripture: "'undecipherable in its fullness and in the multiplicity of its meanings' . . . a deep forest, with innumerable branches, 'an infinite forest of meanings.' . . ."[14] Interpretation, rather, is comprised in the act of bringing into evidence the properties of the text and/or its history. Philosophical questions (e.g., What is the meaning of "meaning"?) raised by such an account aside, such a model of interpretation does not account for the dynamic realities of discourse.

A hermeneutical model of the kind thus proposed by modernity runs aground on at least two points. First, although a text read with due attention to its literary cotext, and with due consideration of its sociohistorical context, places constraints on the range of possible inter-

---

13. John Goldingay, *Models for Scripture* (Grand Rapids: Eerdmans; Carlisle: Paternoster, 1994), p. 215; see pp. 215-19.

14. De Lubac, p. 75; with reference to Blaise Pascal, Jonah of Orleans, Paulinus, Gregory, Jerome, Origen, et al.

pretations that might be regarded as legitimately related to that text, texts require readers for their actualization.[15] And readers bring with them to the text their own protocols, crises, and interests, and the result is different, though presumably related, performances of the one text. Second, the interpretive model to which we object treats the biblical text solely or primarily as a source of data, of knowledge. Meaning is "back there," awaiting our discovery. In the last century we have come to appreciate more a different set of questions: How do these texts impinge on their readers? What processes do they set in motion? In this accounting the text cannot be regarded as mere object; it, too, is a subject in the communicative discourse.[16]

The perspectives on reading from such persons as Wolfgang Iser and Umberto Eco are important here. For them, texts are not self-interpreting, semantically sealed meaning factories.[17] For Eco, texts like those in Scripture are characterized by the invitation for readers "to make the work" together with the author, so that texts might achieve a vitality that cannot be reduced to the cognitive domain. Rather, they are rendered meaningful in personal and communal performance. Iser observes that narrative texts — incapable of delineating every detail, even in plot — are inevitably characterized by gaps that must be filled by readers; even if the text guides this "filling" process, different readers will actualize the text's clues in different ways. For both Eco and Iser, then, texts are capable of a range (though not an infinite number) of possible, valid meanings, depending on who is doing the reading, from what perspectives they read, what reading protocols they prefer, and how they otherwise participate in the production of significance. In their own ways Eco and Iser indicate the absurdity of reading as the "discovery of meaning," substituting in its place the notion of reading as text-guided "production" and "performance." They also show how

---

15. "Cotext" refers to the string of linguistic data within which a text is set, the relationship of, say, a sentence to a paragraph, and a paragraph to the larger whole. "Context" refers to the sociohistorical realities within which the text is set and to which it gives witness.

16. This is developed in Anthony C. Thiselton, *New Horizons in Hermeneutics: The Theory and Practice of Transforming Biblical Reading* (London: Collins; Grand Rapids: Zondervan, 1992).

17. See, e.g., Wolfgang Iser, *The Implied Reader: Patterns of Communication in Prose Fiction from Bunyan to Beckett* (Baltimore: Johns Hopkins University Press, 1974); Umberto Eco, *The Role of the Reader: Explorations in the Semiotics of Texts*, AS (Bloomington: Indiana University Press, 1979; London: Hutchinson, 1981).

our readings of Scripture reflect our own communities of formation, how the differing aims of our interpretive strategies and habits cultivate different readings of Scripture. We should not be surprised to discover, then, that a Pentecostal and a Calvinist construe texts differently; nor should we imagine that this sort of interpretive variety ought to be or can be adjudicated by recourse to better interpretive methods or more conscientious deployment of particular interpretive approaches or the development of an as-yet-unforeseen technology of reading.

Undoubtedly, a comprehensive list of the shortcomings of modernity-sponsored biblical interpretation would not stop at this point. Our agenda lies elsewhere, however. Our purpose has been threefold: to comment on the architectural and engineering ventures whose product is the "iron curtain" separating biblical studies and theological studies; to indicate their shortcomings; and to begin surveying the land for a different sort of edifice in which theology and Bible might find a home together. Our objectives will be served further by sketching a relatively recent, twentieth-century attempt to scale the wall in order to bring the Bible and theology into more intimate conversation.

## 2. From Bible and Theology to Biblical Theology

Although a number of possible bridges have been attempted by way of spanning the distance between these two landmasses, Scripture and theology, here we will focus briefly on one. Our choice of this particular "model" is grounded in its importance in different sectors of the Christian community in the modern period. This discussion, when taken together with our previous discussion of modernity, will then provide the basis for a short list of issues that should be considered in fresh attempts to work at the interface of Scripture and theology.

### 2.1. Biblical Theology

When Krister Stendahl published his essay "Biblical Theology, Contemporary" in *The Interpreter's Dictionary of the Bible* (1962),[18] he acknowledged that biblical scholars at the time shared no common understanding of the

---

18. Krister Stendahl, "Biblical Theology, Contemporary," in *IDB*, 1:418-32.

field of "biblical theology." In ways that he may not have predicted, his account helped to create something of the consensus for which he could find little evidence in the early 1960s. His distinction between the "two tenses" of "meaning" — "'What *did* it mean?' and 'What *does* it mean?'" — or between exegesis (the task of description) and hermeneutics (the task of translation) has become second language to scholars across the theological spectrum. This is particularly true among evangelicals. Introducing only a slight alteration in language, I. Howard Marshall writes, for example, that "the basic principle is that the significance of the text is derived from its original meaning; the meaning determines the significance."[19] And Gordon Fee accepts the dilemma posed by Stendahl, how to move from historical exegesis to contemporary meaning, as "the core of the hermeneutical problem today."[20] Contributions to the genre "a theology of the New Testament" in the past three decades further signify the ascendancy of this way of construing the theological mission of biblical scholars, for invariably they point to the important inaugural step of engagement in the "descriptive task" — which Stendahl presented thus: "[O]ur only concern is to find out what these words meant when uttered or written by the prophet, the priest, the evangelist, or the apostle — and regardless of their meaning in later stages of religious history, our own included."[21]

Many today imagine that the movement from Bible to theology is a three-stage process, from exegesis to (descriptive) biblical theology to (prescriptive) systematic theology. At more popular levels, the same hermeneutic is prescribed in three steps: observation, interpretation, application.

The premier status of this "what it meant/what it means" hermeneutic notwithstanding, it has encountered opposition on numerous fronts, among which four may be mentioned here.

1. The descriptive task of biblical theology has for many run aground on the problem of diversity within the canon. How does one present a descriptive *biblical* theology when the biblical *witnesses* themselves do not seem to agree? One answer has been a kind of harmonization that makes all of the voices speak as though they were one, in spite of the fact that no one voice in Scripture, taken on its own, could ever be heard to speak in just that way. Another answer has been to allow one voice to speak for all;

19. I. Howard Marshall, "How Do We Interpret the Bible Today?" *Themelios* 5, no. 2 (1980): 4-12 (9).

20. Fee, pp. 2-3.

21. Stendahl, p. 422.

in Protestant circles the voice of choice has typically been Pauline, especially as heard in Romans. When thinking of the theology of James or John or Jude, according to this strategy, one is more likely to hear the voice of the Pauline ventriloquist than that of James, John, or Jude. A third answer has focused on the search for the coordinating center of Scripture — "covenant," for example, or "reconciliation" — the effect of which has been to mute alternatives within the canon. A fourth, and perhaps the most promising, has been to focus on Scripture's metanarrative, a unity that lies in the character and activity of God that comes to expression in various but recognizably similar ways in these various texts. Fifth, many have rejected outright the possibility of using Scripture as a normative source in theology and ethics on account of its diversity.

2. Stendahl's proposal and those that have followed from it have fallen on hard times as a consequence of difficulties encountered at the stage of "translation." If we could agree on "what it meant," how might we construe "what it means today"? What ought to be translated? Who does the translation? And on what basis? Why do we translate some passages so that they speak with immediacy within our contemporary contexts, while others are regarded as culturally bound? One group refuses to ordain women but does not engage in foot washing. Another group ordains women, engages in foot washing, but thinks nothing of eating meat sacrificed to idols. Another group refuses to drink alcohol but would never think of passing the "holy kiss." How are we to explain the hermeneutics of appropriation active in such instances where Christians and Christian communities embrace some "clear" scriptural injunctions while neglecting others?

3. The "what it meant/what it means" hermeneutic has made promises it could never keep. It was anchored to a scientific approach to Scripture that assumed the impossible by requiring contemporary readers of Scripture to shed their contemporary clothing and to stand on a nonexistent ledge of neutrality and objectivity in order to delineate the "original meaning" of a biblical text.

4. One of the crucial assumptions of this pervasive biblical-theology hermeneutic, which has not received the critical attention it requires, is that the function of Scripture in theology was and is solely or primarily content oriented and boundary making.[22] This way of conceiving the relationship

22. Ben C. Ollenburger raises a parallel set of issues in his essay "What Krister Stendahl 'Meant' — a Normative Critique of 'Descriptive Biblical Theology,'" *HBT* 8 (1986): 61-98.

between the Bible and theology is to construe the role of the Bible foundationally — i.e., it determines what we should and might believe. Lack of critical reflection on this assumption is remarkable since this way of thinking runs against the grain of some of our actual practices. For example, many of our Christian communities pray *to* the Holy Spirit, sans any biblical precedent for this practice; others render belief in the virginal conception a matter of central importance, in spite of the fact that it is not even mentioned in twenty-four or twenty-five of our New Testament books; and presumably all Christians affirm in some sense the triune character of God, though most agree that trinitarian language is *warranted* rather than *required* by Scripture.[23] In our view, the price we pay for the uncritical application of this assumption is high. Paul's teaching, for example, is unacceptable since he advocates human slavery (else why does he not critique this ancient social institution?). We must read against the text of the Lukan narrative, since the Third Evangelist operated with an antiwoman bias (else why does he not allow women leadership and/or teaching roles?). Such views as these, now current in American NT studies, illustrate the difficulty inherent in the what-it-meant/what-it-means paradigm, since they suggest the ease with which we read biblical texts against a cultural horizon more in line with our own rather than that of (in this case) Roman antiquity.[24] More telling, though, is how such readings assume that the primary or sole role of Scripture in theology is to provide theology's content. There is another way, to which we will turn in section 3 below.

## 2.2. An Inventory of Issues

Prior to moving on, however, it is important that we pause to take stock of the issues before us. Our analysis to this juncture has surfaced, however

23. So, e.g., Charles J. Scalise, *From Scripture to Theology: A Canonical Journey into Hermeneutics* (Downers Grove, Ill.: InterVarsity, 1996), pp. 89-109.

24. As Marshall Sahlins observes in a different context, "Each people knows their own kind of happiness: the culture that is the legacy of their ancestral tradition, transmitted in the distinctive concepts of their language, and adapted to their specific life conditions. It is by means of this tradition, endowed also with the morality of the community and the emotions of the family, that experience is organized, since people do not simply discover the word, they are taught it. They come to it not simply as cognition but as values" (*How "Natives" Think: About Captain Cook, for Example* [Chicago: University of Chicago Press, 1995], p. 12).

implicitly at times, a number of issues that invite reflection in the larger enterprise of integrating biblical and theological studies, including the following (in no particular order of importance):

- the ease with which biblical texts can be and are recruited to our own agenda, and thus the need for systems of self-criticism and mutual accountability;
- the formative and persuasive roles of Scripture;
- the inescapability of the multiple contexts that shape the significance of biblical texts — especially cultural, cotextual, and canonical — as well as the inescapability of our own contexts as those who read and appropriate Scripture;
- the reality of diversity within Scripture;
- the need for models of theological reflection that take seriously the generally narrative content of Scripture;
- the theological unity of Scripture, which takes its point of departure from the character and purpose of Yahweh, and which gives rise to the historical unity of Scripture as the narrative of that purpose being worked out in the cosmos;
- no particular method is guaranteed to enable the building of bridges between Scripture and theology, though priority must be allocated to the status of these texts (and not the histories to which they point) as Scripture; and
- the necessity of resolving the centuries-old complex of issues concerning the relationships between "history" and "theology," and thus between "history" and "text."

Hopefully, it will be obvious that uniting the two so long divided, Scripture and theology, is not a matter of introducing new "techniques." In fact, although some of the issues we have raised can be addressed cognitively, this is not true of all. Pressing, too, is the need for shifts in what we value and how we perceive — that is, transformations at the level of our dispositions and commitments.

## 3. Crossing the Great Divide: Constructing Interdisciplinarity

We have assumed that, today, systematic theology and biblical studies constitute two distinct disciplines, each determined by its own interests and methods. In truth, the picture is not so simple. Professionalism in this case is oriented toward and favors further specialization, with the result, for example, that the title "biblical studies" can be used less with a "discipline" in mind and more as a descriptive heading for another kind of interdisciplinary work involving discourse between the departments of Old Testament studies and New Testament studies.[25] The Bible itself is divided, then, and the same may be said, for example, of the segregation of theological studies and ethics in many curricula. The agenda of the larger project to which this chapter points must work therefore at multiple levels of interdisciplinarity.

In pointing the way forward, we may consider three possibilities: (1) interdisciplinarity as an import-export operation, (2) (genuine) models of interdisciplinarity, and (3) a more organic rapprochement to which we will refer here as theological hermeneutics.[26]

## 3.1. Interdisciplinarity as an Import-Export Operation

According to this proposal, the gap between biblical and theological studies is negotiated by borrowing the insights and/or categories of one discipline for use in another. In this instance the biblical scholar does not actually participate in theological studies but imports what has already been analyzed from one disciplinary system into another. Brevard Childs's own attempt to engage in "biblical theology," in his *Biblical Theology of the Old and New Testaments*, has often been critiqued in this light — both for al-

25. The problem is further exacerbated by references in Christian seminaries to "Hebrew Bible Studies," since this signals an even more significant break from the theologically substantial notion of the Christian Scriptures.

26. The following discussion is indebted to Julie Thompson Klein, *Interdisciplinarity: History, Theory, and Practice* (Detroit: Wayne State University Press, 1990); to conversations with Judith A. Berling, professor of History of Religions at the Graduate Theological Union, who currently convenes the "Interdisciplinary Studies" area of the doctoral program at the Graduate Theological Union; and to my participation from 1995 to 1997 in "Portraits of Human Nature," an interdisciplinary project (involving evolutionary and molecular biologists; cognitive, neuro-, and pastoral psychologists; and persons from philosophy, theological and ethics studies, and biblical studies) funded by the Templeton Foundation through the Lee Edward Travis Institute for Biopsychosocial Research (see *Whatever Happened to the Soul? Scientific and Theological Portraits of Human Nature*, ed. Warren S. Brown, Nancey Murphy, and H. Newton Maloney [Minneapolis: Augsburg Fortress, 1998]).

lowing the categories of "modern theology" to determine his articulation of "biblical theology" and for not pursuing the more constructive agenda of exploring the prophetic and pastoral concerns of Scripture in Childs's own context in the late twentieth-century United States.

This approach is not genuinely interdisciplinary, and is not without its problems. Chief among these are the possibility of distortion and misunderstanding of what is borrowed, the deployment of concepts or data devoid of their context, the sometimes outdated character of what is borrowed, and failure to recognize that what one finds helpful in another discipline may be regarded as idiosyncratic or with caution by those within that discipline.[27] These obstacles can be overcome with increased collaboration — either actual, between scholars of the different disciplines; or metaphorical, as the student of one discipline participates more fully in the discourse of the other — in which case one has moved more in the direction of our second category.

## 3.2. Models of Interdisciplinarity

Negotiating the potential interface of two or more disciplines raises a number of possibilities, the most pervasive of which is probably the model of *balanced disciplinary reference*. In this model two or more fields or disciplines are employed, with each weighted equally in usage. This model goes beyond import-and-export tendencies, as the student acquires more broad, basic grounding in the intellectual substance (methods, models, theories, data, concepts) of each discipline, and as the student holds herself and her work accountable to the standards of each discipline employed.

One example of this kind of work is represented by Hans Schwarz's recent study, *Christology.*[28] Working primarily as a historian, Schwarz examines how the historical Jesus has been depicted in Bible and theology from the first century to the end of the twentieth, showing how different environmental situations have given rise to a diversity of portraits of Jesus. The result is a study that, on the one hand, finds a home in biblical studies and in theological studies and, on the other, raises serious questions against those currently engaged in the quest of the historical Jesus who fail

27. See the helpful discussion in Klein, pp. 85-89.
28. Hans Schwarz, *Christology* (Grand Rapids: Eerdmans, 1998).

to take into account the many historical and theological contexts within which Jesus has (had) significance.

Another form of interdisciplinarity is suggested by recent work in the *hermeneutics of analogy,* represented well in the work of Stephen Farris.[29] Although Farris is concerned with the practice of preaching, his hermeneutical reflections are equally apropos the work of the constructive theologian. Working with the assumption that an important criterion for preaching is coherence with the biblical witness, he helpfully observes that mastery on this point is not guaranteed by quoting biblical texts and/or following closely the text of Scripture. Coherence requires both similarity to the biblical witness and dissimilarity, the latter arising from our attending to the passage of time and the changes that accompany it since a biblical text first served as a particular, concrete word from God. What is required, then, is exegesis of one's own world set in relation to exegesis of the biblical text, so that one can move from text to proclamation. Although he offers a series of steps in the process of "finding the analogies," two are of special significance — the most important question, What is God doing in this text? and the most difficult question, Is God doing something similar in our world? For Farris, then, the hermeneutics of analogy is worked out at various levels, with heavy doses of discernment along with exegetical adeptness.

Richard Hays's discussion of "hermeneutical appropriation" pursues a similar agenda. In his proposal for the use of the NT in ethics, he posits the necessity of "an integrative act of the imagination" in which we place "our community's life imaginatively within the world articulated by the texts."[30] For Hays, the NT is not a depository of "timeless truths" or transcultural "principles," with the result that its interpreters must discern "analogical relations" between the text and their community's life and commit themselves to (re)form their communal lives in ways that make more clearly visible those analogies. "Where faithful interpreters listen patiently to the Word of God in Scripture and discern fresh imaginative links between the biblical story and our time, we confess — always with reverent caution — that the Spirit is inspiring such readings."[31]

These and other forms of interdisciplinarity all assume to varying

29. Stephen Farris, *Preaching That Matters: The Bible and Our Lives* (Louisville: Westminster/John Knox, 1998).

30. Hays, p. 6; see further, pp. 207-312.

31. Hays, pp. 298, 299.

degrees the status quo in theological and biblical studies — that is, they assume the integrity of these two disciplines and, further, the legitimacy of that integrity. Accordingly, such models provide pressure to shape the character of the one discipline so as to ensure significant opportunity for overlap and discourse with the other.

## 3.3. Theological Hermeneutics

Conversely, the more organic approach of theological hermeneutics resists the status quo and asks for a reconceptualization not only of the relationship between these two academic disciplines, theology and Bible, but more fundamentally of their nature and status as discrete disciplines. This does not mean that the brand of theological hermeneutics we have in mind will dispense with (say) study of Scripture, but it does mean that the aims (and thus the interests, values, and procedures) of that study will be sharply reoriented.

How might Scripture function in theology and ethics? As we have observed, answers to this question generally revolve around cognitive concerns with the provision of theology's content or with solutions to ethical "problems" — an approach that severely curtails the normative role of Scripture in the theological enterprise and that runs against the grain of how Scripture actually communicates. Given the content of Scripture, and especially its overwhelmingly narrative character, other possibilities suggest themselves.

Consider, for example, the books of the NT. These are not themselves "the gospel," but are witnesses to the gospel; what is more, they witness to the gospel within specific sociohistorical contexts (e.g., 1 Corinthians, Philemon) or more generally within the ancient Mediterranean world (e.g., Luke-Acts, 1 Peter). None are transcultural per se, even if they have the capacity to speak beyond their contexts of origin, for they articulate within, and against, the cultural mores of the ancient Roman world and (some of) that world's subcultures. These NT materials, then, are not simply or primarily "sources" for theological data, but are themselves already exemplars of the theological task, of representing the implications and working out the ramifications of the gospel.

Their assumptions can invite paradigmatic status, to be sure. For example, they bear witness to such nonnegotiable presuppositions as the continuity of past, present, and future with respect to the Scriptures of Israel and the character of the people of God on account of the one, eternal purpose of God; or the new-age inaugurating advent of the Messiah, Jesus of Nazareth; and so on. Without overlooking the importance of such matters, we must also give appropriate weight to the status of Scripture for how its books, separately and together, while drawing on these paradigmatic presuppositions, model the instantiation of the good news in particular locales and with respect to historical particularities. Here, in the NT already, one finds "theology" both in its critical task of reflection on the practices and affirmations of the people of God to determine their credibility and faithfulness, and in its constructive task of reiteration, restatement, and interpretation of the good news vis-à-vis ever-developing horizons and challenges.

Hence, our task is not simply (and sometimes not at all) to read the content of the message of (say) 1 Peter into our world, as though we were (merely) to adopt its attitudes toward the state or its counsel regarding relations among husbands and wives. We are interested rather (and sometimes only) in inquiring into how 1 Peter itself engages in the task of theology and ethics. These texts, 1 Peter included, have as their objective the formation of communities that discern, embrace, serve, and propagate the character and purpose of Yahweh.

Such an approach is not ahistorical, but actually accords privilege to the formation of a "word on target" within particular social environments. In his *Communities of Discourse,* Wuthnow has drawn attention to what he calls "the problem of articulation" — how ideas and behaviors can both be shaped by their social situations and yet manage to disengage from and even challenge the very contexts in which they were generated. Wuthnow's reflections invite a series of related questions. How is 1 Peter situated in and reflective of a particular sociohistorical environment? What is its response — on the basis of the great story of God's activity in the world, including the world of 1 Peter — to that environment? When read against that mural, what does 1 Peter affirm, deny, reject, undermine, embrace? What strategies for articulating the good news and construing practical faithfulness are portended in those pages? How does this text participate in theological and ethical reflection? How does it invite its readers into the reflective and constructive task of discourse on the nature of faithful discipleship? On what authorities does the text of 1 Peter rest? What vision of the "new world" does it portend? In short, according to the theological-hermeneutical concerns sketched here, if we are concerned with the "theology of 1 Peter," we cannot be satisfied with "description"; rather, we must explore how this letter draws its readers into transformative discourse.

In the mid-1980s Jim McClendon insisted on an account of biblical authority that did not rest on particular affirmations of its explicit authority, but which assumed for Scripture what we may call a more implicit authority, perhaps even an invitation, to which he referred as "a hermeneutical motto": *"the present Christian community is the primitive community and the eschatological community."*[32] For McClendon, it would appear that the fundamental character of the division between the biblical world and our own, or between biblical studies and theological studies, is not *historical.* It is theological. It has to do with a theological vision, the effect of which is our willingness — whether we are biblical scholars or theologians or some other species — to inhabit Scripture's own story.

If we are to believe this story, to embrace it fully, to integrate it wholly into our own lives so that it shapes how we read our own lives in relation to God and to what God has created, the historical distance between Scripture and ourselves posited by the Enlightenment project must be collapsed. This is not to say that we become in this sense "precritical." We cannot go back. Razing the iron curtain cannot be for us a naive act, but, according to this model, involves intercultural discourse and theological formation within the community of God's people.

## 3.4. Finding a Home

The distance between biblical and theological studies is sufficiently wide and professionally valued, and is of such lengthy duration, that the task of building bridges of whatever sort requires a high level of commitment and intentionality. Whether one of the models we have sketched is adopted, or some other, activity aimed at "uniting the two so long divided" ought (1) to proceed by clearly identifying where and how one wants to locate the disciplinary interface, (2) to locate structures of accountability to ensure from a disciplinary perspective that one has met the burden of comprehension of the concerns of both fields, and (3) to locate means for probing the validity of one's work. Given the lay of the land at the turn of the twenty-first century, depending on how comprehensively one per-

---

32. James Wm. McClendon, Jr., *Systematic Theology,* vol. 1, *Ethics* (Nashville: Abingdon, 1986), p. 31.

ceives the nature of this interdisciplinarity and engages in it, one may well find those structures and means far more within ecclesial structures than in professional academic ones.

## 4. Conclusion

Those of us who live in late modernity or postmodernity, whichever label is preferred, face the task of mending much of what was torn apart in the service of the Enlightenment project. This is not because the sundering of things was in all cases erroneous; given the excesses of an earlier period, we may well appreciate past efforts at allowing Scripture to speak with greater clarity with its own voice, so to speak, rather than with the muted and/or embellished voices of officially sanctioned ecclesiastical interpretation. At the same time, as Christopher Seitz helpfully insists, "Having labored for two centuries to free the Bible from dogmatic overlay, Protestant and Catholic critics alike should 'concede victory.'"[33] Having worked to create the resultant gorge, how can we span the distance between Scripture and theology?

A primitivism that longs for the way we were before the onset of modernism is naive both in its veneration of premodern exegesis and in its optimism concerning our own capacity or willingness to depart from our own historical rootedness. We cannot go back, nor need we. What must be faced squarely by modernists such as ourselves, many of us weaned on the idolatry of technique, is that neither is the way forward marked by discovering or acquiring the right method, an exegetical technology, a meaning-making machine into which biblical texts can be dumped and the handle cranked so as to produce at the other end a theologically significant reading of Scripture. What is necessary on the part of students of Scripture is a conversion of sorts, from one set of interests and aims to another, and thus for formation and/or resocialization in communities for whom "meaning" is not reified as the sole property of the past or of the text itself, but belongs rather to the intercultural interplay of discourse within communities of interpretation for whom these biblical texts are invited to speak as Scripture.

---

33. Christopher R. Seitz, *Word without End: The Old Testament as Abiding Theological Witness* (Grand Rapids: Eerdmans, 1998), p. 15.

# CHAPTER 3

## Historical Criticism and Theological Hermeneutics of the New Testament

MAX TURNER

R ecent trends have tended to play down the significance of the "behind the text" questions that dominated biblical scholarship until the 1980s. This essay provisionally reassesses the question of the relevance of "behind the text" questions and approaches in theological readings of NT texts, and how these might be weighed in relation to "in the text" and "in front of the text" questions and approaches. Of course, how they might be weighted will depend very much on whether the reader is simply engaging in spiritual meditation, or whether she is preparing a sermon, or writing a book on "the message of Ephesians" or on "the biblical view" of healing. My principal concern is with the last kind of reading — that is, with the sort of publicly accountable explanations of biblical texts that seek to guide the church at large. As I understand it, the primary task of "theological hermeneutics" in the public domain is an ethically "responsible" reading of the text for its most critically transparent sense and significance.

That, of course, begs such questions as: What is a text? Is there a meaning in this text? How do we grasp and appropriate (or "create") the meaning(s)? and, How secure are the "results"? Some progress has been made in answering these questions, especially through the two major critical reviews of contemporary controversies offered by Thiselton and

Vanhoozer.[1] These provide a convincing critique of the extreme decon-struction/reader-response positions of Derrida and Fish, which collapse the two hermeneutical horizons (those of author/text and reader) into one and throw the reader into a bog of interpretive relativism. Author, text, and reader all have their different parts to play, albeit with differing roles in the variety of writings.

How, then, do we weigh "behind the text" issues with competing "in the text" and "in front of the text" questions? Again, we cannot answer that question in the abstract. Indeed, the attempt by some advocates of the New Criticism to do so (i.e., to treat all texts as though they were works of art, pieces of "literature") has very much been part of the current problem concerning the nature of interpretation. Discernment of authorial mean-ing, for example, may not be very important in reading C. S. Lewis's *Till We Have Faces*, but it is rather more important in reading his critical aca-demic works (cries of "incompetence!" would greet any misrepresentation of him), and it is all-important for his executors in interpreting his last will and testament. In Eco's terms, some texts are "closed," others more "open" to the interpreter. The different types of biblical texts suggest their own agendas and project their own "model readers."[2] This suggests that we should distinguish narrative works, letters, and the book of Revelation (or Apocalypse), and divide the questions of "meaning" accordingly. We shall raise most of the issues first in respect of historical criticism and theologi-cal interpretation of the letters, then deal more briefly with the narrative texts and the Apocalypse. Despite some recommendations to abandon the term "meaning" altogether, I propose to retain it with all its potential fuzz-iness and polysemy (sense, reference, implicature, illocution, significance, etc.), clarifying at different stages which sense(s) of "meaning" we are deal-ing with.

1. Anthony C. Thiselton, *New Horizons in Hermeneutics: The Theory and Practice of Transforming Biblical Reading* (London: HarperCollins; Grand Rapids: Zondervan, 1992); Kevin J. Vanhoozer, *Is There a Meaning in This Text? The Bible, the Reader, and the Morality of Literary Knowledge* (Grand Rapids: Zondervan, 1998).

2. Umberto Eco, *The Role of the Reader: Explorations in the Semiotics of Texts,* AS (Bloomington: Indiana University Press, 1979; London: Hutchinson, 1981), esp. pp. 4-8.

## 1. Historical Criticism and the Letters:
## "Behind the Text" and "In the Text" Issues

We can be clear that the "text" of (say) a Pauline letter is the record of what in semantic terms would be called an "utterance."

> The words "The cat is hungry" form a sentence that could be uttered in many different contexts, and so with quite different meanings — e.g., *(a)* as an excuse to break off conversation (= "Excuse me, I must feed Tibbi!"); *(b)* as a request to someone else to feed the cat (= "John, I am busy; could you please feed Tibbi!"); *(c)* as a warning to keep well clear, for the lion is hunting; or *(d)* as a laconic comment on the impatient twitching of the scourge in the master-at-arms' hand as a hapless sailor is being tied to the gratings for a flogging. Contextless sentences are thus nearly always ambiguous. "Utterance" is the speaking of sentences, which thus embeds the sentence(s) in the specific context of the speaker, the addressee, and what is being spoken about. Utterances are thus relatively determinate in meaning (even when the speaker is deliberately ambiguous). Spoken by a ranger (in a particular tone of voice) following the roar of a lion and spoken to an overconfident tourist armed with a camera, meaning *(c)* would be evoked.

Contra Derrida, for example, a letter is not a collection of polyvalent text "sentences," but the transcription of an extended speech event (often literally, because dictated and read out) in which cotextual and contextual factors provide determinate meaning (= fixed sense, referents, and conventional illocutionary force).[3] To suggest all texts *inevitably* become "detached" from the author and her meaning by time and distance (so Ricoeur) is least convincing with respect to letters. Ricoeur's point, of course, is that, in contrast to the dialogue situation, when the author is absent the reader has no direct access to authorial meaning; he has only "text." But the situation is not essentially different from that of listening to the broadcast of a recorded statement made at the White House earlier in the day. One may not be able to ask the president what he means, but one

---

3. The "cotext" of an utterance is the text before and/or after the utterance. The "context" of an utterance is the real and/or imagined world in which it takes place. The illocutionary force of an utterance is the action conventionally performed through the words said. In the examples of "The cat is hungry" above, *(b)* performs the illocutionary act of *requesting*, *(c)* that of *warning*, etc.

still listens attentively for the *president's* meaning (which may, of course, be subtle and ambiguous on sensitive issues).

It is virtually the universal experience of reading letters that one reads for the writer's intended meaning. Letters function as an intentional projection of the *presence* of the author, in dialogical *communication*, when she must otherwise be absent for some reason. Of all types of writings, letters are among those that most immediately address readers and perform intended actions toward them. Paul's letter to Philemon and his household performs the speech act of publicly *requesting* Philemon's reconciliation with his runaway slave Onesimus (this main "request" being backed by other speech acts taking the form of subtle reminders of obligation, promises to cover financial loss accrued, appeals to love and "fellowship," and so on). Author-less "texts" cannot "request," "promise," and so forth; only *people* can.

It is in this context of the performance of speech acts that we should understand the role of "authorial intention" in relation to the "meaning" of letter texts.[4] When we ask concerning authorial intention, we are not seeking information about Paul's unexpressed psychological motivations (interesting though they may be), which may or may not have been realized. We are inquiring rather about what *intentional acts* he has indeed *performed* in and through what he has actually said, understood within the linguistic/cultural world in which he uttered/inscribed the words of the letter.[5] Essentially the same applies to anonymous texts, such as Hebrews, or letters from authors we know little of, such as Jude.[6] The significances of Paul's letter to Philemon for a theological understanding of slavery, reconciliation, or the nature of Christian community may be plentiful, and po-

---

4. Among those invoking speech-act theory to relate text and author are Thiselton, *New Horizons in Hermeneutics;* Nicholas Wolterstorff, *Divine Discourse: Philosophical Reflections on the Claim That God Speaks* (Cambridge: Cambridge University Press, 1995); and Vanhoozer, *Is There a Meaning in This Text?* In practice, rigorous use of speech-act theory is usually limited to discussion of short utterances. Longer, more complex dialogical discourses used to effect results are usually referred to as "speech events." Cf. George Yule, *Pragmatics,* Oxford Introductions to Language Study (Oxford: Oxford University Press, 1996), pp. 56-58.

5. Here we find the answer to Derrida's complaint that one can never get "outside" language/writing into a world of determinate meaning. Such speech acts "count as" set meanings in the "game" of life (so Wittgenstein, Thiselton, Wolterstorff, and Vanhoozer).

6. See Thiselton, pp. 261-67. In Paul's case, however, what we know from earlier letters may throw light on later letters (and perhaps vice versa).

tentially upbuilding Christian rereadings may even be legion. But the speech acts that Paul actually inscribed or authorized provide the first horizon of meaning. Any fusion of the horizons that occurs without careful delineation of these speech acts may result rather in a *confusion* of horizons — i.e., a failure to locate the more determinate authorial "meaning" that is to be "interpreted" (and thus to become part of a broader "readers' meaning").

In emphasizing the interpreter's task as that of establishing the illocutionary acts actually performed by the writer through the text, we are evidently giving a central place to "in the text issues." All serious exegesis must start there, but it cannot stop there. We need to press on to "behind the text" issues, because (as the disciplines of discourse analysis and pragmatics have abundantly shown) *a large part of discourse meaning* (whether oral or written) *is not actually brought to verbal expression.*[7] All communication would grind to a halt if speakers or writers had to articulate every aspect of their meaning. As it is, speakers do not usually articulate those parts of their meaning that they can assume of their hearers (unless for some special rhetorical function).

> If my car is coughing and spluttering and I wind down the window and shout, "Excuse me, I'm right on empty!" to a sympathetic-looking passerby, she is unlikely to be paralyzed by the potential ambiguities of my utterance. She will probably call back something like, "There is a Shell just round the corner on the left," and continue her way. If one analyzes the "text" of these two utterances in the abstract, there is virtually no formal connection between them. One can imagine the fun a good deconstructionist could have. Yet the conversation would have been eminently successful. I would have been able to assume that the passerby shared with me a sufficient "presupposition pool" about petrol indicators and garages (or gas gauges and stations!) so as to make further explanation unnecessary. And we would both have kept Grice's maxims of cooperation (essentially, Be truthful! Be brief! Be relevant! Be clear!).[8] Intuitively working back from them, the passerby can be expected to understand not only the effective propositional content of my utterance

---

7. See Peter Cotterell and Max Turner, *Linguistics and Biblical Interpretation* (London: SPCK; Downers Grove, Ill.: InterVarsity, 1989), chaps. 2-3; more recently, John Lyons, *Linguistic Semantics* (Cambridge: Cambridge University Press, 1995), pt. 4; Yule, *Pragmatics*.

8. For critical discussion of Grice, see Lyons, *Linguistic Semantics*, chap. 9.

(= I am nearly out of petrol), but also (operating Grice's third maxim) that it constitutes an (indirect) illocutionary act of requesting instructions to the nearest garage. And on the basis of the same principles of cooperation, I would assume her reference to "a s/Shell" had nothing to do with the proximity of the seaside, but everything to do with a location where I might fill up. Similarly, Paul does not feel obliged to "explain" Onesimus's potential peril, the enormity of his own request, the irony of his apostleship from prison, and the obligations hinted at in Philemon 19b-22 against the background of the Greco-Roman social understanding of such matters, because he knows his readers share that knowledge.

If speakers and writers leave much unexpressed, that does not mean that it is the hearer/reader who "fills in the gaps" and thus *creates* meaning; rather it means that the speaker/writer assumes his addressees share with him a presupposition pool — which includes an encyclopedic understanding of the shared social world (including its linguistic and rhetorical conventions) as well as the specific "context" of the communication. It is engagement between the writer's utterance and the implied presupposition pool that establishes the (determinate, even if sometimes ambiguous) authorial discourse meaning. It is important, then, fully to recognize that — insofar as it seeks to elucidate the elements of the first-century presupposition pool directly evoked by a piece of NT discourse — study of so-called "behind the text issues" establishes a substantial part of the discourse meaning itself. The "text" of Philemon (like the text of any utterance) is simply the tip of the iceberg of Paul's discourse meaning. It would only be comprehensible to Philemon at all because he already knows the gospel and quite a lot about Paul and his associates before he receives the letter — and Paul assumes Philemon knows these things. So Paul can leave them as unarticulated elements of their shared presupposition pool. Significant misunderstanding occurs both when the reader/hearer fails to recognize the implied but unarticulated presuppositions and when she brings different presuppositions.

To recognize the importance of rightly identifying the presupposition pool, one only has to imagine Paul's letter being intercepted en route and read by a pagan innkeeper. The latter will have no idea who "Christ Jesus" (v. 1) is, or why Paul (who is he anyway?) is a prisoner for him (v. 1). He will assume this Paul has quite a large family of brothers and sisters (vv. 1, 2, 7, etc.), and probably that Paul himself and his coworkers (vv. 1, 24) are a band of (mercenary?) soldiers (cf. *sustratiōtēs,* v. 2), and that the *ekklēsia* in Philemon's house is perhaps some "assembly" for deciding strategy. He will have no idea what kind of "grace" and "peace" (vv. 3, 25) Paul might anticipate from his gods, nor how many gods he has — but Paul certainly worships at least the *two* first identified in verse 3. There is little point in pursuing the innkeeper's reading further. We are only spared his gross misunderstanding because — from our reading of *other* NT texts — we come to Philemon with some important elements of the presupposition pool shared between Paul and Philemon's household. (Indeed, the so-called "clarity" of Scripture rests largely on this: that the whole of Scripture is part of the presupposition pool we *potentially* engage in reading any single text.) But to say that is to recognize that the "text" (in the sense of the pure wording) of Philemon is only a *part* of the utterance/discourse meaning. And it is the unarticulated and/or allusive (i.e., "behind the text") components that are often *decisive* for correct understanding of the writer's speech act.

To avoid any possible confusion here, let us be quite clear that when pragmatics speaks of "presupposition pools," it is not driving us back to the hidden psychology of the author or reader, but to things that are known by speaker and hearer, writer and reader, because they are conventional to the society of the dialogue partners, or because they are situational elements shared by them. The content of "presupposition pools" is thus a matter of what is in the public context of a speaker's utterance, and so may be taken to count as part of the utterance meaning. This becomes clearest, perhaps, in indirect speech acts. If I utter the "text" "I *do* like the view of your back!" in a context where my son has come to stand in front of the television I was watching, my utterance meaning would situationally be recognized as ironic and conventionally taken to "count as" the request "Please move out of the way." In such instances, to play off any allegedly independent "textual meaning" against authorial discourse meaning (or utterance meaning) would generally be perceived as profound *mis*understanding. In normal discourse, text + relevant situational and conventional elements of the presupposition pool (including maxims of conversational cooperation) together generate the only "meaning" usually taken seriously.

Extensive study of "behind the text" issues will thus inevitably continue, and commentaries filled with scholars' findings will always be with us. Even the very "texts" of the letters — written in *koinē* Greek — are inaccessible for most readers without detailed text-critical and linguistic work. And because these texts represent dialogue with real addressees in particu-

lar circumstances, what some imagine as the "interpreter-neutral" preliminary act of translation needs to be informed by careful assessment of the
implied situation and presupposition pool, including the rhetorical conventions of epistolary writing. One has only to compare the very different
translations of, say, 1 Corinthians 7 to become aware how much "translation" depends on the understanding of the author's discourse meaning in
its historical context. Does 1 Corinthians 7:1b-2 affirm that it is good "not
to marry" (so NIV, GNB) or that it is well for a man "not to touch a
woman" (NRSV), and is this a euphemism for "not to have sexual relations" with one's wife (NIV mg)? Is this advice Paul's, or is he quoting a
Corinthian view, only in order to modify or even to demolish it? Similarly
in verses 25-27 and 36-38, the translations necessarily divide on the basis
of whether they think Paul is speaking about *(a)* how fathers should treat
their virgin *daughters* (the traditional translation), or *(b)* how Christian
husbands should keep their *wives* in celibacy (NEB), or *(c)* how believing
men should relate to their *fiancées* (NRSV).

A nuanced understanding of the "discourse meaning" (including the
propositional content and illocutionary force of each passage, and of the
letters as wholes) demands a wide-ranging and multidisciplined analysis
— or, as Vanhoozer puts it, a "thick description" of the text. Deciding such
"in the text" issues as lexical choice, syntax, text-linguistics (discourse
structuring), discourse coherence and cohesion, and "implicit" development of theme/argument may be the simplest part of the task, but they are
not necessarily the most revealing. We have only to remember the quite
radically different readings of (say) Galatians that result from construing it
against a "background" of Jewish legalism, Gnosticism, or covenantal
nomism to recognize the decisive significance of such issues. Similarly,
socio-anthropological insights may heighten our awareness of the "distance" between ourselves and first-century writers on the relation of the
individual to the community, the importance of honor/shame values, or
ways in which group belonging/exclusion were demarcated and supported, and these may greatly sharpen our perception of a variety of traits
explicit or implicit in the letters.[9] The study of ancient rhetorical conventions may tune our ears to powerful overtones we had not suspected.[10]

9. For good examples, see Philip F. Esler, *Galatians* (London: Routledge, 1998).
10. For the problems involved in applying rhetorical conventions (which belonged to three specialized kinds of public speech) to letters, see R. Dean Anderson,
Jr., *Ancient Rhetorical Theory and Paul,* CBET 18 (Kampen: Kok Pharos, 1996); Esler,
chap. 3.

Historical criticism also attempts to trace a "history" of Christian origins that provides a coherent framework within which to understand the contribution of each letter, and in the case of an author of multiple letters, the "mind of the writer" that may be discerned across the correspondence and allowed (in a controlled way) to "clarify" ambiguous contexts.[11] For all such reasons — but chiefly for the decisive relation of "behind the text" issues to what the text *meant,* understood as a deliberate communicative act — historical criticism (in the inclusive sense) will undoubtedly remain a close handmaid of exegesis.[12]

## 2. Theological Interpretation of the Letters and "In Front of the Text" Issues

Under this heading we need to comment on (1) the interpreter's role in the *description* of authorial meanings, (2) the implications of accepting the letters as "canon," and (3) the relation of both to the task of confessional systematic theology.

### 2.1. The Interpreter's Descriptive Role

Historical-critically informed exegesis has the appearance of great objectivity, especially at the level of morphology, syntax, and sentence. The fur-

11. This is not intrinsically more problematic than clarifying an obscure passage of Bultmann from his other writings, whether earlier or later, as long as due allowance is made for development. In principle it corresponds to requesting a speaker to clarify her own utterance.

12. John Christopher Thomas is suspicious that invoking historical criticism in the name of clarifying presupposition pools actually provides a Procrustean bed on which to distort the text (see his *The Devil, Disease, and Deliverance: Origins of Illness in New Testament Thought,* JPTSup 13 [Sheffield: Sheffield Academic Press, 1998], pp. 15-16). When badly practiced, no doubt it does, and often has. But the cure is not to abandon the search for such "behind the text" issues, but to do it more thoroughly, more critically, and in continuous dialogue with the text. In fact, the history of historical criticism suggests that as a corporate exercise it is self-correcting. Failure to clarify ambiguities in the text from *background* study will often simply mean that the interpreter "fills in the gaps" from his own, contemporary presupposition pools instead (see Max Turner, "Readings and Paradigms: A Response to John Christopher Thomas," *JPT* 12 [1998]: 23-38, esp. pp. 26-34).

ther we move up the semantic hierarchy (to paragraph meaning, "chapter" meaning, and letter meaning), however, the more subjective becomes the interpretive enterprise, and the more complex the meanings of "meaning." Wrede anticipated one might give a full account of Paul's "religion" that one could file confidently in the drawer of "objective historical criticism," but this would now almost certainly be regarded as naive optimism. As Schlatter pointed out, the categories one chose to analyze and how one related them dynamically to each other would inevitably reflect the scholar's own decisions as to what was important, and of what motivates what. Far from being "objective," Wrede's account of Paul's religion would thus bear the imprint of his own liberal Protestant, history-of-religions, anti-theological, and anti-ecclesial agenda. Similar points had been made by Schleiermacher earlier, and were to be made by Bultmann later.[13] Since Gadamer, the essentially *dialogical* nature of interpretation is generally acknowledged. The problems of deciding the "text" of 1 Corinthians 7, alluded to earlier, are those of deciding which of a set of possible senses is justified by a careful mirror-reading and exegesis of the whole letter, rather than of the chapter in isolation. This in turn involves a set of intuitive explorations and exegetical confirmations/disconfirmations that together make up the hermeneutical spiral. Our initial hypotheses about 1 Corinthians are inevitably connected with our preunderstanding of Paul and the issues he addresses, and this preunderstanding involves a matrix of confessional tradition, awareness of the state of NT scholarship, and so forth. Although commitment to the significance of authorial discourse meaning may suggest that there is a determinate meaning to discover, critical self-awareness, the existence of multiple competing interpretations of the letter, and the hermeneutics of suspicion all remind us how difficult it is to recover.

When we turn to the significance of 1 Corinthians (in parts and whole) within a construal of Paul's theology or religion, we meet a host of further complications. One need only call to mind the history of attempts to locate the "center" of Paul's thought over against its "periphery." Or again, the intricacy of the task is well brought out by a recent attempt to define Paul's theology in terms of a series of dialogues between Paul's Judaism (and his Greco-Roman past), his understanding of the Christ event,

---

13. See Edgar V. McKnight, "Presuppositions in New Testament Study," in *Hearing the New Testament: Strategies for Interpretation,* ed. Joel B. Green (Grand Rapids: Eerdmans, 1995), pp. 278-300.

and the traditional kerygma brought about through the Damascus road experience on the one hand, and on the other, the contingent argumentation and development of his thought in specific pastoral and polemical contexts.[14] To take due note of all this risks being all but overwhelmed by the complexity involved in speaking of the apostle's "meaning" in 1 Corinthians, when "meaning" now has more to do with potential significance of what has been said for some more general system of thought than merely "what has been said." This has led some to despair. It need not, however. While we may never be able to give an exhaustive account, we can still recognize false interpretations, and we can rank good ones while recognizing their limitations and provisional status.

## 2.2. The Significance of Canonization

The acceptance of the letters into the canon is perhaps the most significant "in front of the text" issue. On the one hand it is to adopt a specifically confessional stance, and on the other it is to pluck those who penned the letters out of the interpretational limelight and to sit them at a roundtable with other biblical authors. Neither step need require abandoning critical integrity,[15] providing we remember we are talking about a discussion table (in Caird's terms, an "apostolic conference")[16] and not Procrustes' preferred furniture. We must hear each writer give his distinctive and full-blooded witness, yet also make due allowance for undergirding unities (so often played down by historical criticism) and for the canonical principle expressed, e.g., in Paul's affirmations of the *one* gospel shared with the other apostles (Gal. 2; 1 Cor. 15:5, 11, etc.) over against "false" believers and their gospels.[17]

14. James D. G. Dunn, *The Theology of Paul the Apostle* (Grand Rapids: Eerdmans, 1998), chaps. 1, 9.

15. See Max Turner, *The Holy Spirit and Spiritual Gifts: Then and Now* (Carlisle: Paternoster, 1996), chap. 9; Markus Bockmuehl, "Humpty Dumpty on New Testament Theology," *Theology* 101 (1998): 330-38.

16. G. B. Caird, *New Testament Theology,* ed. L. D. Hurst (Oxford: Clarendon, 1994), chap. 1.

17. See I. Howard Marshall, *Jesus the Saviour: Studies in New Testament Theology* (London: SPCK; Downers Grove, Ill.: InterVarsity, 1990), chap. 2; Robert W. Wall and Eugene E. Lemcio, *The New Testament as Canon: A Reader in Canonical Criticism,* JSNTSup 76 (Sheffield: Sheffield Academic Press, 1992), chaps. 8-10.

But how does a canonical perspective relate to "behind the text" concerns discussed above? For a growing number of interpreters, it means that we may safely marginalize the question of authorial discourse meaning. It is not *Paul's* meaning of 1 Corinthians that is significant when we identify the letter as the church's Scripture (so, e.g., Stanley Hauerwas).[18] Either we are saying it is the *divine* voice addressing us through it or the *church's* meaning in accepting this letter (with the rest of the OT and NT) that is significant (and many would say both). Here we must tread cautiously.

1. The canonization process did not clearly marginalize the human authors. Rather the opposite. Had any work been recognized as *not* written by an apostle (or coworker, in the case of Mark and Luke, or brother of the Lord in the case of James and Jude), it would not have gained entry.[19] Moreover, it is hard to believe that 2 and 3 John (say) were eventually accepted as canon for any other reason than that they were thought to have been written by the apostle John (or by the elder John, a close disciple). This is because their contents hardly give these letters some broader "apostolicity of worth," and the history of interpretation shows they have had little influence on the life of the church. Nor may we argue that the canonizing process necessarily marginalized the authorial meaning on the grounds that the letters were now being read by other than the original addressees. The Catholic Epistles were already addressed to a very broad range of Christian communities (cf. 1 Pet. 1:1; James 1:1) or even all such communities (2 Pet. 1:1 and Jude 1), and Paul could anticipate that the letter he had written to Laodicea would be of benefit to the Colossians too, and vice versa (Col. 4:16; even letters such as Romans, Galatians, and the Corinthian correspondence addressed different parties at various points, leaving the others "to listen in"). Although the Colossians' reading of the letter to the Laodiceans would inevitably involve a slightly different interpretive strategy from their reading of the letter addressed to themselves, there is no reason to think their reading of it bracketed out questions of authorial meaning and other background issues.

2. On any view that the letters, appropriated as canon, represent *divine* discourse, we would need to ask about the relationship between God's speaking and (say) Paul's. The major discussion of this issue by Wolterstorff does not suggest any marginalization of authorial discourse

18. For discussion of Hauerwas's position, see Vanhoozer, p. 411.
19. It is also widely agreed that any work that had been *known* to be pseudonymous would almost certainly have been excluded.

meaning. Wolterstorff hesitates over whether the Pauline letters should be regarded as occasions of "representation" of God by an appointed pro- phetic messenger/ambassador, or whether the model of "appropriation" would not be better (God "identifies" with the position spoken by Paul, but less directly — as I might identify my position by saying, "I agree with what Jane and Gregory said"). Either way, however, there is no reason to believe that to speak of divine discourse implies that God abstracted Paul's "text" from his context-embedded discourse meanings in such a way that we can cheerfully refill his words with substantially different meanings, or limit the text's meaning to such as might be provided by canonical cotexts alone.[20] Had Paul written interpreter-open psalms/proverbs/wisdom- speech, designed for all to use in different ways, we could readily make a break with whatever he meant in the context in which he first coined such utterances. But divine appropriation of writings of the *letter* genre itself implies that the context-embedded issues remain relevant to discourse meaning (for that is the very nature of letters).

3. That the Pauline "contextual" meanings are pivotal for canonical/ contemporary meaning can be approached another way. Let us propose that a reader for some reason decides that 1 Corinthians 7:25-38 should be taken as a commendation of asexual platonic marriage (the view attrib- uted to Paul by NEB). If it could be demonstrated to him exegetically that such a view was actually contrary to Paul's own intended meaning — that it was indeed something he intended to correct — would we not expect the reader to relinquish the interpretation?[21] In short, while Paul's discourse

---

20. Wolterstorff, esp. chaps. 3, 11, 12.

21. It is a different case when Christians refuse to attribute to God himself the literal authorial meaning of Ps. 137:8-9, and so treat it in canonical context as a meta- phor cluster expressing God's opposition to whatever opposes his reign. In this case of what Wolterstorff calls "appropriated" (= oblique) divine discourse, conviction that the God revealed in Christ could not express the literal wish of the psalmist (without an inconsistency incompatible with divinity) leads to a distinction between authorial discourse meaning and "canonical" meaning. Similarly, when Paul says, "I, Paul, an apostle of Jesus Christ . . . ," such affirmations are not appropriated directly in "divine discourse"; indeed, Wolterstorff maintains that "it will typically be the case that not ev- erything said by the agent of the mediating discourse is also said by the agent of the mediated discourse" (p. 240; cf. John Goldingay, *Models for Scripture* [Carlisle: Pater- noster; Grand Rapids: Eerdmans, 1994], chap. 18). But Wolterstorff insists that any the- ology of divine "appropriation" of human discourse will necessarily start from the as- sumption of concurrence between authorial and divine meaning, and only modify it when there are strong reasons for so doing (see chaps. 11-13).

meaning may be *less* than the divine/canonical meaning, it is arguably still a fundamentally relevant part of it.

In sum, we may agree with Stephen Fowl that we cannot simply equate authorial meaning with "the whole and determinate meaning of the text" (a phrase itself to which he would strongly object);[22] canonical cotext (or "dialogue partners") and present-day context highlight important aspects of "meaning" (in different senses) of a biblical text. We can nevertheless affirm *(a)* that the authorial discourse meaning (as defined above) of the NT letters is a relatively "determinate" meaning; *(b)* given the reverence accorded to the apostolic circle (within and outside Scripture), their discourse meanings might be expected to be of greater interest/significance for the church than (say) Augustine's or Calvin's (let alone Joe Bloggs's) readings; and *(c)* as other claimed "meanings" of text are in varying degrees moot, it would not be "merely arbitrary" to use the apostolic authors' meanings as a benchmark against which to test twentieth- and twenty-first-century meanings, perhaps even as the most important single benchmark.[23]

## 2.3. Authorial Meaning, Canonical Meaning, and Theology

When we bring the biblical writers to the roundtable, we also come there *ourselves* — to listen in and to learn. A number of aspects of this invite brief clarification.

1. We come to the table as Lutherans, Catholics, Baptists, Pentecostals, and more. Our creeds, confessions, traditions, heroes, and hymns have all provided us with different frameworks from which to read the letters, and inevitably lead us to prioritize different aspects of the theology and ethics of the writings. That this can enable creative and penetrating insight can be seen from, e.g., the Lutheran expositions of Paul by Bultmann and his students. Indeed, we should rather expect that a committed Pentecostal

22. Stephen E. Fowl, *Engaging Scripture: A Model for Theological Interpretation* (Oxford: Blackwell, 1988), chaps. 1-2.

23. See Esler, pp. 24-25. Commenting on Morgan's widely quoted epigram that "texts, like dead men and women, have no rights . . . it is the interests . . . of interpreters that are decisive . . . ," Esler retorts, "While our deceased parents certainly have no rights, who would deny that we have a duty to honour their memory?" Accordingly, there is a case that we should honor our "ancestors in the faith" who composed the NT writings and who received them.

NT scholar might provide a more nuanced pneumatology of the letters than his noncharismatic colleague, all other things (critical powers, mastery of the literature, etc.) being equal. But the same commitments may also lead to eisegesis, selective blindness, and dubious ranking of elements as central or peripheral. So it is hardly surprising that Lutheran interpreters tend to give a more commanding position to "justification by faith alone" in theology and ethics than would their Wesleyan-Holiness colleagues, and their respective views of sanctification differ accordingly. Similarly, a Calvinist's "clear" texts on election and predestination tend to be regarded as "difficult" or "obscure" texts by Methodists and Pentecostals.[24] This does not mean, however, that we are locked up in a tight hermeneutical circle, provided that we both listen and talk *at the table.* It is largely introspective and isolated denominations/groupings that are in that dangerous confinement, and who risk betraying the very principle of the table.

2. We return time and again to the canonical writings. This would itself be strange if all we were doing was an endless and narcissistic reading back of ourselves (and our traditions) into the text. Rather, it has been the church's experience that God has used the letters (and other parts of Scripture) dramatically and innovatively at the beginnings of great new movements (the Reformation, the Radical Reformation, Pentecostalism, etc.), breaking down old (mis)understandings, "shedding new light" on his word, and challenging the church. Such would not be anticipated by a purely reader-response account of hermeneutics (however true may be the claim that changing social factors breed new readings). But believers come to the letters in the hope of learning from them, and experiencing them as the locus of transformative relational grace. That is, the churches have largely understood the letters (and the Bible more generally) as a form of divine discourse that affects (even subverts) and redirects the understanding and the will of the attentive reader.[25] To say that churches come to the letters/Bible to learn (and not merely to remember) is also to say that new readings are not merely different readings, but may constitute advances in reading. Luther's reading of Romans and Galatians was an advance on contemporary ecclesial readings, partly because it afforded greater coherence to central traits of Paul's discourse. That Catholic exegesis has conceded important aspects of Luther's reading of Paul is a measure of the

---

24. See Thiselton, pp. 237-47.

25. See Wolterstorff, *Divine Discourse;* Thiselton, chap. 14; Vanhoozer, pt. II.

critical "advance" involved. Similarly, much of the wider church has come to acknowledge important aspects of Pentecostal/charismatic readings of NT spirituality. But to say so suggests there is a stable discourse meaning to be discovered, of which one reading may provide a more convincing account than another.

3. Protestant emphasis on personal faith and the centrality of the Bible has brokered many individualistic and divisive readings. The confession of the diverse letters and other writings as together one canon of Scripture embodies the ecumenical principle of listening to and learning from other partners at the conference table. This applies both to listening to the full range of the biblical witnesses and to giving a critical but patient hearing to their modern disciples. The danger of many attempts to locate a canon within the canon becomes evident in this context. The idea that one might tease out a general principle (whether salvation history, justification by faith, Christ's lordship, liberation, or some other) or a restricted set of texts to guide readers to the heart of the Scriptures may be sound (though most versions of the "grand vision" turn out to be perilously incomplete). If it becomes a way of silencing other participants at the apostolic conference, however, it is in breach of the canonical principle itself. Not just the voice of the undisputed Paulines, for example, but also the voices of the so-called deutero-Paulines[26] and of the Catholic Epistles have a claim to be fully heard — especially, perhaps, where their voices seem to differ from that of the undisputed Paulines. The principle of the table may also be imperiled by selective methods of reading, which do not command a broad consensus and do not necessarily relate to the usually accepted "literal" meaning of the writings — e.g., by "Pentecostal" and "charismatic" hermeneutics (which are in truth only variations of the "spiritual readings" found more broadly in various brands of pietism).[27]

---

26. The historical-critical exegesis of a suspected pseudonymous letter is interestingly complicated, for the illocutions performed by the real author (effectively a commendation of what an implied author might be *imagined* to say to a projected world) are not straightforwardly those of the implied author. From a canon-critical perspective, however, the inclusion of Ephesians and the Pastorals with the other Paulines begs reading Ephesians as "from Paul." Cf. the discussion by Stanley E. Porter and Kent D. Clarke, "Canonical-Critical Perspective and the Relationship of Colossians and Ephesians," *Bib* 78 (1997): 57-86 (esp. pp. 69-73).

27. For Pentecostal hermeneutics, see the essay by John Christopher Thomas in this volume (below, chap. 6). Such communitarian and experience-based interpretation usually keeps much closer to the literal meaning of Scripture than the kind of

4. We come to the canonical table with our questions about what it means to confess Christ and live for him in our day. As people informed by twentieth-century understandings of the cosmos and humanity, as well as by the history of Christian thought, we naturally have questions both about matters the letters talk of (such as cosmic powers, anthropology, preexistence and divine Christologies, the morality of atonement, the relation of the church to the "Old Testament" and the consequent status of Judaism, and the ethics of authority and the use of force) and about matters they do not — or talk of only so obliquely, and from such a different context, that what is said appears inadequate (such as cosmology, trinitarian relations, feminism, contraception, and monogamous homosexuality). Scholars have queued up since Gabler to tell NT specialists that their task is purely descriptive (so, especially, Wrede, Räisänen, and even Balla), but there is now also a growing recognition that NT scholars need not abandon all hope of taking theological responsibility for their findings.[28]

## 3. History, Historical Criticism, and the Theological Hermeneutics of New Testament Narrative Texts

We have argued above that in the interpretation of letters — at least of genuine letters — issues of authorial discourse meaning are of fundamental relevance to Christian interpretation. As Thiselton tartly observes, one can read them in other ways, just as one can use a chisel as a screwdriver. But a craftsman would not.[29] There is an ethics of reading letters (wills, ac-

---

charismatic exegesis proposed by Mark Stibbe, "This Is That: Some Thoughts Concerning Charismatic Hermeneutics," *Anvil* 15 (1998): 181-93 (cf. John Lyons, "The Fourth Wave and the Approaching Millennium: Some Problems with Charismatic Hermeneutics," *Anvil* 15 [1998]: 169-80). Stibbe, however, does not regard such prophetic reader-response interpretation as a substitute for more conventional exegesis.

28. Cf. A. K. M. Adams, *Making Sense of New Testament Theology: "Modern" Problems and Prospects* (Macon, Ga.: Mercer University Press, 1995); James D. G. Dunn and James P. Mackey, *New Testament Theology in Dialogue* (London: SPCK; Grand Rapids: Eerdmans, 1987); Hans Hübner, *Biblische Theologie des Neuen Testaments,* 3 vols. (Göttingen: Vandenhoeck & Ruprecht, 1990-95); Peter Stuhlmacher, *Vom Verstehen des Neuen Testaments: Eine Hermeneutik* (Göttingen: Vandenhoeck & Ruprecht, 1979); Werner G. Jeanrond, "After Hermeneutics: The Relationship between Theology and Biblical Studies," in *The Open Text: New Directions for Biblical Studies?* ed. Francis Watson (London: SCM, 1993), pp. 85-102; et al.

29. Thiselton, p. 562.

ademic works, etc.) that cannot dismiss the author.[30] But does the same apply to the writers of the Gospels and the Acts of the Apostles? With the exception of allusive references to the "beloved disciple" in the Fourth Gospel, these works are all but anonymous. Even if the traditions about their authorships were substantially trustworthy, the author does not become a "real presence," dialoguing with the reader. Rather he tells a story as a form of witness to Christ, and launches it into the church.

For the postliberals Frei and Lindbeck, the significant issues are thus now the "in the text" and "in front of the text" ones. Rejecting both the old liberal foundationalist claims and their confidence in "objective" historical criticism, Frei has spoken of "the eclipse of biblical narrative."[31] By this Frei and other postmodern liberals mean four things: (1) the attempt to ground religion in historically objective "facts" or in universal realities/truths has led to the analytical approach of historical criticism that has stifled the witness and authority of the canonical narratives; (2) the canonical witnesses together create a narrative "world" in which we (as Christians) are called to live, and which we should use to interpret our world (not the other way around, as in modernism); (3) the canonical witness and the ongoing traditions/confessions of the church are intrasystemically true and binding for us, who read from the Christian tradition of the church, and no objectivizing approach can turn them into more universal truths; (4) the canonical witnesses and the church's confessions are mutually interpretive — so, e.g., it is not Luke's meaning of Luke-Acts that is important, but what the church has come to take it to mean (by accepting it into the canon and its tradition).[32]

While we may applaud the concern to allow Scripture to have its due authority, and its narrative (sharpened by literary approaches) to shape

---

30. On the ethics of reading, see Thiselton, *New Horizons in Hermeneutics;* Werner G. Jeanrond, *Theological Hermeneutics* (London: Macmillan, 1991); and Vanhoozer, esp. chap. 7.

31. Hans W. Frei, *The Eclipse of Biblical Narrative* (New Haven: Yale University Press, 1974).

32. See, e.g., Timothy R. Phillips and Dennis L. Okholm, eds., *The Nature of Confession* (Downers Grove, Ill.: InterVarsity, 1996), chaps. 2, 9. Frei refers to the Gospel accounts as "realistic narrativity," and as containing some historical reference. But for him, they consist primarily not in report but in "history-*like*" portraits of the indispensable savior, which conflate the earthly Jesus and the risen Lord. Frei remains very unclear about the relation of the individual accounts to events in Palestine — i.e., of the Gospel utterances to things-in-the-world to which they appear to refer.

our lives, there are problems with the postliberal approach and its purely confessional reading.

1. The author may be more distant to the reader, but redaction, composition, and narrative criticism have taught us that this certainly does not mean a total absence of the author. It is the author who has selected, shaped, and interpreted the tradition he offers; it is he who has provided the plot, characters, and the narrative insights and asides. It is he who also, no doubt, has published his account, with the intention of being read and thus influencing widely scattered communities.[33] As with the letters, the composition has thus the properties of an utterance, with definable noetic content and illocutionary force.[34] From Luke 1:1-4 (cf. Acts 1:1-2) and John 20:30-31 we even hear the writers' intended perlocutions. And again, as with the letters, the Gospel writers' discourses are replete with allusions and engage culturally determinate presupposition pools. This suggests that to establish the discourse meaning of the parts of Luke-Acts, or of the whole taken as a communicative act, the interpreter needs not only a keen eye for the text's "implied reader" but will also need to pay careful attention to "behind the text" issues that form the most probable joint presupposition pool. Indeed, one only has to note some of the hair-raising interpretations of the Sermon on the Mount/Plain to recognize the problems raised by detaching the texts of these discourses from the essentially Jewish "background" of their rhetorical conventions and the more specifically Palestinian context of Jesus' ministry and of the earliest communities. Similarly, the history of interpretation (scholarly and otherwise) suggests that those who attempt to discern, say, Luke's teaching on reception of the Spirit and conversion-initiation in so ambiguous a narrative as Acts are liable simply to fill in Luke's many "gaps" with the content of their own ecclesial paradigm — whether this be sacramentalist, confirmationist, Pentecostal, or whatever.[35] The postliberal agenda provides no basis for resolving disagreements arising from different readings. Attention to the presupposition pool shared between author and implied reader (in Luke's case, someone sufficiently conversant with Jewish Scriptures and hopes to catch the complex of apocalyptic/Isaianic new exodus allusions) may at

---

33. Cf. the thesis of Richard Bauckham, ed., *The Gospels for All Christians: Rethinking the Gospel Audiences* (Edinburgh: T. & T. Clark; Grand Rapids: Eerdmans, 1998), chaps. 1, 4, 5.

34. So Wolterstorff, chap. 14.

35. Cf. Turner, "Readings and Paradigms," pp. 29-31.

least be expected to highlight more probable interpretations of Luke's discourse meaning.[36]

2. The lack of theological interest in historical issues in the postmodern, postliberal confessional agenda reminds us too closely of Bultmann's kerygmatic emphasis. Believers today cannot remain faithful to the biblical narrative by detaching it from all historical questions and from more universal truth claims. The NT narratives (including those embedded in the letters and Apocalypse) themselves point to a proclamation concerning the one God's ultimate revelation in the person and work of Jesus of Nazareth, crucified under Pontius Pilate, and resurrected from the dead. In addition, they tell a story of a mission to call people away from alternative "confessions," be they Jewish or pagan, which are quite unequivocally branded as false ways and idolatries in the new light of the Christ event. To be true to these NT stories, the confessing community will certainly need to ensure that its life is stamped by them. It cannot afford simply to deliver the Gospels and Acts to historical criticism and then be content to believe and live merely on the basis of the tattered remnant left over as its "assured results." At the same time, the Gospels and Acts belong to a biographical and historical genre of witnessing tradition.[37] If they are to perform their function of witness in the public arena, their truth claims need to be assessed. This certainly does not require the fundamentalist insistence on interpretation-neutral, one-to-one correspondence between narrative detail and reality: ancient

---

36. This raises interesting questions about how Gentile believers might be expected to grasp the nuances of Luke-Acts. The probable answer is that most Christian communities contained Jews and God-fearers who would contribute to the interpretive reading.

37. For the genre, see now Richard Burridge, "About People, by People, for People: Gospel Genre and Audiences," in *The Gospels for All Christians*, pp. 113-45. For the category "witnessing tradition" and its implications for the varying relations between narrative account and factual history, see Goldingay, pt. 1. For the Gospels as "*narrated* history" (with the implications of fictive plot, etc.), see, e.g., Francis Watson, *Text and Truth: Redefining Biblical Theology* (Edinburgh: T. & T. Clark; Grand Rapids: Eerdmans, 1997), chap. 1. Against the view that the Gospels should be compared with historical novels and other more generally fictional genres, see Wolterstorff, chap. 14. Against the early redaction-critical view that the Gospels are primarily theological tracts, using and editing the (generally unhistorical) tradition of Jesus circulating in the churches to address the theological interests of individual churches or related groups thereof, see Francis Watson, "Toward a Literal Reading of the Gospels," in *The Gospels for All Christians*, pp. 195-217.

historical/biographical writings did not work that way.[38] As even Bultmann's own students recognized, however, there needs to be an adequate bridge between the historical Jesus and the Christ of faith: hence the so-called "second quest" of the historical Jesus.

3. Believers who confess that "the Word became flesh" can hardly lack interest in what it was about the whole life and ministry of Jesus which led to his rejection and crucifixion, and why it was that the earliest, predominantly Jewish church, which claimed him to be the fulfillment of all OT hope, separated from Judaism. These are the questions that dominate the so-called "third quest" of the historical Jesus, and its chief method is the critical realism of *(inter alios)* Ben F. Meyer and N. T. Wright.[39] This is a brand of "historical criticism" which is (in Stuhlmacher's terms) "open to transcendence," and it is one seeking the inner coherence of Jesus' ministry in the aims/intentions revealed by his words and actions in the real social, political, and religious context of the Palestine of his day. It is undoubtedly a demanding quest, but unless we attempt it we risk not really understanding Jesus' central agendas, and so being less able authentically to interpret his story for our day and into our lives. People who think they can understand Jesus' words and acts, stripped of the historical Jewish context in which he uttered and performed them, condemn themselves to misunderstand him at least as comprehensively as do those who suppress major emphases of the Gospel narratives (let alone of the church's confessions) in the name of the earlier rationalistic and naively objectivizing kinds of historical criticism.

4. The canonical process asserted the essentially apostolic origin of the Gospels (i.e., that they derived from the circle of apostles and their coworkers), and this was undoubtedly seen as assurance not merely of their theological significance but also of the essential trustworthiness of their historical portraits of Jesus (cf. Luke 1:1-4; John 21:24).

In sum, if Frei was right in 1974 to complain about the eclipse of the narrative by historical criticism, Watson may have had justification in 1997 to complain about the eclipse of history by at least some "narrative" approaches.[40] Fortunately, there are clear signs that literary approaches are

---

38. See Goldingay, pt. 1, esp. chap. 5.

39. See Ben F. Meyer, *Critical Realism and the New Testament*, PTMS 17 (Allison Park, Pa.: Pickwick, 1989); Meyer, *The Aims of Jesus* (London: SCM, 1979); N. T. Wright, *Christian Origins and the Question of God*, vol. 2, *Jesus and the Victory of God* (London: SPCK; Minneapolis: Fortress, 1996).

40. Watson, *Text and Truth*, chap. 1.

also being used to complement historical and redaction-critical interests rather than to supplant them.[41]

Many other issues pertinent to our title have been discussed, at least in principle, in dealing with the letters. Brief mention, however, may be made of four matters. First, on discerning the authorial discourse "meaning" of the Gospels and Acts, it is important to remember that the authors' meaning is far more open-ended than in the letters. It is telling, for example, that Wolterstorff largely restricts his long discussion of the "illocutionary stance" of biblical narratives to an insistence that (Job and Jonah excepted) they involve statements made in the assertive mood, about real worlds, rather than invitations to imagine projected worlds. Whereas the authorial meaning(s) in letters may be read off their many and varied speech acts, and the complex relation between them, the narratives merely "assert" a described world, ostensibly, e.g., to provide assurance (Luke 1:1-4) or to encourage belief (John 20:30-31). Of course, there is far more to it than that. To "assert" that Jesus taught the content of the Sermon on the Mount, with all its sharp challenges and warnings, in a broader cotext where the speaker is revealed as the Son of God who gives the great commission of Matthew 28:19-20, is to perform an indirect speech act (or rather, speech event) exhorting discipleship. To "tell" the story of Jesus' compassion for the "poor" (outsiders, the sick, the demonized, etc.), and to put that in the cotext of *(a)* invitations to disciples to lay down their lives in service and *(b)* an extensive passion narrative and resurrection vindication/commission accounts, is to commend the world described to the reader, and to invite her to step into it. But the point remains that the speech acts (other than of assertion) remain indirect, and often so subtle as to be ambiguous. That need not lead to despair, however, over our capacity to recover the main features of the discourse meaning. This is easiest in John, but it is possible in Matthew, Mark, and Luke too. It can hardly be doubted that the generation of major commentaries from the 1960s onward have together (i.e., in mutually correcting and complementing combination) made significant advances in clarifying authorial discourse meaning.

Second, literary-critical approaches will highlight features of plot,

41. See, e.g., the careful blend of narrative-, historical-, and redaction-critical approaches in David D. Kupp, *Matthew's Emmanuel: Divine Presence and God's People in the First Gospel*, SNTSMS 90 (Cambridge: Cambridge University Press, 1996), and note his methodological discussion of these issues in chap. 1; cf. Joel B. Green, *The Gospel of Luke*, NICNT (Grand Rapids: Eerdmans, 1997), pp. 11-20; John R. Donahue, "The Literary Turn and New Testament Theology: Detour or New Direction?" *JR* 76 (1996): 250-75.

parallels, characterization, thematic "connections," etc., that the author intended, but also (almost inevitably) some or many of which the writer would *not* have been conscious. Such occasions might readily be treated as a type of *sensus plenior* and/or as subconscious workings of the writer's major conscious intentions. They are in any case not problematic for a high view of authorial discourse meaning.

Third, on the relation of the four Gospels, much radical redaction criticism has highlighted the apparent differences between the Gospels in such crucial matters as eschatology, the Law, miracles, Christology, relation to the Gentiles, and so on. It has explained these differences primarily in terms of dialogues between the Evangelists and the distinct theological needs of their particular communities. Such an approach treats the Gospels as theological tracts, where the account of Jesus and his teaching is a subtle allegory of the church's situation. This now seems improbable on purely historical and exegetical grounds.[42] Whether or not that is so, the canonical process certainly subverts such an analysis. The Gospels and Acts are placed before the letters, as the account of the origins of the church. And Luke is separated from Acts and placed with Matthew, Mark, and John as the fourfold Gospel of Jesus, who bridges the Testaments, and whose ministry launches the church. Unruffled by minor disagreements, the church read the Gospels as complementary portraits of their Lord and Master. A canonical perspective will invite the interpreter to spend as much time investigating the unity of the Gospels as has so far been spent on their diversity, and perhaps to give the former the more weight.

Fourth, on relating NT narrative to systematic theology today, narrative is not at first sight a promising resource for systematic theology, even if the Gospels and Acts are much more theologically oriented than, say, Ruth and Esther. But all biblical narratives display a "world" in a way that comments on facets of it, whether on the nature of humanity, the immanence/transcendence of God, the place of "religion" in society, the ethical expectations appropriate of a "people of God," or whatever. And these are all the subject of systematic theology, if the latter is understood sufficiently comprehensively to include practical and applied theology, and the in-depth study of particular aspects of theological discourse, not merely the ranking and logical relationships of cardinal Christian doctrines. Whole monographs have been written on the "theology" of the Gospels and Acts.

42. See Bauckham, *The Gospels for All Christians*, and the more moderate redaction critics.

There is no theoretical problem in discussing, say, the anthropology, soteriology, eschatology, and pneumatology of Acts, and how these relate to each other.[43] Equally there is no problem in saying what these may be considered to contribute to (and what Luke might have learned from) a broader NT theology at the apostolic conference table. Similarly, it is possible, indeed appropriate, to bring Luke-Acts into dialogue with theology today. What would the contribution of its somewhat charismatic and missiologically focused pneumatology be? And how would systematic theology today in turn bring searching questions about the relationship of such a theology to a broader soteriological conception of the Spirit in the community (on which Luke has less to say), or concerning a panentheism of Spirit in creation and humankind (on which Luke, like other NT authors, has nothing to say, but on which the OT and IT literature are more suggestive)? It is appropriate to ask these questions. But theology today can only "dialogue" with Luke when the first horizon of Luke's own perspective has been established as carefully as possible — i.e., when Luke's voice is able to speak clearly as *his* voice.

## 4. "Behind the Text," "In the Text," and "In Front of the Text" Issues in the Theological Hermeneutics of the Apocalypse

Space precludes more than the very briefest comments. The book of Revelation combines the genres of apostolic letter (cf. the form of 1:4-6; 22:21), prophecy (1:3; 22:18-19), and apocalypse (1:1 and passim). John anticipates that his work will be received as from a true martyr/witness (1:9), well known to the churches of Asia, but also as prophetic revelation (cf. 22:18-19). Accordingly, his authorial role varies between direct address, oracle-reports (e.g., to the seven churches), narrations (e.g., of visions, and of his own responses), and final editing of the whole. The history of the interpretation of Revelation suggests it has been sadly misconstrued by those without adequate grasp of such "behind the text" issues as the nature and symbolism of Jewish apocalypses from Daniel onward.[44] Similarly, the so-called "letters to

43. Cf. I. Howard Marshall and David Peterson, eds., *Witness to the Gospel: The Theology of Acts* (Grand Rapids: Eerdmans, 1998).

44. Cf. Christopher Rowland, *The Open Heaven: A Study of Apocalyptic in Judaism and Early Christianity* (London: SPCK; New York: Crossroad, 1982); Richard Bauckham, *The Climax of Prophecy: Studies on the Book of Revelation* (Edinburgh: T. & T. Clark, 1993), chap. 2.

the seven churches" (2:1–3:22) reflect local detail best illuminated by contemporary Greco-Roman literature and by archeology,[45] and the whole writing assumes an awareness of, and provides a radical challenge to, the oppressive Roman sociopolitical, economic, and religious culture of the cities.[46] Equally important, however, are such "in the text" literary-critical issues as structuring, gaps, pauses, repetitions, and parallels — which have perhaps not yet received the attention they deserve,[47] and the internal unfolding and explanation of the symbolism.[48] Turning briefly to "in front of the text issues," we acknowledge that Revelation's place at the end of the canon eminently suits its nature, for the Apocalypse is fundamentally concerned with how the God of all creation fulfills the totality of OT eschatological hopes through the cross, through the (authentic) witness of the church to the nations, and in the final messianic triumph and restoration of creation. Its vivid and profound challenge — both to the church and to the dominant ideology — assures that it will continually and fruitfully be recontextualized (as it has in the past).[49] But the challenge will probably be the sharper and the more authoritative if it is informed by the detail of John's discourse meaning (text + presupposition pool), rather than if this is abandoned in the name of the liberated "text" alone.

## 5. Conclusion

The absolute rule of historical criticism may be over. This essay has briefly assessed the relation of "behind the text," "in the text," and "in front of the text" issues in theological hermeneutics of NT writings in the light of this claim. The different kinds of writings — letter, narrative, and apocalypse

---

45. See especially Colin J. Hemer, *The Letters to the Seven Churches of Asia in Their Local Setting*, JSNTSup 11 (Sheffield: JSOT, 1986).

46. Cf. Bauckham, *The Climax of Prophecy*, chaps. 6, 10, 11.

47. Bauckham, *The Climax of Prophecy*, chap. 1; Alan Garrow, *Revelation* (London: Routledge, 1997).

48. See Rowland, *The Open Heaven*; Bauckham, *The Climax of Prophecy*; Bauckham, *The Theology of the Book of Revelation*, NTT (Cambridge: Cambridge University Press, 1993).

49. See, e.g., Christopher Rowland and Mark Corner, *Liberating Exegesis: The Challenge of Liberation Theology to Biblical Studies* (London: SPCK; Louisville: Westminster/John Knox, 1989), chap. 4; Bauckham, *Theology*, chap. 7; Bauckham, *The Bible in Politics: How to Read the Bible Politically* (Louisville: Westminster/John Knox, 1989), pp. 85-102.

— call forth different answers. Contrary to fashion in some quarters, however, we have found no reason to believe questions of authorial discourse meaning and its closely related "background" issues are dead. They are most vitally relevant in the hermeneutics of letters, but still significant in the other forms of NT literature. The main reason for this is that discourse meaning depends not merely on "text" but greatly on the invoked presupposition pools. Much of what we mean by the "clarity" of Scripture rests on this — that is, we read a "text" such as Philemon against a presupposition pool informed considerably by other biblical (especially Pauline) texts. But we cannot arbitrarily restrict the presupposition pool to the content of biblical texts and to facts about Greek language (a "behind the text" issue!), bracketing out all the rest of our knowledge of the contemporary Greco-Roman and Jewish history and culture in which the NT texts are embedded. Moreover, most would agree that the relation of the Gospels to history is a question with which we can never dispense.

We must welcome the introduction of a variety of literary-critical approaches, which, along with other disciplines such as discourse analysis and structuralism, provide insight into "in the text issues." These are more important for the narrative writings and for the Apocalypse, perhaps, than for the letters, but still significant there too.

We need fully to appreciate the importance of "in front of the text" issues, and how much they can, do, and must shape, not merely our appropriation of texts, but also (to a lesser extent) our exegesis of them. We can thus learn from even the most radical reader-response critics and ardent postliberals — though, in the final analysis, we need to avoid their temptation prematurely to fuse the horizons of author/text and reader. The canonical principle bids us join the apostolic conference table with the NT writers and give them due hearing. It does not invite us to gag and bind the apostolic authors and hustle them into our century, and into our churches, where they are able only to stutter out, in stifled whispers, the things we have already told them to say. We potentially learn perhaps more from those believing communities whose experience of the Spirit and in the world has given sharp insight into aspects of Scripture elsewhere too readily ignored. To mind immediately come *(inter alia)* the Pentecostal/charismatic experience of the Spirit, the African experience of spirits, the South American grassroots experience of oppression and poverty, and women's experience of male domination.[50] But (of "in front of text" ap-

---

50. On spirits, see Keith Ferdinando, *The Triumph of Christ in African Perspective*

proaches) we learn perhaps most by listening respectfully to our various church theological traditions — based in years of experience and reflection — and to the critical discussions of their strengths and weaknesses in the literature of theology. It is these we need to bring back into open dialogue at the apostolic conference table.

---

(Carlisle: Paternoster, 1999). On grassroots communities, see Rowland and Corner, *Liberating Exegesis*. More generally, see John R. Levison and Priscilla Pope-Levison, "Global Perspectives on New Testament Interpretation," in *Hearing the New Testament*, pp. 329-48.

# CHAPTER 4

# The Role of Authorial Intention in the Theological Interpretation of Scripture

## STEPHEN E. FOWL

ebates over the role, significance, and status of authors for interpretation have been hotly contested over the past fifty years.[1] Those who have attacked authors have focused on two main issues. The first concerns whether and how one might uncover the intentions of the author. The other revolves around whether and how authors might be thought of as having some claim or control over how their works are interpreted. Among these critics it is not uncommon to hear people speak of "the death of the author." The French literary critic Roland Barthes has noted that "the birth of the reader must be at the cost of the death of the Author."[2]

1. The classic essay which began this was William K. Wimsatt and Monroe C. Beardsley's 1946 essay, "The Intentional Fallacy." An edition of this can be found in Wimsatt's *The Verbal Icon* (Lexington: University of Kentucky Press, 1954), pp. 3-18.

2. See Roland Barthes, "The Death of the Author," in *Image — Music — Text* (New York: Hill & Wang, 1977), p. 148. Two other names most often associated with this claim are the French philosophers Michel Foucault and Jacques Derrida. While the views of these two are very different from each other in most respects, they do share an antipathy toward authors. Foucault does leave room for what he calls the "author function" (see "What Is an Author?" in *The Foucault Reader,* ed. Paul Rabinow [New York: Pantheon, 1984], pp. 101-20). On the other hand, the attack on "man" as subject, which concludes *The Order of Things* (New York: Vintage, 1973), makes one wonder whether Foucault did not have his sights set on a much bigger enemy than authors. For a good overview of Derrida on authors, which focuses on Derrida's engagements with John

STEPHEN E. FOWL

Of course, authors have also had their defenders. The most vigorous of these has been E. D. Hirsch. In his widely read book *Validity in Interpretation*, Hirsch argued that the best way to make strong claims about the validity of differing interpretations is to make authorial intention the standard to which they must conform.[3] Most recently, Kevin Vanhoozer (following leads in the work of P. D. Juhl, Anthony C. Thiselton, and Nicholas Wolterstorff) has relied on speech-act theory to correct some of the problems in Hirsch's position in order to reemphasize the primacy of authorial intention for theological interpretation.[4]

Debates over authors have largely been carried on in departments of literature and philosophy. Adequate representation of the various strains of these debates goes well beyond the limits of this chapter.[5] Moreover, the aims of this chapter are directed toward helping those interested in reading Scripture theologically to sort out how and why arguments about authors and authorial intentions fit into that larger interest of interpreting Scripture theologically. Hence, more recent work invoking speech-act theory in regard to authorial intention is more directly relevant to my own aims, and in due course I will try to address both what I take to be its strengths and its weaknesses.

What is clear to anyone who enters the debate about authors is that the issues at stake are actually several and diverse. There exists no single position with regard to authors and their role in interpretation with which one either agrees or disagrees. Rather, there are a variety of issues which

Searle in *Limited Inc.* and Hans-Georg Gadamer in *Dialogue and Deconstruction: The Gadamer-Derrida Encounter,* see Reed Dasenbrock, "Taking It Personally: Reading Derrida's Responses," *College English* 56 (1994): 261-79.

3. E. D. Hirsch, *Validity in Interpretation* (New Haven: Yale University Press, 1967). For a concise yet philosophically acute criticism of Hirsch, see Richard Rorty, "Texts and Lumps," *New Literary History* 17 (1985): 1-16.

4. See Kevin Vanhoozer, *Is There a Meaning in This Text? The Bible, the Reader, and the Morality of Literary Knowledge* (Grand Rapids: Zondervan, 1998). See P. D. Juhl, *Interpretation: An Essay in the Philosophy of Literary Criticism* (Princeton: Princeton University Press, 1980). The two primary works by Anthony C. Thiselton in this regard are *The Two Horizons: New Testament Hermeneutics and Philosophical Description* (Grand Rapids: Eerdmans, 1980) and *New Horizons in Hermeneutics: The Theory and Practice of Transforming Biblical Reading* (Grand Rapids: Zondervan; London: Collins, 1992). See also Nicholas Wolterstorff, *Divine Discourse: Philosophical Reflections on the Claim That God Speaks* (Cambridge: Cambridge University Press, 1995).

5. Students are encouraged to engage the arguments and positions of the primary critics (and authors!) on the various sides of these debates. The notes of this chapter are primarily designed to direct students to some of this material.

should, as far as possible, be separated and distinguished from each other. Hence, in this chapter I will argue for several different points in relation to authors and the theological interpretation of Scripture. I begin by articulating a chastened notion of authorial intention, arguing that it is possible to speak in a coherent if constrained way about an author's intention. Moreover, I allow that critics might make serious claims to explicate an author's intention. Having done this, however, I also want to reject the claim that an author's intention is "the meaning" of a text, especially if this claim is made at the expense of other approaches to texts that do not accord privilege to authorial meaning. I want to conclude by arguing that the ends for which Christians are called to interpret, debate, and embody Scripture are to be found in such manifestations as faithful life and worship and ever deeper communion with the triune God and with others, and that these ends neither necessitate any specific critical practice nor accord privilege to the intentions of a scriptural text's human author. I will therefore begin by laying out some claims about authors and their intentions. My hope is that these claims will not be subject to the general criticisms that have led people to claim (prematurely) that the author is dead.

## 1. Reviving Authors

One of the major criticisms of an interest in uncovering an author's intentions is that it presumes an account of human subjectivity which, while characteristic of the Enlightenment, is difficult to maintain today. That is, some ways of talking about authors assume that authors (like other humans) are fully (or substantially) autonomous and aware of themselves and their intentions. Further, it assumes that the texts that authors write (or language more generally) are suitable vehicles for mediating those intentions from one autonomous self-aware mind to another. In the light of the critiques lodged by those masters of suspicion, Nietzsche, Freud, and Marx, this notion of selfhood has come under sustained, vigorous attack. Moreover, from a theological perspective, this account of human selfhood simply does not fit with a view that humans are created in the image of the triune God whose inner life is characterized by its relationships rather than autonomy, a God who creates us for lives of peaceable fellowship with God and each other. Moreover, our creaturely status needs to circumscribe all notions of autonomy and freedom. Further, Christian convictions about sin and sin's manifestations in human habits of self-deception in

73

thought, word, and deed should make Christians wary of any presumptions about humans being fully or substantially present to themselves. Short of the consummation of God's reign, we shall not know as fully as we are known by God. If, therefore, we are to reconstitute notions of authorial intention, we will have to do so in ways that do not presume that via an analysis of a text we can climb inside an author's head and share with the author an immediate and unfettered access to the author's intentions.

The best way to do this is to reshape a notion of intention so that it does not presume problematic notions of selfhood. One way to do this is to try to distinguish authorial motives from an author's communicative intentions.[6] "That is to say, one ought to distinguish between *what* an author is trying to say (which might be called a 'communicative intention') and *why* it is being said (which might be called a motive)."[7] An author might write from any number of motives. She might have a desire for fame and fortune, or failing that, tenure. She might have a deep psychological need to share her thoughts with a wider public. There might be (and probably are) motives at work of which an author is not fully conscious. Alternatively, in the case of lying, an author may be conscious of her motives but wish to conceal them from others. As Mark Brett notes, "any single motive can give rise to a vast range of quite different communicative intentions."[8] In order to get at an author's motives, semantic and historical analysis of her texts is never enough. A desire to discover an author's motives will be quite hard to fulfill in almost all cases. Moreover, in the case of ancient authors an interest in motives will tend to be frustrated by our comprehensive lack of knowledge about these characters.

Alternatively, to render an account of an author's communicative intention one need not attend to an author's motives. Rather, such an account requires attention to matters of semantics, linguistic conventions operative at the time, and matters of implication and inference, to name only three. In the case of dealing with the biblical writers, attention to these matters is inescapably historical. Indeed, in many respects the prac-

6. This distinction is initially made by Quentin Skinner in "Motives, Intentions and the Interpretation of Texts," *New Literary History* 3 (1971): 393-408. For biblical scholars this notion is expertly articulated by Mark Brett in his article, "Motives and Intentions in Genesis 1," *JTS* 42 (1991): 1-16. In what follows I am largely following Brett's work.
7. Brett, p. 5.
8. Brett, p. 5.

tices required to display an author's communicative intention will be familiar to biblical critics even if they do not characterize their work as offering an account of an author's communicative intention. Hence, to this degree, my argument is not so much with any particular current critical practice. Nevertheless, in the course of reviving authors we need to understand, on the one hand, that many of the commonplace practices of professional biblical critics do not deliver the results they have often been thought to deliver. Hence, we need to reformulate our ways of thinking and talking about authors and their intentions to match the sorts of results for which we can reasonably aim. On the other hand, I will ultimately argue that even reformed views about authors and their intentions will only be useful to theological interpretation of Scripture in ad hoc ways.

This notion of an author's communicative intention does not depend on having a textually mediated access to an autonomous, fully aware, authorial self. Rather, it depends on, in the case of Paul, for example, a knowledge of Greek and the linguistic conventions operative in the first century; an ability to detect and explicate allusions, indirect references, implications, and inferences; and a measure of familiarity with the general set of social conventions of which letter writing is a part. No doubt other elements might come into play as well. Further, the exact ways in which to mix and match all of these considerations will always be open to argument and debate. For example, there is no set formula or method that will tell one when to rely more heavily on semantics rather than social conventions, or possible OT allusions. In fact, the great majority of interpretive arguments among professional biblical scholars could be cast as arguments about whether or not these considerations should even count as relevant pieces of evidence and what sort of weight to give each piece of evidence. In adjudicating these arguments a whole range of factors might be considered, but one element that is not relevant is a concern with what was going on in Paul's consciousness at the particular moment he wrote something — assuming we could even know this. It is clearly much easier to talk about an author's communicative intention in regard to epistolary discourse as opposed to narratives such as the Gospels. I think, however, one can argue from analogy that while different factors may need to be brought into play, and while the mix of considerations will be different, one can make provisional claims about the communicative intention of a Gospel or a Gospel passage. Moreover, as with Paul, knowledge of the internal mental states of Matthew, for example, is simply not relevant here.

Needless to say, these are always probability judgments, open to revision in the light of further information and scholarly debate. Given this measure of provisionality, which is the measure within which we generally have to operate, we can expect to make fairly confident claims about an author's communicative intention that will largely be immune to the sorts of criticisms of authors mentioned above.

It is here in regard to establishing an author's communicative intention that my arguments overlap most closely with those who rely on speech-act theory.[9] Like them, I recognize that all utterances are intelligible because they are contextually embedded and that successful communication relies on the knowledge and operation of linguistic and social conventions. To the extent that those who rely on speech-act theory recognize that one needs to make ad hoc arguments about the relative importance of specific conventional and contextual concerns in order to account for specific utterances, I would say that we both recognize the priority of practical reasoning in interpretation.[10] In subsequent sections

9. In this respect, Vanhoozer's constructive arguments in *Is There a Meaning in This Text?* (chap. 5) overlap with my own.

10. This characterization is offered by Merold Westphal in his review of Wolterstorff's *Divine Discourse* in *Modern Theology* 13 (1997): 527. I make this point in the rather circumscribed way that I have because I would argue that there are really two streams of speech-act theory, or rather, two ways of carrying on the views laid out by J. L. Austin in *How to Do Things with Words* (originally the Henry James Lectures for 1955, the volume was posthumously published in 1962 [Oxford: Clarendon]). Philosophers such as Richard Rorty and Jeffrey Stout treat Austin as a therapeutic philosopher, a philosopher who helps us eliminate problems and confusions. This way of reading Austin treats him as one of several philosophers who eliminate confusions about language by showing that words and utterances become intelligible because of the way they are used in context and in the light of various conventions, not because words have meanings as inherent properties. This way of treating Austin places emphasis on the priority of practical reasoning in interpretation. The other way of carrying forward Austin is characterized by John R. Searle's attempt to use Austin's work to develop a philosophy of language and, at least implicitly, a metaphysic or ontology (see *Speech Acts: An Essay in the Philosophy of Language* [Cambridge: Cambridge University Press, 1969]). (Vanhoozer [p. 209] casts Searle as Melanchthon — speech-act theory's systematic theologian — to Austin's Luther.) Given this (overly simplified) account, I would argue that Rorty, Stout, and I stand with Austin, and Thiselton and Vanhoozer stand more with Searle. Both Thiselton *(New Horizons in Hermeneutics)* and Vanhoozer offer criticisms of Rorty and Stout. I am not persuaded by these arguments. In particular, I think Vanhoozer argues primarily against Derrida and assumes too easily that the same arguments work on Rorty and Stout. To read the major criticisms of Searle's approach, see Rorty, *Philosophy and the Mirror of Nature* (Oxford: Blackwell,

of this essay, however, it will become clear that I do not think that speech-act theory can provide either a theory of meaning or the basis for arguing for the interpretive priority of the communicative intention of authors.

## 2. Only Authors?

In the previous section I argued that, in the light of sustained criticisms of the Enlightenment's presumptions and assumptions about human subjectivity, it is possible to preserve a chastened notion of authorial intention. The next set of issues concerns the interpretive status to be given to an author's communicative intention.

Some defenders of authors see the chief end of criticism to be the display of an author's intention. Such critics argue that a text's meaning is coextensive with, or primarily determined by, the author's intentions. The only valid form of interpretation is one which ultimately is determined by judgments about an author's intentions. Many of these critics may also adopt the problematic notions of authorial subjectivity noted above. They could, however, in the face of mounting arguments against that type of authorial subjectivity, adopt the distinction between motives and intentions while still arguing that a text's meaning is coextensive with an author's communicative intention.[11] The results of any and all other critical practices are always subsidiary to the text's meaning as determined by an author's (communicative) intention.

One of the chief concerns that fosters this particular interest in authors is that without a theory of textual meaning tied to something relatively stable and determinable, interpretation will lapse into either vicious or silly relativism. This concern is particularly common among biblical scholars and theologians who worry about deconstructive accounts of interpretation.[12] These deconstructive accounts are primarily concerned to

---

1980), chap. 6; Jacques Derrida, "Signature, Event, Context," in *Limited Inc.* (Evanston, Ill.: Northwestern University Press, 1988); Stanley Fish, "How to Do Things with Austin and Searle," in *Is There a Text in This Class? The Authority of Interpretive Communities* (Cambridge: Harvard University Press, 1980), pp. 197-245.

11. Although he does not use quite this language, I take this to be Vanhoozer's position.

12. To learn more about deconstruction and biblical studies, see the works of Stephen Moore — such as *Literary Criticism and the Gospels: The Theoretical Challenge*

stop a premature shutting down of interpretation. In response to claims that texts have one meaning, deconstruction celebrates the playful and ongoing interactions between texts. Seen against this background, arguments about the primacy of authorial intention are both a way of putting constraints on what can count as textual meaning and of providing some stability for discussion, argument, and debate about the interpretation of any particular text. One might even claim that such stability is crucial for the stability and coherence of Christian doctrine.

Without entering into a more sustained engagement with deconstruction than I have space for here, I do want to note that there are both theoretical and theological reasons against limiting a text's meaning to an account of authorial intention (reconstructed or not).[13]

First the theoretical. Limiting a text's meaning to the author's intention presupposes a definitive account of what the meaning of a text is (or ought to be). Of course, a quick survey of the critical landscape makes it pretty clear that our situation is marked by interminable debate and disagreement about just what the meaning of a text is.[14] Moreover, we should not be confused by the fact that at some times and places there may well be a large degree of interpretive agreement — agreement in terms of what we are talking about when we talk about the meaning of a text, in terms of methods for attaining meaning, and in terms of interpretive results. The fragility and contingency of these agreements become clear as soon as someone asks, "Why should something like the author's intention count as the meaning of the text?"

At such points several things may happen. On the one hand, there will probably be an outpouring of lengthy but ultimately question-begging philosophical polemic designed to show that the author's intention really

(New Haven: Yale University Press, 1989) and *Poststructuralism and the New Testament* (Minneapolis: Fortress, 1994) — and Gary Phillips's "The Ethics of Reading Deconstructively, of Speaking Face to Face: The Samaritan Woman Meets Derrida at the Well," in *The New Literary Criticism and the New Testament,* ed. Edgar V. McKnight and Elizabeth Struthers Malbon, JSNTSup 109 (Sheffield: Sheffield Academic Press, 1994), pp. 283-325; Phillips, "'You Are Either Here, Here, Here, or Here': Deconstruction's Troubling Interplay," *Semeia* 71 (1995): 193-213.

13. Much of what follows here is directly dependent upon my book *Engaging Scripture: A Model for Theological Interpretation* (Oxford: Blackwell, 1998). There I engage more directly the claims of deconstructive critics.

14. This argument is neatly laid out in Jeffrey Stout, "What Is the Meaning of a Text?" *New Literary History* 14 (1982): 1-12. I give a fuller account of Stout's views in *Engaging Scripture,* pp. 56-61.

*is* the meaning of a text. These responses will all be question-begging because they will presuppose some notion of textual meaning which is the very point at issue. Let me state categorically that I am not opposed to people using the word "meaning" in either general conversation or scholarly debate as long as they use it in its everyday, underdetermined sense. What this sense of "meaning" cannot do, however, is resolve an interpretive dispute where the parties involved disagree about the nature of their interpretive tasks.

Of course, on the other hand, when people start arguing about what counts as textual meaning, some authoritative interpreters may exercise their institutional power and decree arbitrarily that meaning equals authorial intention. Those coming under the institutional control of such interpreters must either assent, leave, or be driven out. This phenomenon is as well known in modern academic settings as it is in churches. Displacing one's interpretive opponents may provide a limited amount of institutional stability, but it does not make arguments about textual meaning any more coherent. The problem is that we lack a general, comprehensive theory of textual meaning that is neither arbitrary nor question-begging which would justify privileging authorial intention in this way. This would not be so frustrating if there were evidence that we were moving forward, coming ever closer to our goal by the articulation and reduction of error. In the case of developing a theory of textual meaning without a clear conception of what meaning is, we do not even know what "success" in this venture would look like.

The problem here is that our concerns with textual meaning are confused. The source of this confusion is the term "meaning" itself. Obviously, most of us can use the term "meaning" in informal conversations with relative ease and clarity. This is because the contexts in which the term is used in these informal conversations are so clearly circumscribed (or open to circumscription) that the term poses no impediment to discussion. The problems arise when we move to formal discussions of meaning as such. Take, for example, discussions about a theory of meaning. "What is a theory of meaning a theory of? Evidently, it may be a theory of any number of things. A question of the form, 'What is the meaning of x?' retains all of the ambiguity of its central term but none of the grammatical features that . . . would diminish its tendency to confuse."[15] A notion of authorial intention, no matter how coherent in and of itself, cannot provide us with the

---

15. Stout, p. 3.

"meaning" of a text without begging the question of what textual meaning might be.[16] In the absence of a clear answer to that question, we cannot expect any account of authorial intention to provide the theoretical basis for limiting or authorizing any particular set of interpretive interests at the expense of other interests.

In the light of this situation, we should eliminate talk of "meaning" in favor other terms that will suit our interpretive interests and put a stop to futile discussions. Hence, we should be satisfied with being able to articulate an author's communicative intentions, or a text's contextual connections to the material or gender-based means of its production, or any other type of clearly laid-out interpretive aim. There is no need to cloud the issue further by calling this or that interpretive activity "the meaning of a text" at the expense of other interpretive activities in which one might engage.

Moreover, Christians have theological reasons for arguing against using notions of authorial intention to limit the various ways they are called to engage Scripture. These reasons are largely but not exclusively tied to Christian convictions about the OT. Any attempt to tie a single stable account of meaning to authorial intention will put Christians in an awkward relationship to the OT.

The church has always regarded itself in relationship to Israel. While not continuous in every respect, the church has claimed to be in continuity with Israel. This claim is crucial for Christian affirmations regarding the integrity or righteousness of God. As Paul understood so well, a God who abandons promises to Israel may not be able or willing to keep promises made to Christians. Christians have always maintained the importance of interpreting the Torah, the Prophets, and the Writings as their Scripture. If those texts have a single meaning that is determined by the author's communicative intention, a variety of problems arise. Some of these problems are nicely displayed by the following example:

16. When someone asserts that meaning simply is authorial intention, no matter how loudly and repeatedly the person says this, it is nothing more than an arbitrary assertion that begs the very questions at hand (see, e.g., Vanhoozer, pp. 74-79, in which he discusses Hirsch; or Steven Knapp and Walter Benn Michaels, "Against Theory," in *Against Theory: Literary Studies and the New Pragmatism*, ed. W. J. T. Mitchell [Chicago: University of Chicago Press, 1985], pp. 11-30; Knapp and Michaels, "Against Theory 2: Hermeneutics and Deconstruction," *Critical Inquiry* 14 [1987-88]: 49-68). Vanhoozer seems to be aware that this argument might be used against him, but his very brief excursus on this matter (pp. 253-54) does not suffice. It simply shifts all of the problems with "meaning" onto "interpretation."

80

How was a French parish priest in 1150 to understand Psalm 137, which bemoans captivity in Babylon, makes rude remarks about Edomites, expresses an ineradicable longing for a glimpse of Jerusalem, and pronounces a blessing on anyone who avenges the destruction of the Temple by dashing Babylonian children against a rock? The priest lives in Concale, not Babylon, has no personal quarrel with Edomites, cherishes no ambitions to visit Jerusalem (though he might fancy a holiday in Paris), and is expressly forbidden by Jesus to avenge himself on his enemies. Unless Psalm 137 has more than one possible meaning, it cannot be used as a prayer of the Church and must be rejected as a lament belonging exclusively to the piety of ancient Israel.[17]

Whether or not this situation leads one to adopt the medieval fourfold sense of Scripture, it clearly points out a key theological limitation for those who hold that biblical interpretation is determined by a single meaning that is tied to the human author's intention. Another place where this issue would arise concerns christological readings of various OT texts. A single meaning determined by authorial intention will either force Christians into rather implausible arguments about the communicative intention of Isaiah, for example, or lead them to reduce the christological aspect of these passages into a subsidiary or parasitic role. The first of these options has little to commend it. The second option would put Christians in the odd position of arguing that the "meaning" of these texts is one of their less important aspects.[18]

In addition, these concerns are not limited to the OT. For example, if one is committed to the interpretive primacy of John's communicative intention, it becomes very difficult to locate resources from which to offer a trinitarian account of the Johannine prologue (John 1:1-18) in the face of Arian challenges. To oppose Arian readings of John's prologue, one needs to invoke such things as the *skopos* of Scripture, the Rule of Faith, and theological doctrines about Christology and about how humans might be

17. David Steinmetz, "The Superiority of Pre-Critical Exegesis," in *The Theological Interpretation of Scripture: Classic and Contemporary Readings*, ed. Stephen E. Fowl (Oxford: Blackwell, 1997), p. 28.

18. Vanhoozer, pp. 259-65, addresses this problem by means of a revision of Hirsch's meaning/significance distinction. In particular he makes use of Raymond Brown's thoroughly discredited notion of the *sensus plenior*. The most thorough undermining of this view can be found in Robert Robinson, *Roman Catholic Exegesis since Divino Afflante Spiritu* (Atlanta: Scholars, 1988).

saved.[19] While speech-act theory can helpfully remind us that the intelligibility of language is conventional and contextual, it cannot give any guidance about why, in the face of an Arian Christology, Christians need to employ conventions gleaned from the later theological formulations rather than those that would have been operative at the time of the writing of the Fourth Gospel.

## 3. Authors and the Literal Sense

Someone still wishing to hold on to authorial intention as the meaning of Scripture might respond by noting that even within the medieval fourfold sense of Scripture, the literal sense *(sensus literalis)* of Scripture served as the determinate meaning of the biblical text, a meaning that disciplined and limited all other types of interpretation. Further, the literal sense was often equated with the intention of the author. This would indicate that our discussion of authors and Scripture needs to expand some to discuss notions of the "literal sense" of Scripture.

If an interpretive commitment to authorial intention (communicative or otherwise) is to be supported by arguments about the literal sense of Scripture, it will be important to clarify both what the literal sense of Scripture is or might be, and who the true author of Scripture is.

The first of these tasks is less easy than it might appear. There is no single determinate account of the literal sense of Scripture. Nicholas of Lyra (ca. 1270-1349), for example, seems to hold to a double literal sense which does not really limit interpretation or work to buttress a modern interpretive interest in authors.[20] More contemporary advocates of the literal sense of Scripture such as George Lindbeck, Hans Frei, and Kathryn Tanner treat the literal sense as that meaning established within the community of those who take the Bible to be their Scripture.[21]

---

19. All of these concerns might be part of an account of God's communicative intention as the author of Scripture, but as I will soon show, such a move fits much better with my position than with alternatives.

20. See, for example, the Second Prologue to Lyra's *Postilla litteralis super totam Bibliam*, §14 (translated and introduced by Denys Turner in *Eros and Allegory* [Kalamazoo: Cistercian, 1995], p. 385).

21. George Lindbeck, "The Story-Shaped Church: Critical Exegesis and Theological Interpretation," in *The Theological Interpretation of Scripture*, pp. 39-52. Frei's most concise presentation of his views can be found in "The 'Literal Reading' of Bibli-

Clearly this view is not going to be helpful if one wants to use notions of the literal sense to support an interest in the primacy of authorial intention.

The person most scholars turn to if they want to correlate a notion of the literal sense of Scripture with the author's intention is St. Thomas Aquinas. While Aquinas argued that the literal sense is that which the author intends,[22] "it turns out that Thomas' reflection on the literal sense leaves matters surprisingly underdetermined and that the author's intention functions in his hands more to promote diversity than to contain it."[23] This is because Aquinas recognizes God as the author of Scripture. "Now because the literal sense is that which the author intends, and the author of Holy Scripture is God who comprehends everything all at once in God's understanding, it comes not amiss, as St. Augustine says in *Confessions* XII,

---

cal Narrative in the Christian Tradition: Does It Stretch or Will It Break?" in *The Bible and the Narrative Tradition,* ed. Frank D. McConnell (New York: Oxford University Press, 1986), pp. 36-77. See also Kathryn Tanner, "Theology and the Plain Sense," in *Scriptural Authority and Narrative Interpretation,* ed. Garrett Green (Philadelphia: Fortress, 1987), pp. 59-78. Brevard Childs seeks to distance himself from his erstwhile colleagues in "Toward Recovering Theological Exegesis," *Pro Ecclesia* 6 (1997): 20 n. 8. He claims that their position implicates them in a form of theological liberalism. He contrasts their views with his own position laid out in "The Sensus Literalis of Scripture: An Ancient and Modern Problem," in *Beiträge zur Alttestamentlichen Theologie: Festschrift für Walter Zimmerli,* ed. H. Donner et al. (Göttingen: Vandenhoeck & Ruprecht, 1977), pp. 80-94. It is not clear from this essay why Childs should contrast his position so sharply with Frei's and Tanner's, except that theirs operates with a clearly Thomistic notion of the literal sense and Childs, while misstating Aquinas's views, shows a clear preference for what he takes to be the Reformers' views. In this regard I follow a variety of contemporary historians who treat the Reformation as a late medieval event. Both Luther and Calvin's interpretive habits are much more like those of medieval Catholic interpreters than opposed to them. One need only look at the way Calvin uses his notion of the literal sense of Scripture to refer to christological readings of Isaiah to see that, contra Vanhoozer (pp. 47-48), Calvin's views in this regard are much closer to mine than Vanhoozer's. In fact, one of the basic differences between Vanhoozer and me on the importance of authors is that he holds that there is basically a critical continuity between the interpretive interests of premodern and modern interpreters (see, e.g., p. 74). I argue in *Engaging Scripture* that there are significant ruptures between the premodern and the modern and that it is theologically essential for Christians to recover and revive premodern interests that have largely been eclipsed in modernity.

22. See *Summa theologiae* I.1.10.

23. Eugene Rogers, "How the Virtues of the Interpreter Presuppose and Perfect Hermeneutics: The Case of Thomas Aquinas," *JR* 76 (1996): 65.

if many meanings [*plures sensus*] are present even in the literal sense of one passage of Scripture."[24]

As Eugene Rogers argues, rather than seeing the literal sense as a form of interpretation sharply limited by the author's intention, the literal sense becomes, for Thomas, a "whole category into which many readings may fall. . . . As a whole category the appeal to the author's intention promotes diversity rather than a restriction of readings, particularly since we can point so rarely to relatively independent indications of what it is."[25]

As Thomas argues in *De potentia*, there is further theological importance to maintaining a plurality of readings within the literal sense. Doing so will avoid such a situation,

> [t]hat anyone confine Scripture so to one sense, that other senses be entirely excluded, that in themselves contain truth and are able to be adapted to Scripture, preserving the way the words run; for this pertains to the dignity of divine Scripture, that it contain many senses under one letter, in order that it may both in that way befit diverse intellects of human beings — that all may marvel that they are able to find in divine Scripture the truth that they conceived by their minds — and by this also defend more easily against the infidels, since if anything which someone wants to understand out of sacred Scripture appears to be false, recourse is possible to another of its [literal!] senses. . . . Whence all truth which, preserving the way the words run, can be adapted to divine Scripture, is its sense.[26]

For Thomas, limiting the literal sense to a single determinate meaning would limit edifying scriptural interpretation to the well trained, possibly leaving the untrained at the mercy of the "infidels." Moreover, it would inevitably bring Scripture into disrepute since the literal sense might be forced to teach something obviously false.

Rather than using authorial intention to limit interpretation, a Thomistic account of the literal sense fosters ongoing interpretation within the community of believers. Disputes about the literal sense can only be hashed out through ad hoc argumentation by interpreters guided by the virtue of prudence and by God's providence working through the Spirit.

24. *Summa theologiae* I.1.10.
25. Rogers, p. 72.
26. *De potentia* q.4, a.1, c, *post init.*; quoted in Rogers, p. 74.

It appears, then, that appeals tying an account of authorial intention to a Thomistic account of the literal sense of Scripture will not help defenders of the primacy of authorial intention either to limit interpretation to a single meaning or to overcome the theological objections to such a practice. To argue that the intention of the human authors of Scripture should count as the literal sense of Scripture might secure a sort of determinacy for scriptural interpretation. It would do so, however, by shifting all of the problems associated with the term "meaning" onto the term "literal sense."

## 4. Where Do We Go from Here?

Thus far I have tried to lay out some of the most significant objections to an interest in authorial intention. In the light of those objections, it seems plausible to reconstitute a notion of authorial intention, if by authorial intention one sharply distinguishes motives from communicative intentions and focuses on the latter rather than the former. Even doing this, however, cannot secure a critical primacy for an author's communicative intentions. No matter how one explicates the notion of authorial intention, it is not plausible to argue that an interest in authorial intentions should be the sole or primary interest of theological interpretation. There are two sorts of reasons for this. First, the typical way of doing this, by linking authorial intention to a text's meaning, fails. This is not because we cannot make the notion of authorial intention coherent. Rather, it is because we cannot make the notion of textual meaning strong enough to do the sort of work such a claim needs it to do. Moreover, for Christians, there are significant theological reasons against arguments for the critical supremacy or primacy of authorial intention.

Where does all of this leave interpretation more generally, and theological interpretation of Scripture in particular? In general, interpretation should be seen in terms of the practice of specific and diverse interpretive interests none of which can lay claim to delivering the single determinate meaning of a text at the expense of other interests. Some critics at certain times may want to pursue an interest in authors, but there is no necessity to this interest. Interpretation thus becomes more pragmatic and pluralist. The interesting questions in this regard are more political and moral than hermeneutical. They concern whether or not the institutional and professional bodies within which most scholarly interpretation takes place can provide a sort of order or discipline to the various interpretive practices and interests, thus maintaining institutional and professional coherence.

For theological interpretation of Scripture, the issues are similar yet more complex. This is in part because Christians are called to read, interpret, and embody Scripture in the light of the larger ends of the Christian life. That is, Christians are called to interpret and embody Scripture in the light of their call to live and worship faithfully, thus deepening their communion with the triune God and with others. Theological interpretation of Scripture therefore needs, ultimately, to advance these ends for which Christians are called to interpret Scripture. This will entail a complex and theoretically underdetermined interaction between scriptural interpretation, Christian doctrine, and the practices of the Christian life. Judgments about the quality of any particular theological interpretation, then, have to be rendered in the light of these specific ends.

On the one hand, the clarity of the ends toward which theological interpretation of Scripture is directed provides a sort of order and discipline to the variety of interpretive interests Christians need to bring to scriptural interpretation. Within this order, an interest in the human authors' communicative intentions may well be relevant at specific points in time and for reasons that advance the ends of theological interpretation. Such an interest in authors, while possible and helpful, is not, however, necessary for theological interpretation. Further, as I have indicated above, in some cases a commitment to the interpretive primacy of authorial intention can actually work to frustrate theological interpretation.

While, on the other hand, the ends of Christian living provide an order and discipline for theological interpretation, the way any particular Christian community advances toward that end will always be a matter of ongoing discussion, argument, and debate. This is because neither the particular scriptural texts that Christians seek to interpret and embody nor the various contexts and constraints within which any particular community of Christians finds itself are self-interpreting.[27] Christians should expect that questions about how to interpret Scripture so as to live faithfully before God and to deepen communion with God and others in the specific

27. This claim is not meant to undermine the larger notion that Scripture is its own interpreter. Rather, it is a claim about specific texts. This claim opposes Vanhoozer's assertion, "Biblical texts and works of literature generally, I will say, are themselves 'institutions' with their own sets of constitutive rules" (p. 245).

contexts in which they find themselves will rarely (if ever) admit of easy, straightforward, self-evident answers.

Given this situation, the crucial tasks for Christians are concerned with fostering the sort of common life that will enhance rather than frustrate the prospects for such debates which will issue in their deeper communion with God and others. Within the scope of this larger endeavor, it will be important that some have the skills that will enable them to articulate and explicate an author's communicative intention. For the most part, however, Christians need to subject themselves to other formative processes and practices that will make them wise readers of Scripture if they are to pursue theological interpretation in ways suitable to the ends of Christian living.

CHAPTER 5

# Reading the Bible from within Our Traditions: The "Rule of Faith" in Theological Hermeneutics

ROBERT W. WALL

B ecause Scripture guides its readers toward Christian theological understanding, its texts require our most careful and informed interpretation. When allowed to go forward in an uncritical or uncaring manner,
biblical interpretation not only will distort Scripture's witness to God's
gospel but will ultimately subvert humanity's relationship with God as
well. If the aim of biblical interpretation is to initiate its readers into a life
with God, then Scripture's authorized role in the church's theological enterprise is undermined by careless or cynical readings. This essay proposes
that Scripture's performance as a persuasive word and enriching sacrament depends upon interpretation that constrains the theological teaching
of a biblical text by the church's "Rule of Faith." Simply put, the Rule of
Faith is the grammar of theological agreements which Christians confess
to be true and by which all of Scripture is rendered in forming a truly
Christian faith and life.

As Tertullian (ca. 160–ca. 230) rightly saw, the advent of Jesus was
and is not self-interpreting, and some manner for adjudicating significant
differences of viewpoint is required. "I say that my gospel is the true one,"
Tertullian writes. "Marcion says that his is. I assert that Marcion's gospel is
adulterated. Marcion says that mine is" (*Adv. Marc.* 4.4). If at this point in

his argument Tertullian appeals to the principle of history (i.e., authority lies with the position that is shown to be the more ancient), it is also true that he — and others beginning in the mid–second century, including Irenaeus, Clement of Alexandria, Hippolytus, Origen, and Novatian — appealed to a "Rule of Faith" or "Rule of Truth" in order to determine the soundness of biblical interpretations and theological formulations. Precursors to the later, more formal creeds of the ecumenical church, these "rules" summarized the heart of Christian faith and served as theological boundary markers for Christian identity. Though formally distinct from Scripture, the Rule of Faith formulates the church's attempts to demarcate the significance of what the Jesus of history said and did (Acts 1:1) and also to make sense of the church's ongoing experience with the living Jesus. The results were statements of core theological affirmations, which might continue to serve the church as criteria for assessing the coherence of one's interpretation of Scripture. These formulations are many, but all set out to administer the lines of scriptural faith. Thus, for example, in another place Tertullian writes,

> Now with regard to this rule of faith . . . it is, you must know, that which prescribes the belief that there is only one God, and that he is none other than the creator of the world, who produced all things out of nothing through his own word, first of all sent forth. This word is called his son, and, under the name of God, was seen in diverse manners by the patriarchs, heard at all times in the prophets, and at last brought by the Spirit and power of the Father down into the virgin Mary. He was made flesh in her womb, and, being born of her, went forth as Jesus Christ. Thereafter, he preached the new land and the new promise of the kingdom of heaven, and he worked miracles. Having been crucified, he rose again on the third day. Having ascended into the heavens, he sat at the right hand of the Father. He sent in place of himself the power of the Holy Spirit to lead those who believe. He will come with glory to take the saints to the enjoyment of everlasting life and of the heavenly promises, and to condemn the wicked to everlasting fire. This will take place after the resurrection of both these classes, together with the restoration of their flesh. This rule . . . was taught by Christ, and raises among us no other questions than those which heresies introduce, and which make people heretics. (*De praesc.* 13)

Though from antiquity we find common theological and christological beliefs expressed differently, and fitted together by different grammars (including the one I will suggest later in this chapter), each possesses a narrative quality and confessional tone similar to Tertullian's proposal (cf., e.g., Irenaeus, *Adv. haer.* 1.10). To attend to such a theological canon in biblical interpretation is to take seriously the church's struggle to determine its own theological commitments and to confirm (or condemn) on that basis those interpretations that are formative (or not) of Christian faith and practice.

The crucial assumption of this species of theological hermeneutics, which holds that the church's Rule of Faith constrains the theological teaching of a biblical text, is that Scripture's legal address is the worshiping community, where biblical interpretation helps to determine what Christians should believe and to enrich their relations with God and neighbor. While rejecting a premodern reductionism that sacrifices critical Bible study to theological harmony, the orientation of this chapter toward the interpretive enterprise contrasts sometimes sharply to the interests and aims of much modern scholarship, which often appears uninterested in promoting theological understanding and redemptive results as a strategic part of the church's mission in the world. The tendency of modern biblical criticism to problematize Scripture, sometimes to underscore its inherent unreliability in matters of faith and life, in truth envisages the primacy of human reason and experience in modernity's account of theological hermeneutics. In my judgment, this modern tendency is not only cynical but fundamentally at odds with the aim of a Christian reading of Scripture, which rather seeks to problematize the human situation to underscore the primacy of God's transforming grace.[1] Thus, for all the important gains of the modern period of biblical study, this evident dislocation of Scripture from the church to the academic guilds of biblical and theological scholarship to serve more secular (rather than confessional) interests, funded by a theological hermeneutics of suspicion, actually strips Scripture of its fiduciary claim upon the church.[2] This is especially true in North America, where much of the center of gravity of biblical scholarship has shifted to state-supported departments of religious studies.

1. This is the point made by Francis Watson in his incisive essay, "Bible, Theology and the University: A Response to Philip Davies," *JSOT* 71 (1996): 3-16.

2. Both my criticism of current hermeneutical practice and desire to recover a more sacramental approach to Scripture are similar to those advanced in William J. Abraham's important book, *Canon and Criterion in Christian Theology: From the Fathers to Feminism* (Oxford: Clarendon, 1998); I acknowledge a profound debt to him.

In this light, then, the most crucial move theological hermeneutics must make is to recover Scripture for use in Christian worship and formation. The normative role of Scripture within the church is to "teach, reprove, correct, and train" believers to know God's wisdom more completely and to serve God's purposes more earnestly (2 Tim. 3:15-17). Scripture aims at God as the divinely inspired medium by which the Holy Spirit illumines a people to know God's truth and supplies the grace to perform it in holy living. Yet, the interpretation of Scripture that targets a knowing and faithful relationship with God is no less "critical" than the academy's intentions, since the knowing and faithful reader must still ask whether what one finds in the biblical text actually supplies meaning and direction to a faith that is truly Christian in content and practice. This assessment of the theological problem facing the biblical interpreter is the subtext of the present chapter.

## 1. The Central Concern of Christian Theological Hermeneutics

The truth about God is now known more completely because of Jesus Christ in whom God's word and purposes became flesh and through whom God's grace and truth are mediated to us (John 1:14; Heb. 1:1-2). This conviction remains the central epistemic claim of Christian faith, and it most naturally points us to the central concern of Christian interpretation: *The church can hardly know anything at all of this incarnate Word except by reading those biblical texts about him, and by living in an abiding relationship with him and his people — a relationship that these same sacred texts both monitor and enrich.* The Christian reader of Scripture seeks to know and experience the presence of a God whose truth and grace are personified by God's Son, which now in his personal absence comes to us by his Spirit through these sacred texts when faithfully rendered for theological understanding. Accordingly, the aim of biblical interpretation is to make more clear and viable this divine truth and to excite a robust experience of God's grace, especially for those who have turned to God for salvation through, in, and because of Christ Jesus. Only in this location, then, where God's healing grace is most fully found, can a faithful people reverently approach the Scriptures and presume to find there a subject matter that is true to Jesus in whom believers posit normative truth and from whom they receive a measure of God's healing grace.

Following this statement of the beginning point for theological hermeneutics are five related claims, simply asserted and in broad strokes as the bits and pieces of a more ambitious and qualified discussion of this central concern of biblical interpretation.

1. Especially for Protestant Christians, Scripture is the exclusive (and sometimes the private) medium of God's word for God's people. Scripture, however, is not the only resource the church catholic draws upon to initiate believers into their life with Christ. The entire canonical heritage of the church includes still other "texts" — the great ecumenical creeds, the hymns and prayers of the church, the testimonies of the saints who exemplify faithful living for us all, and the theological writings of faithful tradents — that help to chart the formation of theological ideas and biblical interpretation within the history of the church. To these texts one might add the affective media of theological understanding, such as the sacraments and religious experience of God's people. These all congregate the subject matter of Christian theological reflection, which the interpretive community then relates carefully and self-critically to that word of God made incarnate in Jesus Christ; it is this heritage, interpreted as a mutually informing whole, that is constitutive of what it means to be the church and to do as the church ought.

2. The task of theological interpretation cannot escape the epistemological and social contexts in which it operates. The modern historicism determines the normative meaning of Scripture in terms of "what happened," and so approaches biblical texts as a window, presumed "darkened" by theological conjecture, through which we might find the "real" Jesus within his own historical setting. On this basis, then, truth is mediated through this reconstructed Jesus of history; and biblical texts (especially the synoptic Gospels) serve merely to circumscribe the limits of this quest. The postmodern intellectual situation, however, has challenged the epistemology envisaged by this quest after the historical Jesus in three profoundly important ways.[3] First, we are now more keenly aware of the practical impossibility, even futility of the scientific quest after faith's normative meaning, when it is posited in some recon-

---

3. Joel B. Green has sharply criticized the naïveté of employing a "modern scientific world-view of history" to assess the historiography of biblical writers (see his "In Quest of the Historical: Jesus, the Gospels, and Historicisms Old and New," *CSR* 27 [1999]: 544-60) and has provided a working bibliography as an entry into this question with respect to the historical-critical study of Luke-Acts ("Luke-Acts and Ancient Historiography," in Joel B. Green and Michael C. McKeever, *Luke-Acts and New Testament Historiography*, IBRB 8 [Grand Rapids: Baker, 1994], pp. 91-94).

structed and, ironically, speculative past found someplace "behind" the biblical text. Second, we are now more keenly aware that the execution of historical criticism inhibits — I think mainly because of the method's limited task rather than the interpreter's intent — the interpreter's ability to relate in meaningful ways the theological subject matter of the biblical text and its contemporary implications. Finally, we are now more keenly aware of the rich diversity found in both the biblical witness to God's word and in the indigenous responses to it by faithful interpreters throughout the church catholic.

3. The faith community receives and reads this biblical word as the word of God in terms of its particular place and its particular time in history. In other words, the canonical audience of Scripture is ecclesial and contemporary rather than authorial and ancient. A fully *critical* theological hermeneutic, then, demands that interpreters constantly struggle to discern how the truth of God, mediated through these stable, sacred texts, is ever adaptable for ever-new audiences of readers whose Christian witness is challenged by the changing contingencies of particular moments in time. Interpretation that targets theological understanding is always provisional and unfolding in its details, because the word of God is multivalent and is heard differently and only in part by particular persons in diverse places — in Brueggemann's nice phrase, "interpretation is . . . local praxis."[4] In this sense the word of God disclosed through the reading of the biblical text can never achieve a permanent expression or recover its full meaning. This shift of hermeneutical valence from an authorial to a text's "divine meaning" underscores the dynamism of postmodern biblical interpretation, where interpreters no longer pursue a single meaning they presume will be found fixed in the mind of the human author of a text; rather, we seek to discern some fresh meaning that God intends to convey through that text to its current readers. After all, a biblical writing is no longer the exclusive property of its author(s), any more than its intended audience consists only of those auditors/readers the author originally addressed. A biblical writing is a canonical property with a life of its own, and the privileged setting for its current interpretation is the worshiping community who submits before its biblical canon to hear the word of the Lord Almighty.

Such discernment is not a mystical or magical result. The medium of

---

4. Walter Brueggemann, *Theology of the Old Testament: Testimony, Dispute, Advocacy* (Minneapolis: Fortress, 1997), p. 112.

this revelatory transaction is the biblical text itself, requiring reading strategies that critically scrutinize its literary, rhetorical, and ideological composition. Yet, Scripture's larger meaning also derives from the specific and concrete setting of its current readers — from the faith tradition to which they belong and the social currents that either threaten or empower their faithful response to God.[5] That is, the status of believers in a particular setting requires critical discernment of their present situation so that one meaning of a text may be recovered by the interpreter to "afflict the comfortable" (prophetic meaning) and still another to "comfort the afflicted" (pastoral meaning). The religious location of a particular interpreter helps to determine the thematic accent or pattern of response proposed by an interpretation. For example, the interpreter who seeks after theological understanding within and for a Pentecostal communion of believers will naturally intensify the importance of a believer's responsiveness to God's sanctifying Spirit — an orienting concern of Pentecostal theology. The strong reader who stands within and for a particular Christian communion within the church catholic, then, is ever alert to its particular "rule of faith" which brings to light certain, more apropos dimensions of a text's theological meaning, not to disregard them but to recognize their importance for revitalizing its particular contribution to the whole people of God. This point is nicely illustrated by the next chapter, with which this one is paired.

4. The process of learning about Jesus by reading Scripture in the context of the worshiping community is complemented by the process of learning Jesus in the context of a dynamic, growing relationship with him. In both settings the Spirit of God insinuates itself upon the believer to mediate the truth and grace of Jesus. In either setting one confronts the similar risk of suppressing the diversity of interpretation or reducing God's word to a single, simple conception. The careful study of biblical texts about Jesus, which aims at knowing the truth and grace of God, is both indispensable and incomplete; likewise, the attentive relationship between the trusting believer and the living Jesus is both indispensable and incomplete. At the very least, biblical interpretation is influenced in powerful ways by the faithful interpreter's personal experience of the risen Lord, even as the individual interpreter learns Jesus more fully and accurately within a communal context.

5. For this general point, see Sandra M. Schneiders, *The Revelatory Text: Interpreting the New Testament as Sacred Text* (San Francisco: HarperCollins, 1991).

In making this point, I have in mind Kierkegaard's disquiet over the institutional reification of Jesus, who is known only as a Christian symbol or is objectified in the truth claims of a particular faith tradition or biblical writing. The whole truth of the living Jesus is learned more immediately through his Spirit in our lives. Thus, we make a mistake by supposing that we can only come to know the truth of Jesus by remembering what he once said and did according to the Scriptures. The long and complex process of knowing what manner of truth and grace truly came to us with Jesus must include those ordinary moments of life when we simply and quietly engage and concretely experience the transforming Spirit of Jesus in our lives.[6]

5. Issues of the text's real authority for Christian formation are, of course, decisive in determining the interpreter's approach to the text itself; no less decisive, however, is whether the interpreter has the authority to render Scripture as the authoritative word of God for the people of God. What characterizes, then, the "strong reader"? Suffice it to say that the church should surely expect more of its magisterium than guild-certified mastery of theological ideas and technical tools! If the church has formed Scripture to form the church's theological understanding and Christian living, then it should also have an abiding concern for an interpreter's maturity *as a believer,* deeply rooted in the life of a worshiping community, to insure a discriminating response to Scripture as a sacred medium of God's truth and grace. This more subjective response to the studied text, fashioned by the believer's humility toward others and pious devotion toward God, brings balance to the modern critic's response to this same text, equally subjective, of a dogged suspicion of its sacred intent as well as the subjectivity of its other interpreters. What must be admitted is that faithful readers who approach these texts as Holy Scripture cannot be neutral or objective about what they read; their faith will incline them to make meaning of these sacred writings in order to form (pastoral intent) or reform (prophetic intent) the Christian life and faith of those with whom faith and life is shared. In this sense a "ruled" reading of Scripture is primarily interested in Christian formation.

The practical question of any interpreter's competence to lead in the formation of the faith community rests upon two different although integral credentials. The first is *task oriented:* What skills are characteristic of

---

6. In this regard, see Luke Timothy Johnson's splendid book, *Living Jesus* (San Francisco: HarperCollins, 1999).

the competent interpreter who makes exegetical and interpretive decisions that are true to the plain meaning of the biblical text and the history of its interpretation within the church? Christian understanding, if mediated by biblical texts, is predicated by what these texts actually intend to teach — a discrimination that requires the educated skills of precise dissection and careful analysis. The second credential is *faith oriented:* What beliefs does the competent interpreter possess to find a wider meaning that serves Scripture's theological and soteriological aims, especially for a particular faith tradition? If biblical interpretation is faith seeking understanding, then it is a sacramental as well as an intellectual activity. To the extent that faithful interpreters enjoy a deep and mature relationship with God, then, they will be better able to provide oversight to a history of biblical interpretation that contributes to the theological and spiritual formation of its current audience.

## 2. The Canon of Christian Interpretation

If the central concern of biblical interpretation is to increase the believer's knowledge of God's truth and grace, incarnate in Christ Jesus and now mediated through biblical texts, then the critical question to ask at this point is whether there is available to us a particular interpretation of Scripture that is truly Christian and constitutes a word on target for its students. To say that the truth of God's word is mediated through biblical texts, oft-interpreted over time and in many locations through discoveries of original meaning hitherto undetected, says nothing about whether the content and consequence of that text's interpretation are truly Christian.[7]

The principal contention of this chapter is that the canon that measures the legitimacy and efficacy of the Bible's interpretation is the church's Rule of Faith. The continuing capacity of Scripture to mediate the truth and grace of God must continually be tested by application of this same "grammar of beliefs" which orders the community's confession of faith in God. A Christian conception of theological truth and experienced grace is now disclosed to us through "ruled" interpretations of the Christian Bible, whose content and consequence are roughly analogous to what

7. This is the important concern of Charles M. Wood in *The Formation of Christian Understanding: An Essay in Theological Hermeneutics* (Philadelphia: Westminster, 1981).

the church remembers to be the truth and grace of God instantiated in the Lord Jesus.[8]

Scripture is not self-interpreting, then, but is rather rendered coherent and relevant by faithful interpreters whose interpretations are constrained by this Rule. This claim seems evident to me, since the church's christological "grammar of theological agreements" came first with and was fashioned by the life and teaching of Jesus, not first with and because of the Christian Bible. Scripture's authority for Christians is predicated on the congruence of its subject matter with the revelation of God's Son. One can even imagine that these same "theological agreements" constituted the Lord's own "grammar" when he prepared his apostles to succeed him in ministry (Luke 24:44-46; Acts 1:3), before the earliest Christian creeds were formulated, the NT writings were composed, and the Christian Bible canonized. From the very beginning of the Christian era, the community of Christ's disciples confessed a cache of beliefs and told a story of God's gospel that ordered the protocol of God's salvation they would continue to preach and practice. Under the light shed abroad by this sacred gospel, believed and proclaimed, the subject matter and practical results of the canonical heritage, Scripture included, were recognized (or not) by the church as divinely inspired, and so were preserved and authorized (or not) as "apostolic" texts of one sort or another, divinely inspired for Christian formation.[9]

The struggle for control of Scripture's interpretation, which supplies content for a truly Christian faith, is an ancient one. Of course, it is true that his apostles received the Jewish Scriptures with rabbi Jesus; in this

---

8. See C. Stephen Evans, *The Historical Christ and the Jesus of Faith: The Incarnational Narrative as History* (Oxford: Clarendon, 1996), for the epistemic importance in positing continuity between the life of Jesus remembered and the lives of Jesus subsequently narrated and canonized in Scripture's gospel.

9. I seriously doubt that the apostolicity of a biblical text can be settled on purely historical grounds (i.e., whether a particular apostle wrote a given text or not). The issues at stake are largely theological, and have more to do with the performance of a biblical text in the Christian formation of its recipients. Thus, to say a text is "apostolic" and therefore normative for Christian formation is to speak metaphorically of its *subject matter* and not its human authorship. The content and consequence of a writing cohere with the truth and grace the apostles witnessed in Christ Jesus. Likewise, to speak of a text's "divine inspiration" is not to say that certain authors were "inspired" by God to write down God's word(s); rather, it is to speak of the canonical text's capacity to mediate God's word to its current interpreters, who faithfully seek after theological understanding.

same sense, the faith community has always had a Bible to mediate the word of God to guide its theological formation. Yet, this same biblical people did not always have a *Christian interpretation* of the Bible; this also came with Jesus, but not until his messianic mission was complete and his promised Spirit was given at Pentecost.[10] It is in this wider sense that we can speak of the church's Rule of Faith as existing prior to its Bible; indeed, Scripture took its final canonical shape by analogy to this extant Rule. The church's first sacred writings, gratefully received from the synagogue, came to function as God's first testament for believers only when its apostolic interpretation cohered to the truth and grace revealed to the apostles through the Lord Jesus. To this Scripture were added certain Christian writings, gratefully preserved and received from the earliest church, to form the canonical whole, and for this same reason. Sharply put, then, Scripture was received as God's word by the faith community because its content cohered to the core beliefs of its christological confession; likewise, any interpretation of Scripture is now gladly received as truly Christian when it agrees with this same Rule of Faith.

*1 Clement* 7.2 referred to a "canon" by which to guide Christians in a pervasively non-Christian world; for Clement, this consisted of a grammar of integral Christian beliefs (and not yet Christian writings) to which all true believers cohere. Indeed, the NT already envisages these core beliefs in various creedal formulae and hymnic stanzas (e.g., Luke 1:46-55; Phil. 2:6-11; Col. 1:15-20; 1 Tim. 3:16; Heb. 6:2; Rev. 1:5-8). Suffice it to say that these formulae are mainly fragments from very early confessions of a christological monotheism, whose subtext for Scripture's readers is the gospel narrative of Jesus' life and work. Thus, for Irenaeus, who is usually credited with introducing the idea of a biblical canon in the middle of the second century, the actual Rule of Faith *(regula fidei)* did not yet consist of canonical texts; but still what the church had preserved were sacred texts that mediated the truth and grace of God, precisely because they recalled the precious memories of Jesus for the community and were used in its preaching, singing, confessing, and witnessing (see *Adv. haer.* 3.11.9). These memories of Jesus were received from his apostles (see *Adv. haer.* 1.10.1) and passed on in written form to the church catholic through suc-

---

10. There is, of course, an eschatological horizon to Messiah's mission; in this sense we can only speak proleptically and provisionally of what he will do in the future. This belief in the parousia of Christ supplies a more dynamic quality to the Rule of Faith.

cession of its canonical episcopate (see *Adv. haer.* 3.3.3). It may well be the case that Irenaeus could not imagine how any sacred text could function profitably within the faith community unless guided by a grammar of Christian beliefs. In any case, it is important to note that in the ancient church the Rule of Faith was not identical to the biblical canon, even though both served the common purpose of Christian formation. Clearly by this ancient record, the emergent biblical canon cannot stand alone, independent of the wider canonical heritage, as a self-interpreting text.

It should also be noted by this same record, again, that the normative address for reception of this sacred heritage is the worshiping community where the believer hears and more fully experiences God's truth and grace — not the academy where students come to know the systematics of God's word, whatever its benefits might be. The pietistic bias is sometimes added to this claim that the believer's resolve to follow the church's christological rule is strengthened all the more in context of an abiding (and even mystical) union with the exalted Lord. The function of the biblical canon as originally conceived by Irenaeus, then, was to safeguard this christological memory and confession by which the church is (re)defined; indeed, the canon of truth that first measured faithful living and acceptable teaching in the church is the truth about Jesus as discerned by his apostles and preserved in the traditions of the worshiping community.

While recognizing its historical and theological complexity, this initial point is sharply made to reject two tendencies. The first tendency is of a methodological fundamentalism, which presumes that normative meaning is found only when the methodological rules of accredited scholarship are strictly observed; such a tendency, at least during the modern period, is toward a historicism where theological understanding is fixed in an ancient past. What has always concentrated the church's search for theological understanding is the word of God, incarnate in Jesus, then articulated in the variety of texts that the church recognized as trustworthy witnesses to him. Right interpretation is not determined by whether it is derived by application of critical methods to speculate on the identity of a text's author, the setting of its first readers, or its first meanings; right interpretation is determined by whether the content and consequence of a text's interpretation agree with the church's Rule of Faith.

The second tendency is to equate the church's Rule of Faith with its Scriptures, and it is still prevalent within the conservative Protestant church. Such a tendency leads to a biblicism where meaning is fixed by an uncritical appropriation of text *qua* proof text. To be sure, the equation of the Rule of Faith with the biblical canon was formulated soon enough within the church, when the idea of a biblical canon was accepted from hellenized Judaism. In this subsequent stage, the community's extant christological Rule of Faith was circumscribed concretely by a list of canonical texts consisting of both "prophets" (= OT) and "apostles" (= NT). The authority of the Christian Bible to mediate and localize the revelation of God's word within specific congregations of believers, however, presumed that these sacred writings, now canonized, could be trusted as the trustworthy witness to the incarnate Word of God, in and by whom all truth is ultimately discerned by the believer. Again, my point in briefly rehearsing this history is to separate the Bible from the Rule of Faith: The Christian Bible gives written (and so fixed) expression to the Rule of Faith. The hermeneutics used to decide which writings to preserve (or not), then to canonize (or not), even including the decision to accept Judaism's biblical canon as Christianity's OT, are at every stage of the canonical process explained within this confessional framework. That is, the Bible's original intent (and aim of its interpretation) is formative of a particular faith community whose public life and faith accords with its prior confession that Jesus is Creator's Messiah and creation's Lord.

Walter Brueggemann's recent criticism of Brevard Childs's "canonical approach" to biblical theology, whether warranted or not, underscores the importance of this point.[11] According to Childs, the ancient church's formation of Scripture and the aim of the current church's ongoing theological reflection upon it intend to give shape and direction to this christological rule. Especially troubling for Brueggemann is the implication of Childs's project for a Christian reading of the OT, and indeed, for a Christian reading that seeks to relate OT and NT as two parts of an integral whole. Brueggemann calls Childs a "consensus Protestant" whose reading of OT texts is "hegemonic" and "massively reductionistic," not only because it reads the OT under the light of the church's Rule of Faith but also because it is vested with a christological preemption that excludes all other possible (e.g., secular, Jewish, even non-Reformed Christian) interpretations. Yet, as D. Olson has rightly pointed out, Brueggemann's is not really such a devastating criticism since every biblical interpreter engaged in biblical theological reflection (including Brueggemann) necessarily seeks to localize and summarize the large ideas found in relevant parts of Scripture; every competent biblical theologian is in some sense "guilty"

---

11. Brueggemann, pp. 89-93.

of hermeneutical reductionism since theological reflection upon Scripture is always provisional and contextual. Scripture's clearest and most timely meaning for its readers is always found within a particular history; its full meaning is unfolding to the end of the age.[12]

Yet, if Scripture's interpretation is to remain truly *Christian,* its unfolding meaning for ever-changing ecclesial settings must remain fixed on the core beliefs of *Christian* faith.[13] Even though the history of biblical texts envisages an extraordinarily dynamic and fluid process — beginning with their writing and selective preservation, and their collection, arrangement, and eventual canonization as Scripture, the normative context for Christian theological reflection — these same ancient texts are currently entrusted to the church as the stable medium of God's word for today. What accounts for this remarkable stability, which can bridge ancient and contemporary horizons? In a phrase, the Rule of Faith, which operates at every stage of this canonical process, from composition to canonization, to insure that these Scriptures and their interpretation would help to form a truly Christian faith and life in continuity with the truth and grace that came to us with Jesus, the incarnate Word.

What is the substance of this "Rule of Faith"? What follows is one attempt to summarize, again in broad strokes, its subject. In my judgment the church's Rule of Faith is narrative in shape, trinitarian in substance, and relates the essential beliefs of Christianity together by the grammar of christological monotheism. Accordingly, knowledge of God is inseparable from knowledge of God's Son and Spirit; and such knowledge is impossible apart from its revelation in the events of or actions within history: inaugurated by God's creation of all things, testified to by the prophets, climaxed in and by the life and work of the risen Jesus and the Pentecost of his Spirit, whose work continues in the transformed life and transforming ministry of the one holy catholic and apostolic church, and will be consummated by the Creator's coming triumph at the parousia of the Lord Christ. The catholic and apostolic church's confession and transforming

12. D. Olson, "Biblical Theology as Provisional Monologization: A Dialogue with Childs, Brueggemann and Bakhtin," *BibInt* 6 (1998): 162-80.

13. The important contribution James A. Sanders has made to this current debate over theological hermeneutics is his insistence that the history of biblical interpretation (within and of Scripture) always envisages this dialectic between the "adaptability" of the community's current social context and the "stability" of the community's received/traditional theological norms. See, e.g., James A. Sanders, *From Sacred Story to Sacred Text: Canon as Paradigm* (Philadelphia: Fortress, 1987).

experience of this narrative of God's gospel, deeply rooted in and confirmed by its collective memory, supplies the Rule's raw material. I will leave the details to others and claim only this: The results of biblical interpretation must ever conform to this confession and experience.

The interpretive dialectic between the biblical text and the Rule of Faith in actual practice is implicit — certainly more so than between the text and the interpreter's stated methodological interests in that text. There is a sense in which biblical interpretation that is truly Christian in content and result is the by-product of the interpreter whose theological convictions conform to the Rule of Faith; the theology of an interpreter necessarily informs interpretation and even moves the interpreter discretely and with prejudice, as it were, toward a certain theological understanding of the biblical text. Yet, a critical engagement with the biblical text requires the interpreter to test theological claims by the Rule in a more deliberate manner. If the authorization of the biblical text is made by analogy to the Rule of Faith, so must the interpretation of that text; that is, the "grammar" of any interpretation of Scripture that is truly Christian must agree with the theological typology broadly set forth in the previous paragraph.

Although any interpretation that is truly Christian must envisage these theological agreements, there are those peculiar denominational distinctives that arrange these same agreements differently or place emphasis upon different claims; the ecumenical Rule of Faith is in practice a richly variegated confession. The Rule exists as various "rules" of faith that bear a striking family resemblance to each other. Each rule conforms, more or less, to the core beliefs and deeper logic of the catholic Rule of Faith. Yet, each communion's rule of faith is the product of many small changes that have taken place in every fresh attempt to respond faithfully and often courageously to new contingencies and cultural movements the church catholic has encountered, always in creative and open-ended dialogue with the stable truth claims confessed according to the Rule. The slight discriminations in what a communion of believers confesses as true according to its own rule of faith — the different adjectives and added phrases, the changed ranking of core beliefs or greater emphasis posited on this or another belief — reflect a particular community's struggles to remain faithful to God's word in a space and at a moment in time. These various rules of faith flow from the real experiences and earnest dialogue of believers in their own socioreligious locations that forced new clarity and contemporary understanding of God's word. In my case, the Methodist communion, founded in a historical moment of great social upheaval and religious apathy, presses for a more collaborative notion of salvation — so that in partnership with Christ and mediated through the sacraments (primarily of prayer, Scripture, and Holy Communion) God's grace forgives, heals, transforms, and ultimately sanctifies the believer to respond in active and ever perfecting love toward God and neighbor.[14] Indeed, only in response to God's saving grace can the believer fully experience God's promised blessings, now and in the age to come.

I would argue that these different rules of faith, safeguarded by and transmitted within different communions of believers, shape the theological interpretation of Scripture in particular directions apropos to each. Whether to correct or to nurture the faith of those belonging to a particular tradition, the deeper logic and bias (or "reductionism") of biblical interpretation for its tradents will conform, if only discretely, to their own particular rule of faith. Following Olson, then, one should admire Bakhtin's interest in the sometimes small inflections of a whole but abstracted truth that one discovers *within* a community.[15] Bakhtin supposes, I think rightly, that these variations on a single theme reflect a community's quest for truth, which is essentially partial and ongoing, and made possible only when the community of readers tolerates genuine dialogue between those members holding to competing ideas and lived experiences without ranking one as more or less important or cogent. We need thus to be reminded from time to time that Scripture itself is "many books" in "one book," that these testimonies to the gracious purpose of God stand in complementary and mutually correcting relation to one another; given the nature of these texts, then, we should not be surprised to discover similar variation within and among our various Christian communions. This kind of relativism can be abused, of course, if performed in an uncritical fashion, so that every interpretation is tolerated as equally cogent and important for Christian formation; or if embodied in a provincial fashion, in which congregations or communions adopt a sectarian isolation from other congregations and communions. A critical theological hermeneutic requires that every rule of faith must bear close family resemblance to the catholic Rule of Faith.

At the end of the day, however, the community of interpretation must replace one kind of reductionism, which seeks to conform a text's interpretation to an absolute and abstract belief, with another, more massive

---

14. See Robert W. Wall, "Toward a Wesleyan Hermeneutic of Scripture," *WTJ* 30 (1995): 50-67.

15. Olson, pp. 172-80.

and synthetic one that congregates the rich diversity of all those reductionisms sounded by a complex of interpreters, past and present — each of whom confesses beliefs that are truly Christian, although not with the same emphasis or detail, and lives a life that is truly Christian, but in and for a particular context. Only in such an interpretive community of dialogue, where each inflection maintains its own distinct timbre, can the word be fully vocalized for all to hear, and in hearing, to know what saith the Lord God Almighty.

But what of Scripture? In what sense does the church follow a biblical rule of faith? Again, I do not equate Scripture and the Rule of Faith as though the two are one and the same (see above), nor do I posit divine status for canonical texts as though this is what the church recognized when bestowing canonical authority; rather, the church preserved and canonized certain writings, and then formed the Christian Bible with them, because (when used and used properly) these writings agree with the Rule of Faith in content and consequence. Simply put, Scripture is accepted as a trustworthy source for Christian formation because its content norms and illustrates what is truly Christian.

Ecclesial authority, then, bestows upon Scripture specific roles to perform in forming Christians — nothing more than this, but surely nothing less. These are the two essential roles Scripture is authorized to perform in forming a faith and life that is truly Christian: to *constitute* what the church believes to be truly Christian, and to *correct* it when what it believes to be truly Christian really is not Christian at all. The objectives of biblical interpretation should be apropos to Scripture's canonical functions; that is, the chief aim of biblical interpretation should be the formation of a faith and life that is truly Christian by either nurturing what believers ought to believe or by assessing what believers believe but should not.

## 3. Conclusion

In this chapter I have claimed that a theological reading of Scripture is the primary practice of a diverse community of faithful interpreters who together apply the church's Rule of Faith to the biblical text to lead all believers toward theological understanding. It is also the practice of this same community to evaluate or "rule" their interpretation, whether it renders Scripture in a truly Christian direction. There is, of course, considerable reciprocity in this hermeneutical transaction, since Scripture also supplies a stable setting and normative resource for the church's ongoing theological reflection; thus, the theological maturing of Scripture's interpreter, who is best able to discern God's word in Scripture for the church, is the certain result of steadfast and humble reflection upon these same holy texts. The spiritual calculus is simple: the faithful interpreter who knows Scripture well will more fully learn the Rule's deep logic and its subtle nuances, which in turn inform a more judicious theological reading.

The intended yield of careful, text-centered exegesis is the construction of a biblical theology that is both critically discerning and truly Christian. Theological reflection on Scripture should not therefore reproduce idiosyncratic notions of God's gospel; the theological goods of any biblical writing, carefully considered, should always be true to what the text actually asserts and congruent with what believers confess to be truly Christian — in part because these same biblical texts are canonized as the trustworthy (although not necessarily uniform) analogues of the Rule of Faith. In this sense, then, the move from biblical exegesis to biblical theology is primarily a conservative enterprise, framed in every case by this very "grammar of theological agreements" by which the church has always defined what is truly Christian. Practically, this same grammar of faith should organize the topics and pattern of the interpreter's theological reflection on Scripture. There is a sense in which the dialectic between biblical text and the Rule of Faith is part of the church's wider canonical project. That is, not only is the maturing of the church's theological understanding contextualized by Scripture, but the church's interpretation of Scripture is also constrained by this more mature theological understanding. In this way the Rule of Faith "rules" the interpreter's theological reading of Scripture, constraining it so that it might perform its canonical roles as a word on target. Every interpretation of Scripture, however creative and contemporary it is, must be demonstrably analogous to the Rule of Faith; only then can it effectively mediate the truth and grace of God disclosed in Jesus Christ.

The dialectic between biblical text and the Rule of Faith is not a creation of modern or even postmodern biblical scholarship or theological reflection, but is itself inherent to the relationship between these two. On the one hand, the biblical witness to Jesus is itself already pluriform, with the result that, attempts at harmonization notwithstanding, the biblical and early church traditions *transmit* a complementary and mutually correcting diversity of perspective. Essentially narrative interpretations of Jesus — whether in the form of Gospels such as we find in the NT, in the substratum of the Pauline gospel, or in the form of the rules of faith generated in the early centuries of the church — illuminate not only the possibility but the reality of different practices for negotiating the variety of patterns of interpretation to which the advent of Christ was and remains susceptible. The Rule of Faith thus resides in a reciprocal relationship with Scripture, with the former constraining what can properly be designated as "Christian" readings of the biblical texts and the latter reminding Christians of the heterogeneity of those narrative and confessional formulations that reside not only in Scripture but often also within the "rules." This reciprocity is evident as well in the church's ongoing engagement with biblical texts as it explores the relative faithfulness of these doctrinal formulations to the biblical witness, not least given the reality that the historical contexts and controversies lying behind the conceptual innovations embodied in any particular rule of faith may have defined the content of that "rule" in local ways that are pivotal for its own historical moment but inappropriate to the global church across time. One must always inquire whether such formulations address their own social horizons too closely to serve either as legitimate distillations of biblical faith or as more universal in their appeal to or utility for the church.

The history of the church's interpretation of Scripture demonstrates that a certain depth of clarity and relevance is constantly added to a theological teaching of Scripture whenever interpreters seek to hear a fresh word of God's truth and grace for their own particular settings and faith traditions. If the objective of biblical theology is to universalize Scripture's theological quotient, the objective of constructive or practical theology is to particularize it. The evident multivalency of a biblical text, which the history of its interpretation will surely discover, is not due to the elasticity of its theological subject matter but of its meaning or meaningfulness to different audiences. Neither is any term of the Rule revised, nor any inspired biblical text de-canonized, in light of a new social setting. This dialectic of canonical texts and ecumenical Rule, both integral to the church's theological formation, is worked out in real time and in practical ways. A theological reading of Scripture, which is kept on target by general agreement with the Rule, is translated for specific communicants in a language that allows faith to be formed within particular theological traditions and cultural settings. I would argue that this final move from a consideration of how the biblical text enriches our understanding of the Rule of Faith ("biblical theology") to a consideration of how this enriched theological understanding informs the faith and practice of a particular congregation of believers ("constructive/practical theology") allows the interpreter to explore the full meaning of Scripture.

Finally, let me make two brief suggestions for employing a reading strategy that aims at this more robust theological formation. First, more threatening than the church's biblical illiteracy is its theological ignorance. Whatever epistemology of theological formation is decided upon, its prerequisite is a thorough indoctrination of the core beliefs and moral norms of Christian faith (1 Tim. 6:3). To remove the biblical interpreter from this confessional setting is to nullify both the essential control and the primary aim of biblical interpretation. The results for the church are devastating, not only in tolerating the invasive encroachment of secular norms for reason and experience but also in undermining Scripture's sacramental performance as a means of God's saving grace. Sharply put, the pervasive theological ignorance within today's church makes right faith and holy living real impossibilities. To meet this threat head-on, the church should launch a program of theological catechesis which initiates believers into the grammar of Christian faith (i.e., the Rule of Faith). Such training must emphasize the history of their own faith tradition, and within this history, clarification of their most precious theological and ethical emphases (i.e., their rule of faith). I continue to be impressed by how few in my own faith tradition know of "Christian Perfection"; even their understanding of this most precious feature of the Wesleyan heritage is severely gapped or seriously distorted. Theological education must precede and then lead the community in using Scripture as a blessed sacrament of the church.

Second, while ever concerned about the privatization of Scripture's meaning or the appropriation of Scripture to serve personal or ideological ends, I nevertheless am a fervent champion of the recreational reading of Scripture, reading Scripture simply for the enjoyment of reading about God. As important as Scripture's role is in the theological formation of the church, the old pietistic connection of Scripture with *character* formation is a critical value which today's church must seek to recover. I suspect Scripture's devotional role in nurturing the sorts of persons who simply know (even intuit) God's heart is a tacit yet crucial feature of a cogent epistemology of theology. That is, not only should we press for a devotional reading strategy that "rules" Scripture's present meaning, but also for one that picks up Scripture daily to read its stories in prayerful partnership with the Holy Spirit for no other reason than to grow in Christ. The scholarly concerns for a critical and caring theological hermeneutic are finally secondary to a life brought to maturity by God's grace, which is the ultimate project and purpose of the church's canonical heritage.

# CHAPTER 6

# Reading the Bible from within Our Traditions: A Pentecostal Hermeneutic as Test Case

JOHN CHRISTOPHER THOMAS

## 1. Pentecostalism and the Bible

Pentecostalism is a relatively recent phenomenon in comparison to its Christian siblings, given that its formal origins go back about a hundred years. By any means of calculation it continues to grow very rapidly in many places around the globe and accounts for a not insignificant percentage of the world's Christians. However, Pentecostalism continues to be largely misunderstood by many outside the movement. For example, there are those who "see Pentecostalism as essentially fundamentalist Christianity with a doctrine of Spirit baptism and gifts added on," and others who view it "as an experience which fits equally well in any spirituality or theological system — perhaps adding some needed zest or interest."[1] Yet, those who know the tradition well are aware how far from the truth such assessments are. As Donald W. Dayton and Steven J. Land have demonstrated, standing at the theological heart of Pentecostalism is the message of the fivefold gospel: Jesus is Savior, Sanctifier, Holy Spirit Baptizer, Healer, and

1. Steven J. Land, *Pentecostal Spirituality: A Passion for the Kingdom*, JPTSup 1 (Sheffield: Sheffield Academic Press, 1993), p. 29.

Coming King.[2] This paradigm not only identifies the theological heart of the tradition, but also immediately reveals the ways in which Pentecostalism as a movement is both similar to and dissimilar from others within Christendom. To mention but two examples, when the fivefold gospel paradigm is used as the main point of reference, its near kinship to the Holiness tradition is obvious, as is the fundamental difference with many of those within the more Reformed and evangelical traditions.

Given the ethos of the tradition, it should come as little surprise that many in the movement would have a distinctive approach to the text of Scripture. Several general observations should serve to illustrate this point.

As a para-modern movement,[3] Pentecostalism has been suspicious of the claims made, as a result of the Enlightenment, for rationalism in the interpretation of Scripture. Given this suspicion, it comes as no surprise to Pentecostals that the results of an unbridled rationalism have been anything but uniform, as witnessed in the diversity of current theological thought, which in and of itself suggests that there is more to interpretation than reason.[4]

Unlike many of their Christian siblings, Pentecostals have had a keen interest in, and a place for the role of, the Holy Spirit in the interpretive process. For Pentecostals, it is indeed one of the oddities of modern theological scholarship that across the theological spectrum approaches to Scripture have little or no appreciation for the work of the Holy Spirit in interpretation.[5] As might be expected, such a hermeneutical component is of no little interest to Pentecostals.[6]

---

2. Donald W. Dayton, *The Theological Roots of Pentecostalism* (Peabody, Mass.: Hendrickson, 1991); Land, *Pentecostal Spirituality*.

3. Pentecostals continue to show ambivalence toward both sides in the debates about modernity and postmodernity, and are not fully at home in either. For the term "para-modern" I am indebted to my colleague Jackie Johns. For a helpful analysis of Pentecostalism's place in a postmodern world, see Jackie D. Johns, "Pentecostalism and the Postmodern Worldview," *JPT* 7 (1995): 73-96.

4. This assessment is true even of evangelical theology, where a high view of Scripture has brought little consensus on a variety of interpretive matters — cf. esp. Robert K. Johnston, *Evangelicals at an Impasse: Biblical Authority in Practice* (Atlanta: John Knox, 1979).

5. Clark Pinnock, *The Scripture Principle* (San Francisco: Harper & Row, 1984), p. 155.

6. One of the few academic treatments of this topic among Pentecostals is the work of John W. Wyckoff, "The Relationship of the Holy Spirit to Biblical Hermeneutics" (Ph.D. diss., Baylor University, 1990).

Given the community orientation of Pentecostalism in general, the role of the community in the interpretive process is extremely important as well. Such an emphasis is especially needed owing to the excesses of a somewhat rampant individualism among interpreters generally. For Pentecostals, accountability within the Christian community is crucial in the interpretive process.

From early on Pentecostals have insisted upon the importance of experiential presuppositions in interpretation and the role of narrative in the doing of theology. Recent decades have witnessed paradigm shifts in the field of hermeneutics which have focused on some of these same emphases.

Finally, it should be noted that Pentecostals generally have an extremely high view of Scripture. One of the reasons for such a view is the awareness among Pentecostals of the immediate and direct ministry of the Holy Spirit through Spirit baptism, spiritual gifts, and other manifestations. If, as Pentecostals have come to know, the Holy Spirit could manifest himself in such powerful ways in the lives of ordinary men and women, then it is easy to believe that he could inspire human beings to produce the Bible.[7] Suffice it to say that Pentecostals regard the Scripture as normative and seek to live their lives in light of its teaching.

But what does a Pentecostal hermeneutic look like and, more importantly, how does it function? What are the essential components of such an interpretive approach and how does one settle on them?

---

7. Yet, despite their fervent belief in the inspiration of the Scripture, many Pentecostal groups made very simple statements about inspiration, leaving unsaid many of the things their non-Pentecostal counterparts would have stated. For example, the earliest official Church of God (Cleveland, Tennessee) statement about Scripture (*Evangel* [15 August 1910]) said, "The Church of God stands for the whole Bible rightly divided. The New Testament is the only rule for government and discipline." This brief statement, adopted in the General Assembly of 1911, proved adequate for nearly forty years, until the church adopted a more detailed statement in the Declaration of Faith, which contained a more expansive statement on inspiration similar to that of the National Association of Evangelicals. At the 1948 General Assembly of the Church of God, the following article was adopted: "We believe in the verbal inspiration of the Bible."

Such a history should not be taken to suggest that Pentecostals did not always believe wholeheartedly in the inspiration of Scripture, but that Pentecostals had their own concerns alongside debates that were mostly going on elsewhere within the evangelical community. For a more complete discussion, see John Christopher Thomas, "The Word and the Spirit," in *Ministry and Theology: Studies for the Church and Its Leaders* (Cleveland, Tenn.: Pathway, 1996), pp. 13-20.

This chapter seeks neither to offer an exhaustive overview of the topic of Pentecostal hermeneutics nor to articulate in a detailed fashion a sophisticated theory of interpretation.[8] Rather, it seeks to explore one particular paradigm derived from the NT itself as a model for a Pentecostal hermeneutic.[9]

## 2. Acts 15

It is possible, of course, to find a number of different hermeneutical approaches in the NT, and several full-length studies have been devoted to the use of the OT by various NT writers.[10] Of these, one in particular has

8. For some recent attempts at Pentecostal hermeneutics, cf. the following: Gerald T. Sheppard, "Pentecostalism and the Hermeneutics of Dispensationalism: Anatomy of an Uneasy Relationship," *Pneuma* 6, no. 2 (1984): 5-33; Mark D. McLean, "Toward a Pentecostal Hermeneutic," *Pneuma* 6, no. 2 (1984): 35-56; Howard M. Ervin, "Hermeneutics: A Pentecostal Option," in *Essays on Apostolic Themes,* ed. Paul Elbert (Peabody, Mass.: Hendrickson, 1985), pp. 23-35; French L. Arrington, "Hermeneutics," in *Dictionary of Pentecostal and Charismatic Movements,* ed. Stanley Burgess and Gary B. McGee (Grand Rapids: Zondervan, 1988), pp. 376-89; Roger Stronstad, "Trends in Pentecostal Hermeneutics," *Paraclete* 22, no. 3 (1988): 1-12; Roger Stronstad, "Pentecostal Experience and Hermeneutics," *Paraclete* 26, no. 1 (1992): 14-30; Jackie D. Johns and Cheryl Bridges Johns, "Yielding to the Spirit: A Pentecostal Approach to Group Bible Study," *JPT* 1 (1992): 109-34; Arden C. Autry, "Dimensions of Hermeneutics in Pentecostal Focus," *JPT* 3 (1993): 29-50; Richard Israel, Daniel Albrecht, and Randall G. McNally, "Pentecostals and Hermeneutics: Texts, Rituals and Community," *Pneuma* 15 (1993): 137-61; Timothy B. Cargal, "Beyond the Fundamentalist-Modernist Controversy: Pentecostals and Hermeneutics in a Postmodern Age," *Pneuma* 15 (1993): 163-87; Robert P. Menzies, "Jumping Off the Postmodern Bandwagon," *Pneuma* 16 (1994): 115-20; Gerald T. Sheppard, "Biblical Interpretation after Gadamer," *Pneuma* 16 (1994): 121-41; John McKay, "When the Veil Is Taken Away: The Impact of Prophetic Experience on Biblical Interpretation," *JPT* 5 (1994): 17-40; Rick D. Moore, "Deuteronomy and the Fire of God: A Critical Charismatic Interpretation," *JPT* 7 (1995): 11-33; Robert O. Baker, "Pentecostal Bible Reading: Toward a Model of Reading for the Formation of Christian Affections," *JPT* 7 (1995): 34-48; and Ken J. Archer, "Pentecostal Hermeneutics: Retrospect and Prospect," *JPT* 8 (1996): 63-81.

9. For a more complete discussion, see John Christopher Thomas, "Women, Pentecostals, and the Bible: An Experiment in Pentecostal Hermeneutics," *JPT* 5 (1994): 41-56.

10. Cf., e.g., E. Earle Ellis, *The Old Testament in Early Christianity* (Grand Rapids: Baker, 1992); Richard B. Hays, *Echoes of Scripture in the Letters of Paul* (New Haven: Yale University Press, 1989); Craig A. Evans and James A. Sanders, *Luke and Scripture: The Function of Sacred Tradition in Luke-Acts* (Minneapolis: Fortress, 1993).

had a special appeal for many Pentecostals, especially at the popular level, and has recently appeared also in academic discussions on Pentecostal hermeneutics.[11] This approach is that revealed in the deliberations of the Jerusalem Council as described in Acts 15:1-29.

As is well known, the Jerusalem Council was convened to determine if Gentile believers in Jesus must convert to Judaism in order to become full-fledged Christians. Luke relates that when Paul and Barnabas arrived in Jerusalem with the report regarding the conversion of the Gentiles, certain believers who were members of the religious party of the Pharisees demanded that the Gentile believers (1) be circumcised and (2) keep the Law of Moses. As a result of this report and its somewhat mixed reception, the apostles and elders gathered together to look into this matter.

The first person to speak, Peter, begins by noting the actions of God among them. It was *God* who chose to allow the Gentiles to hear the gospel (through the mouth of Peter) and believe. It was the *God* who knows all hearts who testified to the validity of their faith by giving them the Holy Spirit. *God* had made no distinction between Jew and Gentile either in the giving of the Spirit or in the cleansing of hearts. In the light of such experience, Peter reasons that to place the yoke (of the Law?) upon these Gentiles would be tantamount to testing (πειράζετε) God. In contrast to the bearing of this yoke, Peter says it is by faith that all are saved!

This speech is followed by a report from Barnabas and Paul, which also places emphasis upon God and the things he did through them among the Gentiles, such as signs and wonders.

James now takes center stage and addresses the group. He not only interprets Peter's testimony to mean that God has received the Gentiles as a people unto his name, but he also goes on to argue that this experience of the church is in agreement with the words of the prophets, citing Amos 9:11-12 as evidence. Therefore (διό), in light of what God had done and the agreement of these actions with the words of the prophets, James concludes that those Gentiles who are turning to God should not have their task made more difficult by requiring of them the observance of circumcision and the keeping of the Law of Moses. Rather, these Gentile converts are to be instructed to abstain from food polluted by idols, from sexual immorality, from the meat of strangled animals, and from blood. In the letter

11. Cf. esp. Arrington, pp. 387-88; Rick D. Moore, "Approaching God's Word Biblically: A Pentecostal Perspective" (paper presented at the annual meeting of the Society for Pentecostal Studies, Fresno, Calif., 1989).

written to communicate the findings of this meeting to the church at large, the decision is described as resulting from the Holy Spirit, for verse 28 says, "It seemed good to the Holy Spirit and to us not to burden you with anything beyond the following requirements" (NIV).

Several things are significant from Acts 15 for the purposes of this essay. First, it is remarkable how often the experience of the church through the hand of God is appealed to in the discussion. Clearly, this (somewhat unexpected?) move of God in the life of the church (the inclusion of the Gentiles) was understood to be the result of the Holy Spirit's activity. It is particularly significant that the church seems to have begun with its experience and only later moves to a consideration of the Scripture.

Second, Peter's experience in the matter of Gentile conversions has led him to the conclusion that even to question the Gentile converts' place in or means of admission to the church draws dangerously close to testing God. Apparently Peter means that to question the validity of the Gentile believers' standing before God, in the face of what the Spirit has done, is to come dangerously close to experiencing the judgment of God for such undiscerning disobedience. In this regard it is probably not without significance that earlier in Acts (5:9) Peter asked Sapphira how she could agree to test the Spirit of the Lord (πειράσαι τὸ πνεῦμα κυρίου) through her lie. The results of her testing are well known. Is Peter implying a similar fate for those who stand in the way of the Gentile converts?

Third, Barnabas and Paul are portrayed as discussing primarily, if not exclusively, their experience of the signs and wonders that God had performed among them as a basis for the acceptance of the Gentiles. That such a statement would stand on its own says a great deal about the role of the community's experience of God in their decision-making process.

Fourth, James also emphasizes the experience of the church through the activity of God as a reason for accepting the Gentile converts. It is clear that Luke intends the readers to understand that James adds his own support to the experience of the Spirit in the church; James does not simply restate Peter's earlier words, but actually puts his own interpretive spin upon them.

Fifth, it is at this point that Scripture is appealed to for the first time in the discussion. One of the interesting things about the passage cited (Amos 9:11-12) is that its attraction seems primarily to have been that it agreed with their experience of God in the church.[12] But how did James

12. As Luke Timothy Johnson (*Scripture and Discernment: Decision Making in*

(and the church with him) settle on this particular text? Did Amos intend what James claims that the text means? Could not the believers from the religious party of the Pharisees have appealed with equal or greater validity to other texts that speak about Israel's exclusivity and the Gentiles' relationship to Israel (cf. esp. Exod. 19:5; Deut. 7:6; 14:2; 26:18-19)?

When one reads the Hebrew text of Amos 9:11-12, or a translation based upon the Hebrew text, it becomes immediately obvious that there is no explicit reference to the inclusion of Gentiles as part of the people of God. In point of fact, in the Hebrew text Amos says God will work on behalf of the descendants of David "so that they may possess the remnant of Edom and all the nations, which are called by the name, says the Lord that does this." Although it is possible to read the reference to Edom and the other nations in a negative or retaliatory sense, it is also possible to see here an implicit promise concerning how Edom (one of the most hostile enemies of Israel) and other nations will themselves be brought into the (messianic) reign of a future Davidic king.[13] Whether or not such a meaning was intended by Amos is unclear.

By way of contrast, the LXX rendering of Amos 9:11-12 seems to intend a message about the inclusion of other individuals and nations that seek to follow God. At this crucial point, the text of Acts is much closer to the LXX, which reads, "That the remnant of people and all the Gentiles, upon whom my name is called, may seek after (me), says the Lord who does these things." The difference between the Hebrew text and the LXX seems to have resulted, in part, from reading Edom (אדום) as Adam (אדם) and taking the verb "they shall possess (יירשו)" as "they shall seek (ידרשו)."[14] Whatever may account for this rendering,[15] it is clear that

---

the Church [Nashville: Abingdon, 1996], p. 105) observes, "What is remarkable, however, is that the text is confirmed by the narrative [events previously narrated in Acts], not the narrative by Scripture."

13. So argues Walter C. Kaiser, "The Davidic Promise and the Inclusion of the Gentiles (Amos 9:9-15 and Acts 15:13-18): A Test Passage for Theological Systems," *JETS* 20 (1977): 102.

14. Carl Friedrich Keil, *Minor Prophets* (Grand Rapids: Eerdmans, 1975), p. 334 n. 1; David A. Hubbard, *Joel and Amos* (Leicester: Inter-Varsity, 1989), p. 242.

15. Some wish to argue that a Hebrew text that challenges the MT at this point lies behind the LXX. Cf. Michael A. Braun, "James' Use of Amos at the Jerusalem Council: Steps toward a Possible Solution of the Textual and Theological Problems," *JETS* 20 (1977): 116. Richard J. Bauckham ("James and the Jerusalem Church," in *The Book of Acts in Its Palestinian Setting*, ed. Richard J. Bauckham, A1CS 4 [Grand Rapids: Eerdmans, 1995], pp. 415-80) insists that "the scriptural quotation in 15:16-18 is composed

James, as described in Acts 15:17, shows a decided preference for the LXX's more inclusive reading.

But why did James choose this particular text for support, when other OT passages (e.g., Isa. 2:3; 42:6; Mic. 4:2; and esp. Zech. 2:11) appear to offer better and clearer support for the inclusion of Gentiles within the people of God? Such a choice is difficult to understand until one views it within the broader context of the Lukan narratives. Specifically, Luke seems concerned to demonstrate that the promises made to David are fulfilled in Jesus and thus have implications for the church.[16]

In the Gospel, Joseph is identified as a descendant of David (Luke 1:27). The angel speaks to Mary regarding Jesus, saying, "The Lord God will give him the throne of his father David, and he will reign over the house of Jacob forever; his kingdom will never end" (1:32-33 NIV). Zechariah (apparently) speaks of Jesus when he says,

> He has raised up a horn of salvation for us
> in the house of his servant David. (1:69 NIV)

Joseph and Mary go to the city of David for the census because Joseph is of the house and line of David (2:4). Later, the angels direct the shepherds to the city of David to find Christ the Lord (2:11). In Luke's genealogy of Jesus, David is mentioned (3:31). In a dispute over the Sabbath, Jesus appeals to the actions of David (6:3). The blind beggar near Jericho addresses Jesus as the Son of David when he calls for help (18:38-39). In a discussion with the Sadducees and teachers of the Law, Jesus says that although the Messiah is called Son of David, David calls him Lord (20:41-44).

This same emphasis continues in the book of Acts. Peter states that the Holy Spirit spoke Scripture through the mouth of David (1:16). In the Pentecost sermon Peter attributes Scripture to David again (2:25) and says that he foretold the resurrection of Jesus (2:29-36). A little later in the narrative David is again identified as one through whom the Holy Spirit spoke (4:25). In Stephen's speech David is described as one who enjoyed God's

---

and interpreted by the skillful use of contemporary Jewish exegetical methods," and that one must take seriously how "the quotation is exegetically linked with the terms of the apostolic decree" (p. 453; see further, Bauckham, "James and the Gentiles," in *History, Literature, and Society in the Book of Acts,* ed. Ben Witherington III [Cambridge: Cambridge University Press, 1996], pp. 154-84).

16. On this theme cf. Mark L. Strauss, *The Davidic Messiah in Luke-Acts: The Promise and Its Fulfillment in Lukan Christology,* JSNTSup 110 (Sheffield: Sheffield Academic Press, 1995).

favor (7:45-46). Several references to David are found in Acts 13, in Paul's sermon at Pisidian Antioch. David is said to have been a man after God's own heart whose descendant is the Savior Jesus (13:22-23). Jesus is said to have been given "the holy and sure blessings promised to David" (13:34 NIV), and his death is contrasted with that of David (13:36).

The reader of Luke's narratives would not be surprised at this continued emphasis on David, nor that James would bring it to its culmination. It would appear, then, that part of the reason for the choice of this particular text from Amos is to continue the emphasis on the continuity between David and Jesus. It may also be significant that the first citation of Amos (5:25-27) in Acts (7:42-44) speaks of exile, while Acts 15 speaks of restoration.[17] To cite the rebuilding of David's fallen tent as the context for the admission of Gentiles into Israel was perhaps the most effective way of making this point.

Sixth, James clearly speaks with authority as he discloses his decision. That the decision is closely tied to the previous discussions is indicated by the use of "therefore" (διό). That James has the authority to render a verdict is suggested by the emphatic use of the personal pronoun "I" (ἐγὼ κρίνω). But as the epistle itself reveals (Acts 15:24), the decision was one that involved the whole group and the guidance of the Holy Spirit.

Seventh, several stipulations were imposed upon the Gentile converts. Significantly, reference to the necessity of circumcision is omitted from these. Aside from the directive to abstain from sexual immorality, the other commands refer to food laws. Although there is some evidence that their origin is in the regulations regarding aliens who lived among the Hebrews, as found in Leviticus 17–18, their intent is a bit puzzling. Are they to be seen as the lowest common denominator of the Torah's dietary laws or as the true meaning of the food laws? Are they intended to be seen as universally valid? The practice of the later church (and perhaps Paul's own advice in 1 Cor. 8:1-13) has not viewed the food laws as binding, how-

---

17. For a comprehensive discussion of this approach, cf. Pierre-Antoine Peulo, *Le problème ecclésial des Acts à la lumière de deux prophéties d'Amos* (Paris: Cerf, 1985). Cf. also Jacques Dupont, "'Je rebâtirai la cabane de David qui est tombée' (Ac 15,16 = Am 9,11)," in *Glaube und Eschatologie,* ed. Erich Grässer and Otto Merk (Tübingen: J. C. B. Mohr [Paul Siebeck], 1985), pp. 19-32. Max Turner (*Power from on High: The Spirit in Israel's Restoration and Witness in Luke-Acts,* JPTSup 9 [Sheffield: Sheffield Academic Press, 1996], pp. 314-15) argues strongly for an interpretation that emphasizes "that Zion's restoration is *well under way* as a consequence of Jesus' exaltation to David's throne."

ever.[18] Perhaps it is best to view them as (temporary) steps to ensure table fellowship between Jewish and Gentile believers. When the composition of the church changed to a predominantly Gentile constituency, it appears that these directives regarding food were disregarded.

### 3. The Hermeneutic of Acts 15

What sort of hermeneutical paradigm is revealed from the method of the Jerusalem Council, and what are the components of this model? Of the many things that might be said, perhaps the most obvious is the role of the community in the interpretive process. Several indicators in the text justify this conclusion. (1) It is the community that has gathered together in Acts 15. Such a gathering suggests that for the author of Acts it was absolutely essential at least for representatives of the community to be in on the interpretive decision reached. (2) It is the community that is able to give and receive testimony as well as assess the reports of God's activity in the lives of those who are part of the community. (3) Despite James's leading role in the process, it is evident that the author of Acts regarded the decision as coming from the community under the leadership of the Holy Spirit. All of this evidence suggests that any model of hermeneutics that seeks to build upon Acts 15 cannot afford to ignore the significant role of the community of believers in that process.

A second element is the role the Holy Spirit plays in this interpretive event. In point of fact, appeal is made to the action of God and/or the Holy Spirit so often in this pericope that it is somewhat startling to many modern readers. Not only is the final decision of the council described as seeming good to the Holy Spirit, but the previous activity of the Spirit in the community also spoke very loudly to the group, being in part responsible for the text chosen as most appropriate for this particular context.

The final prominent component in this interpretive paradigm is the place of the biblical text itself. Several observations are called for here. (1) The methodology revealed in Acts 15 is far removed from the modern-

18. There is some evidence that the decree regarding food was still followed as late as 177 C.E. in Gaul. Eusebius's report (*Hist. eccl.* 5.1.26) of one female Christian's response to her tormentor, shortly before her martyrdom, illustrates this point. She said, "How would such men eat children, when they are not allowed to eat the blood even of irrational animals?" (cited according to the translation of Kirsopp Lake: *Eusebius, Ecclesiastical History* I [London: Heinemann, 1926], p. 419).

looking historical-critical or historical-grammatical approaches where one moves from text to context. On this occasion the interpreters moved from their context to the biblical text.[19] (2) The passage cited in Acts 15 was chosen out of a much larger group of OT texts that were, at the very least, diverse in terms of their perspective on whether Gentiles were to be included or excluded from the people of God. It appears that the experience of the Spirit in the community helped the church make its way through this hermeneutical maze. In other words, despite the fact that there were plenty of texts that appeared to allow no place for the Gentiles as Gentiles in the people of God, and that there were also texts where Gentiles had a place but not as equal partners, the Spirit's witness heavily influenced the choice and use of Scripture. (3) Scripture was also apparently drawn on in the construction of certain stipulations imposed upon the Gentile converts to ensure table fellowship between Jewish Christian and Gentile Christian believers. This step seems to have been a temporary one, and these stipulations in no way treat the Gentile converts as less than Christian nor as inferior to their Jewish Christian brothers and sisters. These points unmistakably reveal that the biblical text was assigned and functioned with significant authority in this hermeneutical approach. However, in contrast to the way in which propositional approaches to the issue of authority function, Acts 15 reveals that the text's authority is not unrelated to its relevance to the community, its own diversity of teaching on a given topic, and the role that the Scripture plays in the construction of temporary or transitional stipulations for the sake of fellowship in the community.

In sum, the hermeneutic revealed in Acts 15 has three primary components: the believing community, the activity of the Spirit, and the Scripture.

## 4. Toward a Pentecostal Hermeneutic

A Pentecostal hermeneutic has much in common with the paradigm revealed in Acts 15. Several observations are here offered as to its shape and nature.

19. Cf. the perceptive comments on moving from context to text by William A. Dyrness, "How Does the Bible Function in the Christian Life?" in *The Use of the Bible in Theology: Evangelical Options,* ed. Robert K. Johnston (Atlanta: John Knox, 1985), pp. 159-74.

First, this study suggests that what has been going on in much of Pentecostal hermeneutics actually has good basis in Scripture (though other approaches might also be supported in Scripture). Three elements are crucial for this approach to Scripture: the role of the believing community, the role of the Holy Spirit, and the role of Scripture.

Second, the community functions as the place where the Spirit of God acts and where testimony regarding God's activity is offered, assessed, and accepted or rejected. It also provides the forum for serious and sensitive discussions about the acts of God and the Scripture. The community can offer balance, accountability, and support. It can guard against rampant individualism and uncontrolled subjectivism. A more serious appreciation for the role of the community among Pentecostals generally, and Pentecostal scholars specifically, might perhaps result in less isolationism, on the one hand, and a serious corporate engagement with the biblical text rather than equating a majority vote with the will of God, on the other hand.

Third, the explicit dependence upon the Spirit in the interpretive process as witnessed to in Acts 15 clearly goes far beyond the rather tame claims regarding "illumination" often made regarding the Spirit's role in interpretation. For Pentecostals, the Holy Spirit's role in interpretation cannot be reduced to some vague talk of illumination, for the Holy Spirit creates the context for interpretation through his actions and, as a result, guides the church in the determination of which texts are most relevant in a particular situation and clarifies how they might best be approached. This approach *does* make room for illumination in the Spirit's work, but it includes a far greater role for the work of the Spirit in the community as the context for interpretation, offering guidance in the community's dialogue about the Scripture. Although concerns about the dangers of subjectivism must be duly noted, the evidence of Acts 15 simply will not allow for a more restrained approach.

Fourth, in this hermeneutical approach the text does not function in a static fashion but in a dynamic manner making necessary a more intensive engagement with the text in order to discover its truths in ways that transcend the mere cognitive.

Fifth, this approach clearly regards Scripture as authoritative, for ultimately the experience of the church must be measured against the biblical text and, in that light, practices or views for which there is no biblical support would be deemed as illegitimate. Thus, a Pentecostal hermeneutic is unwilling to embrace theological and ethical positions that are unable to

119

find support in the biblical text. Here again, then, we find protection from rampant subjectivism. Instead of understanding the authority of Scripture as lying in the uniform propositions to which Scripture is sometimes reduced, however, in this paradigm an understanding of authority includes a respect for the text's literary genre and the diversity as well as the unity of Scripture. Therefore, this method regards Scripture as authoritative but allows the form and the content of the canon to define the nature of biblical authority, and consequently one might say that it approaches the issue of biblical authority more biblically.

Sixth, this interpretive model offers a way forward for the church when faced with issues about which the biblical evidence is (or appears to be) divided. Just as the Spirit's activity in the community was able to lead the church to a decision regarding the inclusion of Gentiles, despite the diversity of the biblical statements on this topic, so it would seem that this paradigm could assist the (Pentecostal) church in grappling with significant issues that simply will not disappear (for example, the issues of women in ministry,[20] divorce, and the relationship between the church and civil governments).

## 5. Final Thoughts

Before closing this essay, let me make explicit some of the implications of this hermeneutical approach for a Pentecostal contribution to the project to which this volume points, a commentary series explicitly engaged in theological hermeneutics. These final remarks will rely in part upon testimony, a mode of discourse much at home in my tradition.

Simply put, it is my intention to write the volume on the book of Revelation, or Apocalypse, for the Two Horizons Commentary with a focus on the multidimensional meaning of Scripture, within the context of a worshiping and believing Pentecostal community, and with an intentional sensitivity to what the Spirit is saying to the church. Given the limitations of space, only a few brief comments may be offered here.

My first encounters with the book came early in my life through my own reading of Revelation and via prophecy preachers who used the book

---

20. For an example of the way application of this paradigm addresses the issue of women in ministry for Pentecostals, see Thomas, "Women, Pentecostals, and the Bible."

to calculate the end time. Although fascinating, the ultimate result was to reduce the book to end-time speculation that had little or nothing to do with the contemporary church and believer. Growing up in an apocalyptic community like Pentecostalism, where Jesus as Coming King was regularly preached, made me aware of the great distance between approaching the book to calculate the Lord's return and embracing the passion and heart of the book itself. Two specific events helped create within me a greater desire to think about the Apocalypse in a more intentional fashion. One day in chapel at the seminary where I teach, a student from the former Soviet Union gave a testimony about his life and ministry. This student, Vladimir Mourashkine, who had experienced imprisonment and other forms of persecution at the hands of the communist government for being a Pentecostal Christian, began to rehearse the history of Russia by means of the story line found in the Apocalypse. Although there were aspects of the story that did not seem to fit for me as well as they did for him, I was enraptured by his words and began to think more deeply about how the book sounds and what it means in parts of the world where people do not have the luxury of spending large amounts of time speculating about end-time events. The second event that influenced me significantly was reading Richard Bauckham's *The Theology of the Book of Revelation*.[21] This was far and away the best thing I had ever read on the Apocalypse, and has given me reason to ponder the book from a more deliberately theological vantage point.

A Pentecostal hermeneutic necessitates that my commentary work be contextualized within the local communities of which I am part. At my local church this contextualization includes extended and numerous times of prayer on my behalf and for the various research projects in which I am involved, dialogue with those in the community about the process and results, and times of interaction where insights from a variety of sources are processed. Just as it is difficult to put into words the effects one's family has upon one's scholarship, so it is difficult for me to describe the community's role. I have learned that the Spirit can and does speak in and through a variety of unexpected contexts and individuals. It has amazed me over the years that in my local church, a congregation where there is a place for many of those on society's margins (the poor, the severely retarded, ex-convicts, ex-addicts, etc.), the Spirit speaks about certain issues that, while

---

21. Richard J. Bauckham, *The Theology of the Book of Revelation*, NTT (Cambridge: Cambridge University Press, 1993).

not always directly related to my scholarly work, often have a profound impact upon it. At the seminary where I teach, additional prayer and reflection about these projects takes place. It is within this context that a variety of interpretive matters are examined and debated. The context of Pentecostalism generally, a movement that historically has very much been on society's fringe, should inform the commentary in powerful ways. A final community-oriented component of this project should be mentioned. This volume is to be coauthored with Frank D. Macchia, a theologian in the Pentecostal tradition. Despite the geographical distance that separates us, our intention is to arrange periodic meetings to talk through and pray through the entire project in order that it will be a true joint effort.

While more could be said, these few comments are offered in the attempt to make concrete some of the implications of this Pentecostal hermeneutic for our undertaking of a Two Horizons volume on the Apocalypse.

CHAPTER 7

# Biblical Narrative and Systematic Theology

## JOHN GOLDINGAY

## 1. Narrative and Theology

When I watch a film or listen to music or read a novel, as a narrow-minded intellectual I cannot help thinking about it — about its significance, about its insight on life and God. Indeed, I am such an ivory-towered academic that I cannot stop myself from reflecting on what my wife calls "waste-of-time" films or music, by which she means popular art designed simply to entertain or make money or make someone famous.

I indulge in this weakness during the film or song or novel, grinning to myself or uttering some exclamation under my breath. I did so recently in the film *The Truman Show.* Tru(e)man has just discovered that his whole life has been lived on a soap opera set; all the people he thought loved him have been playing parts. The God/Devil/Director figure, Christoph (at least one syllable short of being a Christ-bearer), then tells him, "It's all deception out here in the real world, too, you know" (I reproduce the quotation from memory and may have sharpened its import to match my agenda, rather in the manner of the NT's use of the OT).

But then, after listening to the song a few times, or completing the novel, or leaving the cinema, I will probably be compelled to think back over the lyrics or the novel or the film as a whole. I do it every time I play to a class the song about God and David called "Hallelujah," whether sung by Leonard Cohen as the songwriter or by Jeff Buckley in the definitive version or by Sheryl Crow in her recent tribute performance after Buckley's

death. I do it every time I watch *When Harry Met Sally,* still wondering
whether it is true that men and women can never be friends because sex
will always get in the way (and still not sure what is the film's own implicit
take on that). I did it after I first saw *Leaving Las Vegas* in Britain, as I spent
three hours (with a break for pizza) attempting to explain to a seminarian
why her seminary principal should want to see such an unchristian film;
and I did it again after watching the video with a small group of seminari-
ans down the freeway from Las Vegas (the answer being that it expresses
such gloomy realism yet also such hope in its portrayal of the difference
loving and being loved can make to a man who has sentenced himself to
death and to a woman whom life has sentenced to a living death). I did it
on leaving the cinema openmouthed at *The Truman Show*'s breathtaking
discussion of whether it is best to live in a clean, unquestioning, problem-
free, hermetically sealed world such as a film set or a Garden of Eden, or
whether it is best to live a "real" life outside, with all its ambiguity.

In films the plot also counts, though as I come to think about it, the
plots tend to be simple (man goes to Las Vegas to drink himself to death,
and does so). We know that George Clooney will get the woman in some
sense, in *One Fine Day* or *Out of Sight;* the question is how and how far and
for how long. We suspect that Tom Hanks will succeed in *Saving Private
Ryan,* despite the false clue when we see a Ryan dead on the Normandy
seashore; the only question is how.

Further, films depend on believable characters (well, some films do),
though film is a tough medium for the conveying of character, and character comes out more in novels. Perhaps this is partly because characterization in films comes via the character of the actor, and most actors are playing themselves. I reflected on this recently when re-watching *Sophie's
Choice* on television and seeing Kevin Kline behave the same way he would
a decade later in *A Fish Called Wanda;* and I reflected on how much more
the novel *Sophie's Choice* conveyed than the film did.

Doing theology on the basis of biblical narrative parallels one's reflection on a film, a novel, or a song. One may do it in the same four ways.

First, individual moments in a narrative convey insights. A famous
reflection by Günther Bornkamm on the story of Jesus' stilling of the
storm, in its two forms in Mark and Matthew, brings out this event's message in the different versions of these two Evangelists.[1] In Genesis, three

1. See Günther Bornkamm, Gerhard Barth, and Heinz Joachim Held, *Tradition
and Interpretation in Matthew* (Philadelphia: Westminster; London: SCM, 1963).

stories about one of Israel's father figures passing off his wife as his sister seem to comprise attempts to come to terms with male ambivalence at female sexuality.[2] In Exodus 19–40 there is a long series of attempts to find ways of speaking about God's presence as real, while recognizing the fact of God's transcendence; John Durham has suggested that God's presence is the theme of Exodus 19–40, as God's activity is the theme of Exodus 1–18.[3] Exodus 19–40 is thus an exercise in narrative theology.

Second, biblical narratives have plots, and a key aspect of their theological significance will be conveyed by their plot. On the large scale, the plots of the four or five NT narratives (is Luke-Acts one or two?) are at one level simple, like those of many films. There are two of these plots, the story of the beginnings, ministry, killing, and renewed life of Jesus of Nazareth, and the story of the spreading of his story from Jerusalem to Rome. But these simple plots are theologically crucial. The NT theological message is contained in the plot about Jesus, because that message is a gospel. And the NT ecclesiology is contained in that plot about the spread of the gospel.

Yet, there being several versions of the first plot draws attention to the fact that there are many ways of bringing out its theological significance. To put it another way, it has many subplots. It is also the story of how Jesus starts as a wonder-worker and ends up a martyr. It thus raises the question of the relationship between these two. Is the former the real aim and the latter a deviation and a way of ultimately achieving the former? Or is the former a dead end succeeded by the latter? Or do the two stand in dialectic tension? Again, the Gospel story portrays Jesus choosing twelve men as members of his inner circle, which might confirm men's special status in the leadership of the people of God. It then portrays him watching them misunderstand, betray, and abandon him, so that the people who accompany his martyrdom and first learn of his transformation are women — which might subvert men's special status in the leadership of the people of God.

Third, biblical narratives portray characters. From a theological angle, they concern themselves with two correlative pairs of characters: God

2. See Jo Cheryl Exum, "Who's Afraid of 'The Endangered Ancestress'?" in *The New Literary Criticism and the Hebrew Bible*, ed. Jo Cheryl Exum and David J. A. Clines, JSOTSup 143 (Sheffield: Sheffield Academic Press, 1993), pp. 91-113; also in Jo Cheryl Exum, *Fragmented Women*, JSOTSup 163 (Sheffield: Sheffield Academic Press, 1993), pp. 148-69.

3. John I. Durham, *Exodus*, WBC 3 (Waco, Tex.: Word, 1985).

and Israel, Jesus and the church. They "render" these characters sometimes by offering titles for them (El Shaddai, Yahweh; holy nation, royal priesthood; Son of God, Son of Man; body of Christ, flock of God). They render them by describing them by means of adjectives or nouns ("gracious," "long-tempered"; "family," "servant"; "good shepherd," "true vine"; "household," "temple" — the examples show that the boundary between "title" and "description" is fuzzy). They render them most by describing them in action — because that is the way character emerges. It has become customary to distinguish between "showing" and "telling." The Gospels rarely "tell" us things about Jesus (e.g., "Jesus was a compassionate person"). Instead they "show" us things. They portray Jesus in action (and in speech) and leave us to infer what kind of person Jesus therefore was. In this respect they are much more like films than novels; in general, films have to "show" rather than "tell."

Fourth, biblical narratives discuss themes. I have suggested two examples from the Gospels: Mark discusses the relative position of women and men in leadership in the church and the relationship between what Jesus achieves by works of power and what he achieves by letting people kill him. In the OT, Esther is directly a discussion of how Yahweh's commitment to the Jewish people works itself out. It also implicitly makes theological statements or raises theological questions about the nature of God's involvement in the world and the significance of human acts in accepting responsibility for history; about the nature of manhood and womanhood; about human weakness and sin (pride, greed, sexism, cruelty); about the potentials and the temptations of power; about civil authority, civil obedience, and civil disobedience; and about the significance of humor. Jonah is about the disobedience of prophets and Yahweh's relationship with the nations and the possible fruitfulness of turning to God. The stories in Daniel constitute a narrative politics that discusses the interrelationship of the sovereignty of Yahweh, the sovereignty of human kings, and the significance of the political involvement of members of God's people.

The task of exegeting biblical narratives includes the teasing out of the theological issues in such works.

It has not commonly been assumed to be so. A school friend of mine is now a professor of Latin; in comparing his textual work and that of biblical exegetes some years ago, I was depressingly struck by the similarity in the apparent aims and procedures. One might never have guessed that biblical narratives had a different set of concerns from those of Ovid.

Biblical narratives came into being to address theological questions, or at least religious questions. The teasing out of their religious and theological implications is inherent in their exegesis; it is not an optional, additional task that the exegete may responsibly ignore if so inclined. Greek or Roman, English or American literature, and Russian or French films will of course always have an implicit theology, but teasing this out may not always be an essential aspect of their study. With biblical narrative, theological issues are the texts' major concern, and the exegete who fails to pay attention to them, and focuses on (for instance) merely historical questions, has not left the starting line as an exegete.

The exegete may undertake the task by the four means suggested above. First, it involves teasing out the theological implications of individual stories within the larger narrative. The agenda here cannot be predicted: discerning it depends on the exegete's sensitivity to recognizing a theological issue. Second, it involves standing back and giving an account of the distinctive plot of the story (e.g., that of Chronicles as opposed to Kings or that of Matthew as opposed to Mark) so as to show what is the gospel according to this Gospel. Third, it involves realizing a portrayal of the two or four characters in the story. According to this narrative as a whole, Who is God? and, Who is Israel? And in the case of a NT narrative, in addition, Who is Jesus? and, Who is the church? Fourth, it is a matter of analyzing the narrative's various insights on its own specific theme(s).

There is no method for doing this, no more than there is for the interpreting of a film or for any other aspect of the interpretive task — for I have suggested that it is no more or no less than an aspect of that. It requires a more-or-less inspired guess as to what the theological freight of this narrative might be, and then discussion with other people (perhaps via their writings) to discover whether my guess says less or more than the narrative — whether they can help me notice things I have missed or eliminate things I am reading into the text. This guess comes from me as a person living in the culture in which I live, and it needs to recognize the specificity of that (so that my reading fellowship needs to embrace people from other ages and other cultures, and people of other beliefs and of the opposite sex). But it can also benefit from the possibility that this enables me to see something of how this narrative speaks to people like me in my culture in the context of its debates.

## 2. The Difference between Systematic Theology and Biblical Narrative

The theological work I have just described will stand somewhat short of interaction with systematic theology.

Systematic theology means different things to different people.[4] Traditionally, it has denoted the discipline that gives a coherent account of Christian theology as a whole, showing how the parts constitute a whole. Consciously or unconsciously, it undertakes this task in light of the culture, language, thought forms, and questions of its time; it is not written once-for-all.[5]

Such descriptions of systematic theology's task suggest several observations from the perspective of biblical studies. First, it is a telling fact that "systematic" and "theology" are both Greek-based words. The discipline emerged from the attempt to think through the gospel's significance in the framework of Greek thinking. Thus the key issues in the theological thinking of the patristic period concerned God's nature and Christ's person, and these were framed in terms of concepts such as "person" and "nature" as these were understood against the background of Greek thinking. Subsequent theological explication of the atonement and the doctrine of Scripture similarly took place in terms of concepts and categories of the medieval period and the Enlightenment. Theoogians' being able to use scriptural terms may obscure the fact that their framework of thinking is that of another culture.

This points us toward the awareness that not only are individual ventures in systematic theology contextual but also that the enterprise is inherently so, dependent as it is on that collocation of Jewish gospel and Greek forms of thinking. Thus Alister McGrath has noted that ancient Greece and traditional African cultures resemble the scriptural writers in tending to use stories as a way of making sense of the world. But just before the time of Plato a decisive shift occurred; "ideas took the place of stories"

---

4. See Colin E. Gunton, "Historical and Systematic Theology," in *The Cambridge Companion to Christian Doctrine,* ed. Colin E. Gunton, Cambridge Companions to Religion (Cambridge: Cambridge University Press, 1997), pp. 3-20.

5. See, e.g., the definitions in *New Dictionary of Theology,* ed. Sinclair B. Ferguson and David F. Wright (Leicester: Inter-Varsity; Downers Grove, Ill.: InterVarsity, 1988), pp. 671-72; *The New Handbook of Theology,* ed. Donald W. Musser and Joseph L. Price (Nashville: Abingdon, 1992), p. 469.

and a conceptual way of thinking gained the upper hand and came to dominate Western culture.[6]

The arrival of postmodernity has then brought implications for systematic theology. While one great contemporary German theologian, Wolfhart Pannenberg, has written a three-volume systematic theology on something like the traditional model, another great contemporary German theologian, Jürgen Moltmann, has written a series of "systematic contributions to theology" on a similar scale but declines to call these "systematic theology."[7] Admirers may nevertheless see them as suggesting the way forward in systematic theology, insisting as they do on creativity, coherence, rigor, critical thinking, and the conversation between the modern world and the Christian tradition, but being suspicious of grand schemes. If "systematic theology" seems a misguided enterprise, one response is thus to replace it by a wiser enterprise. But another is to assume that this will simply leave the term "systematic theology" with its value status to unwise exponents of it, and therefore rather to set about the different task that one does approve of and to appropriate the term "systematic theology" for that.

Perhaps it is indeed the case that humanity's rationality necessitates analytic reflection on the nature of the faith; at least, the importance of rationality to intellectuals necessitates our analytic reflection on the nature of the faith as one of the less important aspects of the life of Christ's body. Yet such rational and disciplined reflection need not take the form of systematic theology, of the old form or the new. For long it did not do so in Judaism, where the two key forms of reflection were *haggadah* and *halakah*. This reflection took the form of the retelling of biblical narrative in such a way as to clarify its difficulties and answer contemporary questions, and the working out of what behavioral practice was required by life with God. We need to distinguish between the possible necessity that the church reflects deeply, sharply, coherently, and critically on its faith, and the culture-relative fact that this has generally been done in a world of thought decisively influenced by Greek thinking in general as well as in particular (e.g., Platonic or Aristotelian).

The nature of reflection in Judaism thus draws attention to the need

6. Alister E. McGrath, *Understanding Doctrine* (London: Hodder, 1990; Grand Rapids: Zondervan, 1992), p. 34.

7. Wolfhart Pannenberg, *Systematic Theology*, 3 vols. (Edinburgh: T. & T. Clark; Grand Rapids: Eerdmans, 1991-98). With regard to Jürgen Moltmann's work, see, e.g., *God in Creation* (London: SCM; Philadelphia: Fortress, 1985), p. xv.

for systematic theology to do justice to the essentially narrative character of the OT and NT gospel if it is to do justice to the nature of biblical faith. Old Testament faith centrally concerns the way in which God related to Israel over time. It relates the story of the way Yahweh did certain things, such as create the world, make promises to Israel's ancestors, deliver their descendants from Egypt, bring them into a sealed relationship at Sinai, persevere with them in chastisement and mercy in the wilderness, bring them into their own land, persevere with them in chastisement and mercy through another period of unfaithfulness in the land itself, agree to their having human kings and make a commitment to a line of kings, interact with them over centuries of inclination to rebellion until they were reduced to a shadow of their former self, cleanse their land, and begin a process of renewal there. New Testament faith sees itself as the continuing of that story. Like the OT, the NT takes predominantly narrative form, and the form corresponds to the nature of the faith. Its gospel is not essentially or distinctively a statement that takes the form "God is love," but one that takes the form "God so loved that he gave. . . ."

Second-century Christians found the need of a "rule for the faith," an outline summary of Christian truth that could (among other things) guide their reading of Scripture. The two great creeds that issued from the fulfilling of that need, the Apostles' Creed and the Nicene Creed, do not actually summarize the fundamentals of biblical faith (neither mentions Israel, for example),[8] but they are noteworthy for the fact that at least they take a broadly narrative form. In this respect they are a far cry from the Westminster Confession or the Thirty-nine Articles of Religion. Similarly, systematic theology has commonly been shaped by the doctrine of the Trinity, and recent years have seen an increased emphasis on the importance and fruitfulness of thinking trinitarianly.

This highlights the problem of seeking to work at the relationship of systematic theology to Scripture in general, and to biblical narrative in particular. Let us grant that the doctrine of the Trinity is a (even the) logical outworking within a Greek framework of the implications of statements of the more Greek-thinking writers within the NT. That means it is two stages removed from most of the NT narratives (because they are narrative, and because they are less inclined to think in Greek forms). Further,

---

8. It is noteworthy that "The Jewish People and Christian Theology" has become one of the topics that needs to be considered in *The Cambridge Companion to Christian Doctrine* (pp. 81-100, by Bruce D. Marshall).

it is three stages removed from most biblical narrative (which was written before Bethlehem and Pentecost made trinitarian thinking possible, let alone necessary). If one starts from biblical narratives and asks after their theological freight, the vast bulk of their theological implications does not emerge within a trinitarian framework.

That is even true (perhaps especially true) if we are interested in theological implications in the narrowest sense, in what biblical narrative tells us about God. For all its truth and fruitfulness, the doctrine of the Trinity seriously skews our theological reading of Scripture. It excludes most of the insight expressed in the biblical narrative's portrayal of the person and its working out of the plot. There is a paradox here. Some of the key figures in the development of the doctrine of the Trinity emphasized how little we may directly say about God, particularly God's inner nature. Yet theology nevertheless involves the venture to think the unthinkable and say the unsayable. Yet in doing so it ignores the theological potential of the things that Scripture does say.

There is a further sense in which scriptural reflection on God's nature is inextricably tied to narrative, recently expressed in Jack Miles's *God: A Biography*.[9] To use systematic theology's own terms, it applies to revelation as well as to redemption. God's person emerges in a series of contexts. God is a creator, then a destroyer. God relates to a family in the concerns of its ongoing family life, such as the finding of a home, the birth of children, and the arranging of marriages; God then relates to a nation in the different demands of its life, which include God's becoming a war-maker. Entering into a formal relationship with this people takes God into becoming a lawmaker and into becoming a deity identified by a shrine (albeit a movable one) and not merely by a relationship with a people. The "revelation" of God's person is inextricably tied to the events in which God becomes different things, in a way that any person does; it is thus inextricably tied to narrative.

Systematic theology's theological and philosophical framework imposes on it a broader difficulty in doing justice to much of the biblical material. By its nature traditional systematic theology, in particular, is concerned with the unequivocal; it presupposes a quest for unity. Biblical faith indeed emphasizes that Yahweh is one, but then relaxes in implying paradox within that oneness. For instance, it emphasizes God's power, but generally portrays events in the world as working themselves out not by God's

9. Jack Miles, *God: A Biography* (New York: Simon & Schuster, 1995).

will but in ways that reflect human and other this-worldly considerations (indeed, the emphasis in biblical narrative in particular is very predominantly on the latter). It emphasizes God's wisdom and knowledge, but it also portrays God asking questions and experiencing surprise and regret. Starting from its Greek framework, traditional systematic theology affirms God's power and knowledge ("omnipotence" and "omniscience") and then has to subordinate any theological account of the reality of human decision making (except insofar as it emphasizes the "necessity" for God to give human beings "free will," some further alien ideas imported into Scripture) and/or has to offer an allegorical interpretation of statements in scriptural narrative that indicate God's ignorance or God's having a change of mind.

Narrative is by nature open-ended, allusive, and capable of embracing questions and ambiguity. I have noted two features of Mark's Gospel that illustrate this. It is also a feature of Genesis 1–4, where the three stories (1:1–2:3; 2:4–3:24; and 4:1-26) keep offering different perspectives on what God is like and what human beings are like and on the goodness or otherwise of life in the world. These keep the reader ricocheting between them in a way that is simultaneously bewildering and enriching — or at least they would do that if we were able to escape the lenses the categories of systematic theology impose on these chapters.

While concerned to work out the implications of biblical narrative, by its nature systematic theology (traditional or postmodern) does not take narrative form. It thereby has difficulty in maintaining touch with the narrative nature of the faith upon which it seeks to reflect, and therefore with the object of its concern. And it has difficulty in maintaining touch with the narrative contexts out of which aspects of God's character emerge, and thereby in understanding the significance of these aspects of this character.

From the side of biblical studies, over the past two decades there have been two powerful attempts to relate the Bible to the concerns of systematic theology, on the part of Brevard Childs and Francis Watson. There is something wrong with me, because I find Childs's work in particular profoundly disappointing. The opening chapter headings for his *Old Testament Theology in a Canonical Context*[10] expose one major problem here, for they indicate that the chapters concern "The Old Testament as Revela-

10. Brevard S. Childs, *Old Testament Theology in a Canonical Context* (London: SCM, 1985; Philadelphia: Fortress, 1986).

tion," "How God Is Known," and "God's Purpose in Revelation." The entire framework of thinking is introduced into biblical study from elsewhere, in this case not from the Greek thinking of the patristic period but from the agenda of the Enlightenment age. In turn, Watson opens his *Text, Church, and World* with his concern for "an exegesis oriented primarily towards theological issues" but clarifies that, "at least in my usage, the terms 'theology' and 'theological' relate to a distinct discipline — that of 'systematic theology' or 'Christian doctrine.'"[11] He restates the point at the opening of his *Text and Truth*.[12] The exegete who expounds the theological significance of the text expects to do so in the terms of the existent Christian doctrinal tradition.

Jon D. Levenson has tartly commented on Gerhard von Rad's famous study of "faith reckoned as righteousness" (Gen. 15:6): "Within the limited context of theological interpretation informed by historical criticism — the context von Rad intended — his essay must be judged unsuccessful. Within another limited context, however — the confessional elucidation of scripture for purposes of Lutheran reaffirmation — it is an impressive success." It is for this reason that Jews are not interested in biblical theology.[13] In other words, Christian theological interpretation of Scripture is always inclined to come down to the elucidation of our already-determined Christian doctrines (and lifestyles) by Scripture, either accidentally (von Rad) or deliberately (Childs, Watson).

## 3. From Narrative to Theology

Scripture's focus on narrative might seem to imply that the whole enterprise of thinking critically and analytically about biblical faith is doomed

11. Francis Watson, *Text, Church, and World: Biblical Interpretation in Theological Perspective* (Edinburgh: T. & T. Clark; Grand Rapids: Eerdmans, 1994), p. 1.

12. Francis Watson, *Text and Truth: Redefining Biblical Theology* (Edinburgh: T. & T. Clark; Grand Rapids: Eerdmans, 1997), pp. 2-4.

13. Jon D. Levenson, *The Hebrew Bible, the Old Testament, and Historical Criticism* (Louisville: Westminster/John Knox, 1993), p. 61. Von Rad's essay, "Die Anrechnung des Glaubens zur Gerechtigkeit," first appeared in *TLZ* 27 (1951): 129-32; then in his *Gesammelte Studien zum Alten Testament* (Munich: Kaiser, 1958), pp. 130-35; then in English in *The Problem of the Hexateuch and Other Essays* (Edinburgh: Oliver & Boyd; New York: McGraw-Hill, 1966), pp. 125-30. R. W. L. Moberly also makes the point in "Abraham's Righteousness," in *Studies in the Pentateuch*, ed. J. A. Emerton, VTSup 41 (Leiden: E. J. Brill, 1990), pp. 103-30 (111).

to failure. Pointers within Scripture suggest that this is an unnecessary fear.

First, nonnarrative books such as the Psalms, the Prophets, and the Epistles abound in material that has taken the first step from narrative to discursive statement, while keeping its implicit and explicit links with the gospel, with the OT and NT story. Thus the statement "God is love" is grounded in a narrative statement about the way "God showed his love among us" (1 John 4:8-9 NIV). The statement "Yahweh our God Yahweh one" (Deut. 6:4) is implicitly grounded in narrative statements such as "I am Yahweh your God who brought you out of Egypt" (Deut. 5:6).

This example illustrates how the point can be made in terms of Hebrew syntax. Biblical narrative is conveniently able to express itself by means of the finite verbs characteristic of Hebrew and Greek. But the OT also makes use of Hebrew's "noun clauses" which lack verbs, such as "Yahweh our God Yahweh one." I do not imply the fallacy that the language's syntax reflects distinctive ways of thinking, only that the use of this particular syntax in theological statements shows that theological thinking does not have to be confined to narrative statements.

Second, narratives themselves incorporate discursive statements. Exodus tells of moments when God offers some self-description in response to questions from Moses. Before the exodus God declares, "I am who I am," and speaks as "Yahweh, the God of your ancestors, the God of Abraham, the God of Isaac, and the God of Jacob." After the exodus and the people's faithlessness, God offers an extensive adjectival self-identification as compassionate and gracious, long-tempered, big in commitment and faithfulness, keeping commitment for 25,000 years, and forgiving — yet not ignoring wrongdoing (presumably that of people who do not seek forgiveness) but punishing it for 75 or 100 years. In both cases the statements are inextricably linked to narrative; they gain their meaning from the narrative contexts in which they are set. But they are open to being reflected on as statements offering insights on God's nature that hold beyond their narrative context.

In between these two is a narrative such as John's Gospel. A film may sometimes seek to escape its form by having a narrator "tell" us things or by putting instructive speeches on its characters' lips. The *Pasadena Weekly* commented on the way *You've Got Mail* incorporates Nora Ephron's "digressions into social commentary about the computer age, commercialism and blah, blah, blah." The Deuteronomists work like that, but John does it most systematically. He and Paul are the two biblical thinkers who have most in common with systematic theology's way of thinking, but this technique enables John to do his theology in the writing of narrative as Paul does in writing discursively.

Scripture includes fundamentally factual narratives such as Kings and Mark, and fundamentally fictional narratives such as Ruth and Jesus' parables. By "fundamentally" factual or fictional, I indicate a recognition that factual narratives in Scripture (like factual narratives elsewhere) include fictional elements, while fictional narratives incorporate factual elements (and are arguably always based on factual human experience). My working assumption is that most biblical narratives, like most other narratives, stand in the space between bare fact and pure fiction. The latter two are ideal or notional types — extremes that are useful to define but of which there are no instances. Outside Scripture, both fact and fiction can be the means of conveying truth and depth, untruth and triviality. Every night I watch television news, which is breathtaking in its combination of factuality and triviality. Most weeks I watch one or two films, which may be breathtaking in their combination of fiction and deep truth. Within Scripture, fact and fiction are both entirely true narratives and deeply significant ones. The truth of the fact is that which can be conveyed through facts, while the truth of fiction is that which can be conveyed through fiction.

The two then have differing relationships with systematic theology. A factual narrative needs to keep systematic theology on the narrative straight-and-narrow, to drive it to keep thinking narratively, on the basis of the nature of the gospel that systematic theology is seeking to explicate. Fictional narrative is more inclined to be the discussion of a theme, or the interweaving of several themes, and it needs to keep systematic theology from its traditional besetting temptation to be too straight and narrow, to be rationalist. I have noted that part of narrative's genius is its capacity to embrace ambiguity, to discuss complexity, to embrace mystery. Traditional systematic theology's strength is its analytic rigor and its emphasis on the law of noncontradiction, but that is also its limitation. Taking biblical narrative seriously has the capacity to release it from this limitation. Systematic theology could construct a discursive equivalent to the narrative discussion of the notion of God's presence and of God's transcendence and immanence such as appears in Exodus 19–40, but it would need to be one that preserved the richness and paradoxicality of what a narrative presentation makes possible.

The reader will have noted that by this example I have subverted my distinction between factual and fictional narrative and demonstrated the point that this distinction is a notional one; observations I have made about Mark also establish the point. I assume that Exodus is telling us about historical facts in a sense that Jonah or the parable about the Good Samaritan is not, but the nature of its narrative shows that it has fiction's strengths and not merely the narrowness of factual narrative.

If the Prophets and the Epistles show Scripture taking a step toward the way of thinking more characteristic of systematic theology, their nature also lays down another marker for the enterprise. They are also parts of Scripture especially concerned with the commitment of God's people to the gospel's behavioral implications. They thus suggest the need for systematic theology to be kept in relationship with commitment.[14] The collocation of *haggadah* and *halakah* as Judaism's two traditional ways of undertaking sustained reflection on Scripture coheres with this observation.

Biblical narrative itself has practical concerns. The Torah and the Gospels, for instance, incorporate much material that explicitly delineates the way of life expected of Israel and of disciples. Further, the narrative itself is designed to shape a worldview, but a worldview within which people then live. The point can be illustrated from its handling of the theme of God's creation of the world. Scripture frequently takes up the theme of creation, but never for its own sake. In retelling the creation story, it always has some world shaping to do. A work such as Moltmann's *God in Creation* is thus likewise concerned to work out the significance of creation in our own context.

There is a point to be safeguarded here. I have noted that biblical narrative talks more about human acts than about God's acts. Nevertheless, its understanding of the significance of these human acts is generally rather gloomy. It is like that of *film noir* such as *L.A. Confidential*. In the end, *film noir* declares, everyone has their weaknesses; there are no unmitigated heroes. Biblical narrative agrees, but adds that God is also decisively involved in its story. In this sense Scripture puts its emphasis on God's acts rather than on human acts. We leave church less sombered than we leave the cinema.

Perhaps narrative can decisively shape human character. Certainly people who want to shape character often try to do so by telling stories, and people who want to have their characters shaped often seek this by reading them, though they often then find that biblical narrative is differ-

14. See, e.g., Stanley Hauerwas, "On Doctrine and Ethics," in *The Cambridge Companion to Christian Doctrine*, pp. 21-40.

ent from what they expected (but what would be the point of the Bible if it were what we expected?). Even the biblical narrative that is nearest to *film noir,* 1 and 2 Samuel, does shape character by portraying for us people with weaknesses and strengths like ours (Hannah, Peninnah, Eli, Samuel, Saul, Michal, Jonathan, David, Abigail . . .), handling pressures and crises that are usually greater than ours, and inviting us to set their stories along-side ours. Yet the shaping of character is rarely the direct aim of biblical narrative; we are not told stories about Abraham, Moses, Jesus, or Paul chiefly in order that we may let our characters be shaped by theirs. The primary concern of biblical narrative is to expound the gospel, to talk about God and what God has done, rather than to talk about the human characters who appear in God's story. The commonsense view that biblical narrative is concerned to shape character is surely right, but the narrative assumes that expounding the gospel is the way to do that.

The narrative also interweaves imperatives, in a variety of ways. Yahweh's promises to Israel's ancestors give them a responsibility they are to exercise for other peoples (Gen. 18:17-33). Or, Yahweh's acts on Israel's behalf are sovereign deeds that establish Yahweh's lordship over Israel and look for a submissive response that takes certain forms ("I am Yahweh your God who brought you out of the land of Egypt: you are to have no other gods . . ."). Or, Yahweh's acts embody priorities that Israel is expected to share ("I delivered you from slavery; you are not to treat people the way you were treated there"). Or, Yahweh's acts establish a distinctiveness about Israel, mirroring Yahweh's distinctiveness and requiring them to be embodied in its life ("You are to be holy as I am holy").

Biblical narrative thus suggests for systematic theology a context of concern about a relationship with God and a life lived for God. It is not merely an exercise in describing abstract truth. Nor is this merely a matter of acknowledging that systematic truths need to be applied. As happens in human relationships, the apprehension of truths about the person and the expression of these in relationship is dialogical. Apprehending truths about the person feeds the relationship, but living in the relationship unveils truths about the person. As liberation theology has shown, a commitment to right living generates insight on the theological interpretation of Scripture as well as the other way around. Biblical narrative suggests that insight on theology and on lifestyle cannot be pursued separately. This awareness of the context of relationship leads to a further observation, that the Psalms (arguably the densest theology in Scripture, at least in the OT) hint that an appropriate form for systematic theology is that of adoration, thanksgiving, and lament, or at least that a context in the life of adoration, thanksgiving, and lament ought to be a fruitful one for theological reflection on biblical narrative.[15]

At least that is so in theory. In practice it is not evident that piety produces profound theology or serious interaction with biblical narrative. I am not yet ready to give up the hope that Christian doctrine and lifestyles might be shaped by Scripture, though I do not have great expectation that this will ever happen. If it is to do so, however, of key importance will be not the reading of scriptural narrative in light of what we know already and how we live already, but the reading of scriptural narrative through the eyes of people such as Jack Miles and Jon Levenson who do not believe what we believe or do not practice what we practice.

## 4. Reflecting on Theology in Light of Narrative

If systematic theology did not exist, it might seem unwise to invent it — at least, unwise to begin the devising of grand schemes that are bound to skew our reading of Scripture and from which postmodernity delivers us. But systematic theology does exist, and it fundamentally shapes the church's thinking. In the context of our interest in the relationship between scriptural narrative and systematic theology, this suggests three functions for it.

First, systematic theology has the task of critical reflection on the theological tradition in such a way as to tweak the latter so that it does better justice to the prominence of narrative in Scripture.

The doctrine of Scripture itself suggests an example. Tradition has bequeathed to us a series of concepts that have shaped its formulation of Scripture's theological status and significance, concepts such as authority, canon, inspiration, inerrancy, infallibility, and revelation. Like the concept of Trinity, none of these appear in so many words in Scripture (at least, not with reference to Scripture, except for one possible reference to inspiration in 2 Tim. 3:16), and their significance in theology derives from questions that have arisen over the centuries such as the problem of authority, the question about reason and revelation, and the development of historical criticism.

---

15. Geoffrey Wainwright's *Doxology* (London: Epworth; New York: Oxford University Press, 1980) is "a systematic theology written from a liturgical perspective" (p. ix).

This need not make the use of these concepts unjustifiable; concepts from outside Scripture might enable us to articulate Scripture's own thinking. In practice, however, these concepts obscure Scripture's own implications regarding its nature, and do this in particular with regard to the prominence of narrative in Scripture. Authority, revelation, and inspiration are not concepts well fitted to bring out the theological status of a body of Scriptures that is dominated by narrative (they suit the Qur'an and the Book of Mormon rather better). I have suggested in *Models for Scripture* that the concepts of "witness" and "tradition" have more capacity to do this.[16] The nature of scriptural narrative makes it necessary for systematic theology to reflect on matters such as the nature of narrative itself and the nature of history, on narrative interpretation and on historical criticism, and these have more capacity to help theology do that.

Second, systematic theology has the capacity to encourage reflection in light of scriptural narrative on the church's more everyday assumptions regarding a topic such as the nature of God's involvement in the world and the implications of this for the practice of prayer. Christians commonly emphasize the omniscience, omnipotence, omnipresence, and timelessness of God, assume that God had a detailed plan for the world and for their lives, and reckon that God works out in history a sovereign will framed before all eternity. That is part of their implicit systematic theology. Thus prayer never really involves informing God of something that God did not know (even of our own feelings), nor does it involve overcoming God or causing God to do something different from what God intended (such as show mercy when God did not intend to do so).[17]

The understanding of God implicit in such convictions derives from the same meeting of the Christian faith with Greek thought that we considered in section 2 above. Such Greek thinking essentially emphasizes that God is the great absolute, independent of the world and unaffected by constraints. Such an understanding of God could perhaps not have come to shape Christian thinking unless there had been overlapping statements in scriptural material such as the Psalms and the Epistles. On the other hand,

16. John Goldingay, *Models for Scripture* (Grand Rapids: Eerdmans; Carlisle: Paternoster, 1994).

17. See, e.g., Jonathan Edwards, "The Most High a Prayer Hearing God," Sermon XXXV in *The Works of President Edwards* (New York: Leavitt, 1854), 4:561-72. I am told that this is the text that most shapes thinking about prayer and the practice of prayer by Christian students throughout the Greater Los Angeles universities and colleges.

quite different assumptions about God feature prominently in biblical narrative. Here God is committed to the achievement of certain long-term aims, and sometimes acts in history, but does not decide how most events work out in history. If sovereignty means that what happens is what God wants to happen, God is not sovereign. As we have noted, specifically, God is capable of being surprised, frustrated, grieved, and angered by events, and of becoming aware of failure to realize some intent. God thus has changes of mind and tries one plan after another. In responding to events and making new plans, God consults with human beings and as a result does things that would otherwise not have happened or refrains from doing things that otherwise would have happened.

In Christian thinking the first kind of statement about God (as omniscient, outside of time, etc.) is allowed to determine an allegorical interpretation of the perspective of biblical narrative, which is not allowed to mean what it says. Like the "rule for the faith," "doctrine provides the conceptual framework by which the scriptural narrative is interpreted." In theory "it is not an arbitrary framework, however, but one which is suggested by that narrative. . . . It is to be discerned within, rather than imposed upon, that narrative."[18] In practice, in this instance, this process is short-circuited; the relationship between scriptural narrative and Christian doctrine becomes a vicious circle in which the narrative's significance is narrowed down to what doctrine allows it to say.

One result is that prayer which involves asking for things becomes much less significant than prayer as portrayed in biblical narrative. Indeed, the relationship between God and humanity becomes much less than is portrayed in biblical narrative. We never say anything that God does not know already or anything that makes a difference to God; the relationship becomes one-sided and in this sense not really a relationship at all. Biblical narrative has a dynamic understanding of humanity's relationship with God and of humanity's involvement in God's purpose in the world. God acts in interaction with human activity and speech. In reflection on biblical narrative, systematic theology has the opportunity to encourage Christian thinking toward a more whole understanding of our relationship with God and of prayer's possibilities.[19]

18. Alister E. McGrath, *The Genesis of Doctrine: A Study in the Foundation of Doctrinal Criticism* (Oxford: Blackwell; Grand Rapids: Eerdmans, 1990), pp. 58-59.

19. See further John Goldingay, "The Logic of Intercession," *Theology* 99 (1998): 262-70.

Third, systematic theology has the capacity to facilitate reflection in light of scriptural narrative on current issues.

Recent decades have seen urgent questioning about what it means to be human in light of differences between the sexes, between races, and more recently between able-bodied people and handicapped people.[20] In reflecting on what it means to be human, traditional systematic theology has commonly emphasized the notion that we are made in God's image. The difficulty with this procedure is that "in God's image" is an extremely opaque expression, open to our reading into it whatever we wanted to emphasize about humanity's nature. Thus traditional systematic theology assumed that the divine image lay in human reason or morality or human capacity to have a spiritual relationship with God. One place where the image certainly did not lie was in the body, despite the fact that images are usually physical. More recently the divine image has been seen in the capacity for relationship, which suits our concern about relationship in the late twentieth century. The disadvantage of Genesis's description of humanity as made in the divine image is that this phrase is not further explained in the context (or only allusively so). It is open to being understood in whatever way suits us.

A more positive way to put it is to see God's image, like God's reign, as a symbol rather than a concept. It is thus open-ended and dynamic, a stimulus to thought as much as a constraint on thought. If the description of humanity as made in God's image had appeared in a discursive work such as Deuteronomy or Romans, it might have been explained discursively (as happens in connection with talk of images in Deut. 4). In contrast, we have noted that the nature of narrative is to "show" rather than "tell." Placed at the beginning of the biblical narrative, the declaration that human beings are made in God's image is not to be understood as an isolated comment, but neither is it simply a blank screen on which we are invited to project whatever suits us. It is to be understood in light of the narrative of whose introduction it forms part. As is the case with the word "God" itself, it is the narrative as a whole (e.g., from Genesis to Kings) that tells us what is "the image of God" and thus what it is to be human. Sys-

---

20. I have discussed the last in "Being Human," in *Encounter with Mystery*, ed. Frances M. Young (London: Darton, Longman & Todd, 1997), pp. 133-51, 183-84. Alistair I. McFadyen's systematic reflections on what it means to be a human person begin with his experience as a psychiatric nurse; see *The Call to Personhood: A Christian Theory of the Individual in Social Relationships* (Cambridge: Cambridge University Press, 1990), pp. 1-2.

tematic reflection on the nature of humanity as made in God's image needs to be reflection on this narrative, not merely reflection on this opaque but stimulating phrase. So systematic reflection on what it means to be human will involve reflection on the succeeding biblical narrative of the lives of people such as Cain and Abel; Abraham, Sarah, and Hagar; Jacob and Esau; Ruth and Naomi; Saul, David, and Jonathan. All these lives raise issues about what it means to be human that can contribute to a systematic understanding of what it means to be human. Indeed, I assume that this is why they are there.

CHAPTER 8

# Two Testaments, One Biblical Theology

## STEVE MOTYER

There is no question mark after the title above, a fact that gives this essay a programmatic quality. Many regard as an open question whether there is one "biblical theology" that holds together all the literature of the Bible. This essay proceeds from the assumption that, despite the grand variety of biblical texts and themes, there is a unified "theology" to be discerned and affirmed in the Bible.

But what is it? And how is it discerned? We need to explore the implications of the confession of the Bible as Christian Scripture. Let us, in effect, put an unprinted question mark at the end of the title, and ask: (1) What are the difficulties in the way of that affirmation? (2) In the light of these difficulties, what are the different ways of formulating a "biblical theology"? (and what are their pitfalls?), and finally (3) What really is the best option? How may we think ourselves forward, and be confident in our affirmation?

## 1. Challenges to a Unified Biblical Theology

In a nutshell, challenges arise from the *historical particularity* of the different writings that make up our Bible. At the most basic level, we must recognize that, from a Christian point of view, most of this "book" (or collection of "books") is not "about" Jesus Christ, even though we want to recognize him as the supreme Word of God. The contrast between Jesus as the Word and the many "words of God" that preceded him opens the letter to the Hebrews (1:1-2), and thus raises within the NT itself the paradox that, as Graham Hughes puts it, "previous forms of God's Word were and remain God's Word and yet can now be obsolete."[1]

Historical criticism is not bothered by the theological problems raised by this, but biblical theology can hardly be sanguine about it. For instance, between the covers of the Bible, there is one line of thought that regards the covenant with Israel as secure forever (e.g., Gen. 17:7; 2 Sam. 7:14-16; Rom. 11:28-29), another that proclaims its end because of Israel's sin (e.g., Amos 8:1-3; 9:7-8; Matt. 21:33-44), another that marginalizes covenant and law in favor of "wisdom" (the wisdom tradition), and another that proclaims the covenant with Israel "obsolete" (Heb. 8:13) because God has now acted to create a new people for himself in Christ — including Gentiles (e.g., Gal. 3:28). How can we come to terms *theologically* with such diversity?

So historical criticism and biblical theology have usually been at daggers drawn with each other. Gerhard Ebeling locates the origin of biblical theology as a distinct discipline in the seventeenth century, when it arose in reaction to scholasticism (both medieval and Protestant) by reasserting the simplicity and originality of the biblical message over against the complexities of orthodox systematics. But gradually, he suggests, biblical theology was undermined by a growing awareness of the problems inherent in seeking a unified statement of the message of the Bible, and of the historical inappropriateness of studying only the books within the canon as specially related to each other — and indeed of the unsuitability of the word "theology" to describe the content of the Bible at all (for theology was taken to be the scientific explication of the biblical revelation, to be distinguished from the *content* of the Bible, theology's raw material).[2]

In the history of the relationship between biblical theology and the historical criticism of the Bible, William Wrede's 1897 lecture, "The Task and Methods of So-called 'New Testament Theology,'" is notorious.[3]

1. Graham Hughes, *Hebrews and Hermeneutics: The Epistle to the Hebrews as a New Testament Example of Biblical Interpretation,* SNTSMS 36 (Cambridge: Cambridge University Press, 1979), p. 28.
2. Gerhard Ebeling, "The Meaning of 'Biblical Theology,'" in *Word and Faith* (London: SCM; Philadelphia: Fortress, 1963), pp. 79-97.
3. William Wrede, "The Task and Methods of So-called 'New Testament Theology,'" in Robert Morgan, *The Nature of New Testament Theology: The Contribution of William Wrede and Adolf Schlatter,* SBT, 2nd ser., 25 (London: SCM, 1973), pp. 68-116.

Wrede argued that the only proper, scientific object of study was "early Christian history of religion" — which dissolves both "New Testament" and "Theology": "New Testament," because the collection of writings to which we give that name is a dogmatic creation of the church, and is only a selection from the wider literature relevant to the study of early Christian religion; and "Theology," because the dogmatic tradition of the church only began *after* the NT period, and early Christian religion shows such variety both in form and ideology.

Wrede thus left NT theologians with a severe identity crisis. The historical criticism accepted as legitimate by almost everyone seemed to deny them the right to exist. And if that were true for the NT, then how much more for the Bible as a whole?

The problem remains. None of us can deny that the Bible comes to us as a series of texts rooted in history — in many different times, circumstances, and cultures (as reflected in its various genres). The Bible we hold in our hands points in two apparently incompatible directions. On the one hand, it oozes history — the history of each of its separate periods, in which its various books arose out of complex circumstances and relationships with other writings. On the other hand, it oozes theology — simply by the collection of *these* writings (and not others), and by the names of the two parts that bring them into deep relationship with each other. The first part is not "the Hebrew Bible," to be distinguished from "the Christian Bible" in the second part. These names would actually drive them apart, recognizing (implicitly) that the first part is properly *Jewish* rather than Christian. Rather, they are for us "Old Testament" and "New Testament," names that assert a mutual belonging as two parts of *one* literature claiming as a whole to be "testament" (witness) from God, divided into two sequential sections.[4]

The question that teases us is this: Granted the history of biblical criticism over the last two hundred years, in which the study of the Bible as *history* has seemed to undermine any claim to unified theological testimony, how are we to make sense of the Bibles in our hands, which present us with both history and a claim to unity?

---

4. For an excellent reflection on this, see Christopher R. Seitz, "Old Testament or Hebrew Bible? Some Theological Considerations," in *Word without End: The Old Testament as Abiding Theological Witness* (Grand Rapids: Eerdmans, 1998), pp. 61-74.

## 2. Attempts at a Unified Biblical Theology

Among the chief exponents of "biblical theology" in this century we can distinguish five ways in which, as Christians, they have sought to come to terms with this dilemma. A brief review and analysis of these approaches will help to set the scene for our own constructive proposals.

### 2.1. Biblical Theology apart from Historical Criticism

The first approach solves the problem by discounting the whole historical-critical project for biblical theology. We find an example in Geerhardus Vos, who adopted a highly systematic approach, defining biblical theology as "that branch of Exegetical Theology which deals with the process of the self-revelation of God deposited in the Bible."[5] He presupposes the full inspiration and infallibility of the biblical texts, because they are bound up with God's revelatory acts as their essential interpretation, and therefore lifts the Bible out of the realm of historical criticism. Our access to biblical history is fully guaranteed by the biblical texts, which not only *report* it, but also *interpret* it authoritatively. For Vos, then, doing biblical theology means retelling the story of the Bible, tracing the acts of God behind and within its texts. Wilhelm Vischer adopts a similar approach in his famous book, *The Witness of the Old Testament to Christ*.[6] Writing in a strongly Lutheran tradition, Vischer attempts to show how the whole OT is preparatory for Christ, by retelling the story in such a way as to make Jesus its necessary climax and fulfillment.

Vos insists that "Exegetical Theology" comes first, before systematics,[7] yet he and Vischer clearly work out of strong systematic presuppositions. We cannot say this is wrong in principle, but the way in which this works out in their case faces grave difficulties. First, we must in honesty ask at what point the doctrine of inspiration from which they work comes under criticism. Second, historical criticism, in some form, is surely unavoidable on any conception of the nature of "biblical theology." Vos appeals to historical-critical work in order to illumine (for instance) the in-

5. Geerhardus Vos, *Biblical Theology: Old and New Testaments* (Grand Rapids: Eerdmans, 1948), p. 13.

6. Wilhelm Vischer, *The Witness of the Old Testament to Christ* (London: Lutterworth, 1949).

7. Vos, p. 12.

ner dynamic of the purity laws,[8] and the nature of prophecy in Israel.[9] Opening the door to historical criticism where it can be helpful while excluding it where it might undermine one's fundamental assumptions creates an inescapable tension within the work.

Third, this approach tends to value the texts not for their sparkling *variety* in themselves, but for their infallible testimony to the history behind them. As it happens, however, not all biblical texts claim to be infallible records inspired by God. Fourth, and most significantly, the very nature of the OT compels us to ask, To what extent do these texts have validity for us, as Christians, apart from their testimony to God's "acts" or their "foreshadowing" of Jesus Christ? Large segments of the OT are not concerned with God's acts in history — e.g., many of the legal texts and psalms, the whole wisdom tradition, and all of the undated prophetic oracles. Moreover, much of the history writing found in the OT neither relates to the *central* saving acts of God nor foreshadows Jesus. Surely such texts must have a role in "biblical theology." But what?

## 2.2. Biblical Theology Arising out of Historical Criticism

This approach is the exact opposite of the last. Gerhard von Rad's *Old Testament Theology* represents a sustained attempt to build biblical theology out of historical criticism, and thus to solve the dilemma of their relationship.[10]

Von Rad started from the standard historical-critical reconstruction of OT history — briefly, that we know nothing of the ultimate origins of Israel; that something involving a journey from Egypt to Palestine must lie behind the exodus stories but we cannot know exactly what; that Israel's shaping into a twelve-tribe federation took place within the Promised Land, not before; and that the Deuteronomic history is a fundamental rereading of events according to later principles. Similarly, the prophets represented a radical new departure in Israel's history, challenging the very basis on which the tribes belonged together in covenant with God.

8. Vos, pp. 190-200.
9. Vos, pp. 216-29.
10. Gerhard von Rad, *Old Testament Theology,* 2 vols. (London: Oliver & Boyd; New York: Harper & Row, 1962/65).

Von Rad brilliantly turned this standard historical-critical picture into the basis of a biblical theology. The proper subject of OT theology, he suggested, was not the actual history underlying Israel's existence, but rather the *confessions* by which Israel told its story and thus made sense of its existence. This confessional history, of course, focused upon "the mighty acts of Yahweh" and the relationship he had thereby entered with Israel.

When the history of Israel's confessions was traced, von Rad maintained that a typological pattern emerged, whereby earlier traditions were taken up and reread in later situations, thus creating new traditions in line with the old, and yet transformed. For example, the prophets reread and reapplied the exodus traditions in the light of the Babylonian exile. They turned the old traditions into something like predictions, and "looked for a new David, a new Exodus, a new covenant, a new city of God: the old had thus become a type of the new."[11]

In line with this typological pattern of constant rereading and development, von Rad suggested that the NT simply follows on in the same process. "A new name was once again proclaimed over the ancient tradition of Israel: like one who enters into an ancient heritage, Christ the Kyrios claimed the ancient writings for himself."[12] Here the word "writings" is important. By its writings Israel explained itself to itself in ever fresh ways, in light of its ongoing experience. Now, in the light of Jesus, the traditions are reread yet again.

This dramatic theory has had profound influence on biblical scholarship. Oscar Cullmann builds upon it in his notion of "salvation history" as crucial to NT theology.[13] G. Ernest Wright's *God Who Acts* popularized it for several generations of students.[14] Krister Stendahl's famous essay on biblical theology in the *Interpreter's Dictionary of the Bible* also builds upon von Rad's model.[15]

Nevertheless, critics have drawn attention to at least four problems with this approach. (1) Can we really live with this marginalizing of "real"

11. Von Rad, *Old Testament Theology,* 2:323.

12. Von Rad, *Old Testament Theology,* 2:327.

13. Oscar Cullmann, *Salvation in History* (London: SCM, 1967) — anticipated in his *Christ and Time: The Primitive Christian Conception of Time and History* (London: SCM; Philadelphia: Westminster, 1951).

14. G. Ernest Wright, *God Who Acts: Biblical Theology as Recital* (London: SCM, 1952).

15. Krister Stendahl, "Biblical Theology, Contemporary," in *IDB,* 1:418-32.

history, and its substitution by *confessed* history? No, says Walther Eichrodt, who takes an altogether different path in his discussion of OT theology.[16] If we cannot dissolve the real history of the incarnation, death, and resurrection of Christ into mere "confession," no more can we allow Israel's real history to disappear down the tubes of historical skepticism. (2) If *historical recital* is at the heart of biblical theology, as von Rad suggests, does this not marginalize the whole wisdom tradition? Walter Brueggemann makes this criticism in his recent reevaluation of von Rad.[17] The wisdom tradition makes little of "the mighty acts of God" by which Israel's existence was secured, and to some extent even blurs the distinction between Israel and the surrounding cultures by drawing upon "international" wisdom themes and texts. But since the wisdom tradition is so important for NT Christology, it would seem vital to involve it, somehow, in whatever "center" we find for biblical theology.

(3) Is von Rad's typological model able to cope with discontinuity, as well as continuity, between the Testaments? In a penetrating analysis Christopher Seitz probes the famous essay in which von Rad tried to defend his historical-typological model by resting it upon Troeltsch's principle of analogy.[18] Analogy depends on a fundamental similarity between type and antitype, but von Rad himself recognizes the great extent to which discontinuity is a feature of the relation of the New to the Old.[19] Finally, the connection between the Testaments is theological, as well as historical. (4) On what grounds does this typological model permit a limitation to the texts of "Old Testament" and "New Testament," and to the typological appropriation of the OT by the first Christian community? Jewish appropriation of the Tanakh in the Mishnaic traditions must be allowed, by historical criticism, to be an *antitype* on von Rad's model just as much as the NT. Similarly, on what historical-critical grounds does the

---

16. Walther Eichrodt, "The Problem of Old Testament Theology," in *Theology of the Old Testament,* 2 vols. (London: SCM; Philadelphia: Westminster, 1961/67), 1:512-20.

17. Walter Brueggemann, *Theology of the Old Testament: Testimony, Dispute, Advocacy* (Minneapolis: Fortress, 1997), pp. 36-37.

18. Von Rad, "Typological Interpretation of the Old Testament," in *Essays on Old Testament Hermeneutics,* ed. Claus Westermann (Atlanta: John Knox, 1963), pp. 17-39; critiqued by Seitz, "The Historical-Critical Endeavor as Theology: The Legacy of Gerhard von Rad," in *Word without End,* pp. 28-40.

19. See, e.g., von Rad, *Old Testament Theology,* 2:330; von Rad, "Typological Interpretation," p. 36.

story stop with the Christian texts of the "New Testament" and not continue into the rest of Christian history? Von Rad's typological model provides no justification for a limitation of purview to the books of the Christian canon, although that is the extent of his own application of it. Again, his theological substratum is revealed.

## 2.3. Biblical Theology Abstracted from History

Vos and von Rad are united in seeking the focus, or organizing center, of biblical theology in the history of Israel, either confessed (von Rad) or revealed (Vos). But should the focus be sought rather behind Israel's history, perhaps in an idea or experience that serves to hold the OT texts together in all their variety? If the texts of the Christian canon really do belong together in some ultimate sense, then it might be possible to discern in them an integrating principle, something by which their uniqueness together really is signaled. There are three scholars who have made significant contributions along these lines, two from OT studies, one from NT study.

Walther Eichrodt's *Theology of the Old Testament* was published in the 1930s but was not translated for thirty years. Though writing before von Rad, he could almost be replying to him when he writes that OT theology needs to move beyond "the historical method" in the direction of "systematic analysis, if we are to make more progress toward an interpretation of the outstanding religious phenomena of the OT in their deepest significance."[20] By "systematic analysis" of the "deepest significance" of the "religious phenomena" of the OT, he means a kind of "dipstick" approach that measures the inner, spiritual life of Israel at various points in its history. What was the quality of its relationship with Yahweh in the cult, under the kings, under the prophets, after the exile, etc.?

Eichrodt has often been described as organizing OT theology around the idea of "covenant." It is not covenant as an idea that matters for him, however, but "the covenant relationship" — something that exists throughout the OT, even where the term "covenant" is not mentioned. He seeks to show that Israel enjoyed a unique relationship with God, and thus displayed a unique quality of religious experience, although its depth varied. It was at its most profound under and through the ministry of the

20. Eichrodt, *Theology of the Old Testament*, 1:27-28.

great prophets, but then tailed off in the exile and postexilic period as the vibrancy of the prophets' relationship with Yahweh was lost.

This is how Eichrodt seeks to build the bridge into the NT — which he announces as one of the chief aims of his *Theology*,[21] but to which in fact he devotes little space. He makes experience of God the vital, behind-the-text factor that constitutes the focus of biblical theology, an experience traceable through all the ups and downs of Israel's history until finally Jesus brings it to its climax.

At first this is very suggestive. If it is really possible to show that both Testaments point to a unique, and (relatively) consistent, experience of God, reaching a climax in the Christian experience of the Spirit through Christ, then we might have found the key to "biblical theology."

But flaws soon appear. How does one measure the "quality" of religious experience? Against what objective scale? Even if we had such a scale, do these texts provide sufficient information to allow us accurately to discern the underlying experience of God? Most damaging of all, from a biblical-theological perspective, what does this approach do to Christ? At best, it makes him the supreme example of a God-conscious individual (shades of Schleiermacher), experiencing God more deeply than any other. In fact, Eichrodt had already found the "religious confidence, capable of overcoming the world" (an allusion to John 16:33 and 1 John 5:4!) in the OT prophets.[22] We could also find it reflected in the Qumran Hymns, wonderful expressions of trusting piety. But if this is true, where is the need for Jesus, the Word become flesh?[23] On this analysis the Judaizers were right, and Paul was wrong!

The other two scholars to mention here are Peter Stuhlmacher and Brevard Childs.[24] They both seek to locate the subject matter of biblical theology in core ideas that lie both after and behind the texts — after, because they are essentially related to the church's dogmatic tradition; and behind, because these ideas are the essential content of the Scriptures, even where they do not come to explicit expression.

Stuhlmacher's two-volume *Biblical Theology of the New Testament*

---

21. Eichrodt, *Theology of the Old Testament,* 1:26.

22. Eichrodt, *Theology of the Old Testament,* 2:228.

23. This criticism is powerfully voiced by Francis Watson, *Text and Truth: Redefining Biblical Theology* (Grand Rapids: Eerdmans, 1997), pp. 196-97.

24. We could also classify here the recent contribution of Christopher Seitz, who confesses his indebtedness to Childs (see "'We Are Not Prophets or Apostles': The *Biblical Theology* of B. S. Childs," in *Word without End*, pp. 102-9).

is still in the process of production, but we know enough about it to be able to judge its main lines.[25] For Stuhlmacher, the task of biblical theology is to identify "the center of Scripture" [*die Mitte der Schrift*], which he defines as the ideas that form the unifying heart not just of the NT but of the whole Bible. In seeking this "center," he starts from dogmatic presuppositions, recognizing that, for Christians, the canon forms a given which we identify as containing "the truth of the Gospel, as God's redeeming revelation."[26]

For Stuhlmacher this vital "center of Scripture" is soteriological. It is essentially the gospel and its testimony to the nature of "the one God, who made the world, chose Israel for his special people, and has acted sufficiently for the salvation of Jews and Gentiles in the sending of Jesus as the Christ."[27] So it is the gospel as the story of salvation that forms the heart of biblical theology. Stuhlmacher recognizes that this means choosing between texts — highlighting the significance of those that are especially important for telling the story, downgrading those that are not.

Childs does not make such a distinction between texts in his massive *Biblical Theology* published in 1993.[28] This is because, more than Stuhlmacher, he wants to emphasize the independent, self-standing "witness" of each of the Testaments in its own right. But, like Stuhlmacher, he starts from dogmatic presuppositions concerning the role of the canon within the Christian church, so that the goal of biblical theology is "to understand the various voices within the whole Christian Bible, New and Old Testament alike, as a witness to the one Lord Jesus Christ, the selfsame divine reality."[29] He recognizes the tension between these two impulses — on the one hand wanting the texts to preserve their independence and variety, on the other seeing Jesus Christ as in some sense their real subject. How can they be reconciled? One of Childs's most recent critics, Francis Watson, suggests that they are in fact irreconcilable, and that a Christian

---

25. Peter Stuhlmacher, *Biblische Theologie des Neuen Testaments*, vol. 1, *Grundlegung: Von Jesus zu Paulus* (Göttingen: Vandenhoeck & Ruprecht, 1992). The second volume has not yet been published. See also his *How to Do Biblical Theology*, PTMS 38 (Allison Park, Pa.: Pickwick, 1995).

26. Stuhlmacher, *Biblische Theologie*, pp. 2-4.

27. Stuhlmacher, *Biblische Theologie*, p. 38. Stuhlmacher gives a slightly fuller statement of the "center" in *How to Do Biblical Theology*, p. 63.

28. Brevard S. Childs, *Biblical Theology of the Old and New Testaments: Theological Reflection on the Christian Bible* (Minneapolis: Fortress, 1993).

29. Childs, p. 85.

approach to the OT cannot make sense of a biblical testimony indepen-dent of Christ.[30]

Whether it is Jesus Christ, or the gospel of salvation, or the covenant relationship with God, what are we to make of this approach which seeks the focus of biblical theology in an abstraction from the text? John Goldingay fires some acute criticisms at it. Such abstractions are "one step removed from a living reality" — the actual life reflected within the texts themselves. By this means, he suggests, the problem of theological diversity within the Bible is bypassed, because the variations become inessential. This approach ends up looking for the lowest common denominator (i.e., the chief, most pertinent texts) and ignoring the rest. And the fact that several different centers have been identified rather undermines the whole ap-proach.[31]

From a Christian theological perspective, it is something of a truism to say that the Bible tells the story of God's plan of salvation, climaxing in Jesus Christ. This is biblical theology done simply from the perspective of the use of the OT by the NT writers. But if biblical theology is, as Ebeling says, reflection upon the biblical tradition, then it must move beyond merely retelling the story. It must probe it with questions. Why is the story in two parts? What does this imply for our understanding of God, and for our relations with Jews? How do we conceive the relation between the two parts? What of the many sections of both Testaments that do not relate di-rectly to that overarching story? What do they contribute to biblical theol-ogy? And how do they contribute? How do we handle diversity within the Bible? And — perhaps the biggest question of all — what role in biblical theology do our contemporary interests play? We wrestle with issues of power and powerlessness, poverty and injustice, wealth and paternalism; and questions of gender, race and culture, religious and ideological plural-ism, sexual morality, globalism, consumerism, individualism — to name but a few! These are all issues not specifically (or only tangentially) ad-dressed by the biblical "story" of salvation in the Bible. Can biblical theol-ogy help us to hear the voice of the Bible on these issues, too?

30. Watson, *Text and Truth*, pp. 213-16.
31. John Goldingay, *Theological Diversity and the Authority of the Old Testament* (Grand Rapids: Eerdmans, 1987), pp. 169-72.

## 2.4. Biblical Theology Founded upon a New "History"

Here we draw on some very recent contributions. Francis Watson is putting us in his debt with some creative and stimulating reflections on biblical theology and its relation to the church's dogmatic tradition, on the one hand, and to biblical history on the other.[32] He too suggests, like Childs and Stuhlmacher, that biblical theology must be conceived as a discipline undertaken within the church by Christians, for whom a priori the whole Bible is Christian Scripture. He too thinks that this commits us, a priori, to seeing the whole Scripture as testimony to Jesus Christ, although he has not as yet shown how this may be done in any detail.[33]

Watson starts to address the vexed issue of the relationship between biblical theology and history with the essay "The Gospels as Narrated History."[34] Here he begins to feel his way, building upon Frei and Ricoeur, toward a view of history that avoids a sharp dichotomy between history writing as a (true or untrue) record of events and fiction as an imaginative construct bearing no necessary relation to the "real" world. Watson proposes that the Gospels can be regarded as "narrated history," that is, as imaginative presentations of Jesus that, for all their quality as literary products, can yet exert a powerful truth claim upon us as descriptions of the "real" Jesus.

Jesus, he says, is for us inescapably textual. The search for the real Jesus "behind" the text always leaves us prey to the vagaries of historical reconstruction, and thus provides no secure basis for Christian access to him. But why should we wish away the Jesus before us, resident in the Gospel texts themselves?

Watson's reflections parallel those of Christopher Seitz on the nature of authorship within biblical theology. Discussing the authorship of Isaiah, Seitz seeks to move away from the old search for a historical Isaiah which was motivated by a desire to distinguish between original and secondary parts of the Isaianic corpus. This search has left its legacy, he suggests, in recent unitary readings of the book which approach it "as if" it were of single authorship and thus written from a single perspective. Rather, in the case of Mosaic authorship of the Pentateuch, "single authorship is linked

---

32. Watson, *Text and Truth*, building on his earlier work, *Text, Church, and World: Biblical Interpretation in Theological Perspective* (Edinburgh: T. & T. Clark, 1994).

33. For some preliminary theses, see Watson, *Text and Truth*, pp. 216-18.

34. Watson, *Text and Truth*, pp. 33-69.

[in Jewish thinking] to an expectation of larger coherence despite a complex and varied range of texts and perspectives" — and a similar approach can be fruitful in the case of Isaiah. Seitz recognizes that this is a theological view of authorship drawing on Childs's canonical perspective, and building upon the recognition given by the receiving community within which the texts were inspired.[35]

In Watson and Seitz we are finding new workings of an older approach. Indeed, Watson recognizes that his proposal is a restatement, in terms of modern literary theory, of Martin Kähler's refusal to distinguish between "the historical Jesus" and "the real, biblical Christ."[36] Against nineteenth-century attempts to reconstruct the psychology of Jesus (and thus to domesticate him), Kähler powerfully insisted that, for us as Christians, the "historical" Jesus *is* the Jesus presented to us by the Gospels. Similarly, Adolf Schlatter famously sought to circumscribe the power of so-called historical investigation to create imaginative reconstructions that run contrary to the flow of the NT texts and their own natural relationships among themselves. His 1909 essay[37] anticipates many of the emphases of the "critical realism" for which Ben Meyer and Tom Wright have powerfully argued.[38] This seeks to tread a careful path between the Scylla of positivism (meaning is "out there" and can be objectively determined) and the Charybdis of subjectivism (meaning is a function of readers and reading-effects only).

Building on all of this, Watson proposes a view of the Gospels that, in theory, could allow biblical history generally to function in a new way within biblical theology. Christians (apart from Marcion and his followers) have always claimed biblical history as "their" story — or rather, have believed that it exerted a powerful claim over them. It tells us who we are

35. Seitz, "Isaiah and the Search for a New Paradigm," in *Word without End*, pp. 113-29 (128).

36. Watson, *Text and Truth*, p. 64 n. 5. Martin Kähler's 1892 lecture, *Der sogenannte historische Jesus und der geschichtliche, biblische Christus* (Munich: Chr. Kaiser, 1969), has exercised considerable influence and fascination in twentieth-century NT scholarship. I think it is appropriate to translate *geschichtlich* as "real" in this context.

37. Adolf Schlatter, "The Theology of the New Testament and Dogmatics," in *The Nature of New Testament Theology*, pp. 117-66.

38. Ben F. Meyer, *Critical Realism and the New Testament*, PTMS 17 (Allison Park, Pa.: Pickwick, 1989); N. T. Wright, *Christian Origins and the Question of God*, vol. 1, *The New Testament and the People of God* (London: SPCK; Minneapolis: Fortress, 1992), pp. 61-65.

by revealing *our* past. We do not regard the written deposits of the OT as "someone else's mail," to allude to the evocative title of Paul van Buren's fundamentally wrongheaded article.[39] They are *ours*. And therefore we are not finally dependent upon a historical reconstruction of that history before we can truly inhabit it.

At the heart of this sense of self-identification with Israel's history lies the historical Jesus. We belong, because he belongs. The God whom he teaches us to call "Father" is the God of Israel. And therefore — whatever the implications may be for our relations with Jews — we regard ourselves as the people of that God, and those Scriptures as ours.

## 2.5. Biblical Theology in Engagement and Dialogue

Finally we review an approach associated with two names in particular, John Goldingay and Walter Brueggemann. Goldingay's *Theological Diversity and the Authority of the Old Testament* is a profound work, reviewing various approaches to the diversity of the OT and then making positive proposals for a "unifying or constructive approach." His Christian starting point is clear throughout, and so inevitably he sets his discussion of OT diversity within a *biblical* context. "A Christian writing OT *theology* cannot avoid writing in the light of the NT, because he cannot make *theological* judgments without reference to the NT."[40] Christians therefore may rightly presuppose the canon as the context of the texts and of their work. At the same time, they must take great care to allow each part to be its distinctive and diverse self. Differences within the OT must be faced, and not blurred. This makes OT theology "a constructive, not merely a reconstructive, task."[41] By "doing" OT theology, we put the varied building blocks of the literature into new, constructive shape, and thus say *more* than each of the biblical authors was individually saying. By this means, Goldingay turns the diversity of the OT into a positive thing: Biblical theology is the task by which the diverse presentations within Scripture are seen as complementary to each other, and not finally contradictory.

39. Paul M. van Buren, "On Reading Someone Else's Mail: The Church and Israel's Scriptures," in *Die Hebräische Bibel und ihre zweifache Nachgeschichte: Festschrift für Rolf Rendtorff zum 65. Geburtstag*, ed. Erhard Blum et al. (Neukirchen-Vluyn: Neukirchener, 1990), pp. 595-606.

40. Goldingay, pp. 186-87; Goldingay's emphasis.

41. Goldingay, p. 183.

This is fundamentally the approach adopted also by Walter Brueggemann, although he does not have the same integrative motivation. Brueggemann's recent *Theology of the Old Testament* will surely be one of the major biblical works of this century — or perhaps we should say, of the next — for Brueggemann's approach represents a radical departure from the traditions of von Rad and Eichrodt. He too writes explicitly as a Christian, referring throughout to "the Old Testament," although he nowhere discusses explicitly how the presence of the NT shapes "the Old Testament" for Christians. Perhaps this is because, within the postmodern world he inhabits, diversity is the furniture of the living space — not a problem to overcome, but a colorful quality to be enjoyed.

For Brueggemann (as for Goldingay), the proper subject matter of OT theology is simply the text within which Israel's "testimony" comes to voice. He adopts a largely synchronic treatment, not ignoring the sweep of OT history but moving it to the theological sidelines. It is through this synchronic approach that he is able to escape Ebeling's charge that the Bible does not contain "theology."[42] By reading the OT "flat," he is able to set Israel's "testimony" over against its own "counter-testimony" and let these perspectives debate with each other. For instance, the fact of Yahweh's self-revelation, so fundamental to Israel's existence, is subverted by Yahweh's hiddenness, a prominent theme in Psalms and prophecy. "I want to insist," he writes, "against any unilateral rendering of Yahweh's life, or against any systematic portrayal of Yahweh, that Yahweh in the horizon and utterance of Israel is inescapably disputatious and disjunctive."[43]

He finds this "disjunction" not between rival texts in different parts of the OT, but within Israel's central confessions, especially Exodus 34:6-7. Here Israel confesses Yahweh to be unpredictable. On the one hand his "steadfast love" seems to be absolute, but no one can tell when suddenly Yahweh may switch to mode B and start "visiting the iniquity of the parents upon the children. . . ." David still received grace after many sins, but Saul was rejected after one.

Brueggemann builds many links between the OT and the world of today, as he allows each perspective and text to challenge not just other OT perspectives, but also the ideologies and assumptions of the modern world. This gives his work much freshness. But we need to ask, From the perspective of Christian theology, where is Christ in this vivid to-and-fro

42. See Ebeling, "The Meaning of 'Biblical Theology.'"
43. Brueggemann, p. 715.

between rival perspectives on Israel's God and his dealings with his people and the world? At the very least, we may comment that Exodus 34:6-7 is crucially rerendered in the NT, not least in the prologue of John's Gospel. Romans 1–3 has a lot to say about the integration of wrath and mercy within the one God who is the Father of our Lord Jesus Christ.

But to ask this question is potentially to subvert Brueggemann's postmodern perspective, which resists all attempts to resolve disjunctions and to seek normative (Christian) readings of disputed texts and OT tensions.

### 3. What Is "Biblical Theology"? How May We Do It?

Finally we focus our review and reflections in a definition of "biblical theology," five theses about its nature and practice, and then a brief example.

We may define biblical theology as *that creative theological discipline whereby the church seeks to hear the integrated voice of the whole Bible addressing us today.* It arises from the self-consciousness of the Christian church as the people of the God of Abraham. We make this claim in full awareness of the parallel Jewish claim, but we can do no other, because of the nature of Jesus and the NT. He interpreted his mission in OT terms, and built his self-understanding on the categories made available to him by first-century Judaism. Similarly the NT authors lived out of "the Scriptures," wrestling with the relation of new to old as they sought to integrate their experience of forgiveness, new life, and the Spirit, given through Jesus, with their prior understanding of God, covenant, kingdom, and law.

This integration was built into Christian identity from the first. It was not "bolted on" at the time of the "parting of the ways" between church and synagogue (contra van Buren). For us, inescapably, the whole Scripture is word of God, and therefore we stand alongside the author to the Hebrews in seeking its unity around "the Son."

How can we do this? There now follow five theses about the process of "biblical theology." It is important to underscore that the hermeneutical process continues, as it always has. Von Rad, Eichrodt, and Brueggemann all emphasize the constant recontextualization of earlier traditions within the biblical process. God's people are prepared by the past to live responsively and creatively in the present. And so we engage with the texts in the light of the challenges that face us today.

1. *Biblical theology needs an explicit Christian starting point.* For us,

the texts of the OT have a different identity from the texts of the Tanakh, because of their friendship with the NT, and the role they play in enabling the NT writers to formulate their understanding of Christ. However, a Christian starting point for biblical theology does not imply that biblical theology can only be conducted through a study of the use of the OT in the New. Far from it.

2. *Biblical theology needs to operate with a clear text-focus,* one that allows the texts of both Testaments to "be themselves," within their own historical setting, taking that history seriously but not allowing it to be a straitjacket. Eichrodt and Brueggemann help us here with their encouragement to employ a sensitive synchronic approach. Text sensitivity allows real connections of substance to be made across considerable time gaps. And Seitz helpfully traces how the "per se witness" of the OT may continue to speak powerfully even when it is *not* taken up by the NT.[44]

3. *Biblical theology needs to adopt a "trajectory" approach to tradition history.* The "trajectory" model is more helpful than the "typology" model in allowing real developmental links to be discerned without having to demonstrate an actual causal pathway. Trajectories have a point of origin, a high point, and a point of touchdown. In relation to some biblical themes (e.g., creation and social justice), the high point may well lie within the OT, rather than in the New.[45] Biblical symbolism can be a creative center of study here, generating further reflections today as we see how symbols function and expand within the biblical tradition.

4. *Biblical theology needs to be conceived as a bright focus within systematic theology* — that is to say, within that process of sustained intellectual and spiritual dialogue by which Christians seek to achieve an integrated understanding of God, of themselves, and of the world. In this process biblical theology plays a vital role because of what the Bible is for us — "the oracles of God." We come to the Bible out of our theological agenda — with the questions and motivations that impel us as Christians today — and we "do" biblical theology as we engage the text with these questions. We do not force the texts anachronistically into our agenda, but allow them to address us on the basis of our shared humanity and our shared knowledge of God.

This is the proper basis on which Troeltsch's principle of analogy

44. Seitz, *Word without End,* pp. 213-28.
45. I am indebted to my London Bible College colleague Deryck Sheriffs for this observation.

plays a role within biblical theology. The difficulties, ambiguity, and contradictions of our experience today, with which theology wrestles, become the basis for our handling of the diversities we discover within the Bible.

5. *So the proper center or focus of biblical theology* is not to be found behind the text in its history, nor is it any abstracted experience or theme, nor any "canon within the canon" (not even Jesus Christ, central though he is to Christian Scripture), but it *is the contemporary theological agenda*, motivating us in our engagement with the texts of both Testaments in their historical relatedness and particularity. The raw material is, of course, these texts. But we encounter the texts with our probing questions, as faith seeks understanding. And therefore inevitably our questions become the focus of this particular exercise.

I believe that, applied together as a coherent set, these principles work creatively, and with integrity. For examples of the kind of study they generate, I mention Chris Wright's *Walking in the Ways of the Lord*, or Alan Kreider's *Journey towards Holiness*, or Deryck Sheriffs's recent study of OT spirituality, or Christopher Seitz's discussions of the homosexual issue in *Word without End*.[46]

Finally we briefly propose an application of this approach to a particular text. Studies on this model can be thematic or text focused, though they must always retain an integrative, whole-Scripture awareness of diversity and development. I follow the lead of Brevard Childs and take the story of the sacrifice of Isaac in Genesis 22:1-19.[47] It is interesting to see how this model of exegesis in the context of biblical theology extends his.[48]

Childs pursues his emphasis on the "discreet" testimony of OT and NT, and then summarizes the main lines of the history of exegesis before his concluding "biblical-theological" reflections. He notes the privileging of the reader, who knows from the outset what Abraham does not — namely, that this is a test (22:1). He treats the tradition history within the OT and into the NT in a standard way — noting the special position of

46. Christopher J. H. Wright, *Walking in the Ways of the Lord: The Ethical Authority of the Old Testament* (Leicester: Apollos; Downers Grove, Ill.: InterVarsity, 1995); Alan Kreider, *Journey towards Holiness: A Way of Living for God's Nation* (London: Marshall Pickering; Scottdale, Pa.: Herald, 1986); Deryck C. T. Sheriffs, *The Friendship of the Lord: An Old Testament Spirituality* (Carlisle: Paternoster, 1996); Seitz, *Word without End*, pp. 263-75 (esp. pp. 319-39).

47. Childs, pp. 325-36.

48. "Exegesis in the Context of Biblical Theology" is the title of the section of Childs's book in which his treatment of Gen. 22 is set.

this narrative within the Genesis story, the use of "revelation" terms (22:14), the intertextual echo with the sacrificial terminology of Leviticus, and the allusions to the story in Romans 8:32 and Hebrews 11:17-19.[49] In his summary of the history of exegesis, he notes the typological treatment of the wood as prefiguring the cross, common until the Reformation when the emphasis fell on the testing of Abraham and his justifying faith.[50]

In his final, "biblical-theological" reflection, Childs exercises great caution because of the need to avoid "a biblicist, external appropriation" of the text like the typological treatment of the wood carried by Isaac.[51] He thus tentatively comments on the faithfulness of God (whose provision of the ram points ahead to the cult), on the theme of testing, on the dialectic of reward and grace that emerges when Genesis 22:15-18 and Romans 4:2 are set alongside each other, and on the ultimate need for a Christian "reader response" to the passage (which he does not illustrate). In spite of the perspective provided by Hebrews 11:17-19, Childs makes no comments about resurrection, presumably because this is not within the horizon of Genesis 22.

The approach suggested in this essay is ready to be more adventurous, because of the role it gives to our *dialogue* with the text. We seek to let the text be fully itself, as part of Christian Scripture, but to probe it with our concerns. What might this produce? I offer four reflections.

1. *The theology of God.* The narrative dramatically poses a question about God. Even the privileged reader, who knows it is a test, does not know why God wants to set this test. Pagan practices of child sacrifice are not specifically alluded to, but readers ancient and modern all make the connection. Suddenly Abraham's God looks like the pagan gods around, demanding human sacrifice.[52] Brueggemann emphasizes the paradox of revelation and *hiddenness* within the OT,[53] and this story illustrates it as profoundly as any. It is not difficult to move to reflections on the way in which God requires us to testify to a faith that looks like self-deception, or like the mere product of our social background or psychology. We agonize too over the hiddenness of God in the suffering of the world, and the story

49. Childs, pp. 326-30.
50. Childs, pp. 330-32.
51. Childs, p. 336.
52. See Jon D. Levenson, *The Death and Resurrection of the Beloved Son: The Transformation of Child Sacrifice in Judaism and Christianity* (New Haven: Yale University Press, 1993).
53. E.g., Brueggemann, pp. 333-58.

resonates strongly with the victimization of children by those whom they have a right to trust. Where is God in all of this?

From a Christian perspective, the story points to the answer at the End. Abraham's faith — and his questions and agony — are stretched to the very last moment. This thought of the postponement of the answer, so that our lives are structured around the need to hope, and believe, and persevere in love, takes us straight into NT eschatology.

2. *The theology of sacrifice.* There are intertextual echoes not just with cultic language in Leviticus but also with Jesus' call to his disciples to give up everything, including children, for his and the gospel's sake (e.g., Mark 10:29-30). The use of cultic sacrificial language ("ram," "burnt offering," and "appear" — cf. Lev. 9:1-7; 16:2-5) connects Abraham's private experience with the public worship of Israel, as Childs notes.[54] But Abraham is essentially called to *self*-sacrifice, as are Jesus' disciples. He must give up the thing he loves most (22:2), and the ram is no substitute for the sacrifice he has already made in mind and heart before it appears in the thicket. Within biblical theology, then, the provision of Christ actually makes it possible for God to call us to go the same way as Abraham.

We live in a world in which ghastly acts of self-sacrifice have brought grief to thousands. What is the difference between the self-sacrifice of a suicide bomber and that of Abraham? Chiefly, the absence of the promise of reward. Islam promises certainty of paradise to those who sacrifice themselves for Allah. But Abraham acts simply out of "fear" of God (22:12) — that is, his loyalty and love to God exceed everything else. He is then promised a reward (22:16-18), and similarly Jesus offers "eternal life" to those who give up everything for him (Mark 10:30). But the "reward" is what Abraham has already been promised, before ever the test took place (Gen. 17:5-8), and "eternal life" is given to all who believe (John 3:16). We are all called to the inner struggle for faithfulness and obedience, through which Abraham passes, irrespective of any particular reward (Rom. 6:17; 12:1-2).

3. *The theology of bereavement.* Here we have a father facing the death of his child, and even his own complicity in it. More broadly, many have to cope with anticipated bereavement, and then with agonizing questions afterward: If I had acted differently, would she have died? What does the story say, within biblical theology, to such situations? It encourages us to think of bereavement as sacrifice, as voluntary surrender, as willing gift —

54. Childs, pp. 327-28.

chiefly because of the way in which this story is handled in the NT. "You have not withheld your son" (22:16) is echoed in Romans 8:32, with reference to God's gift of his Son "for us all." Similarly in Hebrews 11:17-19 and in James 2:21-23 the note of entrusting is clearly sounded. The severing of relationship in bereavement can be conceived as grave loss, or as great gift. The way in which Genesis 22 is caught up in the NT points us clearly in the latter direction. Bereavement can be a giving up in which we meet with the wonderful provision of God, at the End.

The author of Hebrews speculates that Abraham expected God to raise Isaac from death (Heb. 11:19). In so doing he follows the lead of the story, which makes no comments about Abraham's state of mind and thus leaves readers to fill this vital "narrative gap." Abraham's words to his two young men, "We will come back to you" (22:5), could well have prompted the speculation about resurrection. Granted that this line of thought is already present within the Bible, it lies to hand to extend it and to conceive of Christian bereavement as gift in hope of resurrection.

4. *The theology of testing.* The "now I know" of 22:12 inevitably makes us ask why God needed to discover the depth of Abraham's faithfulness, as if he did not know it already. But such questions arise from an understanding of the omniscience of God with which the passage is not working. The story tells us that we must think of our relationship to God not in terms of finite to infinite, but of person to person, servant to Lord. As in all intimate relationships, he needs to know how much we love him, and our lives need to be structured around opportunities to show how much we love him. Bereavement is such an opportunity. It is not difficult to trace a trajectory through the Bible on this issue, and to ask exactly what such experiences of testing contribute to our relationship with God. Paul addresses this with great suggestiveness in Romans 5:3-5, a passage in which quite possibly he is still thinking of Abraham, who has been the focus of his discussion in Romans 4.

## 4. Conclusion

We conclude where we began. What of that vision of a unified biblical theology — the fundamental conviction expressed in the title of this essay? If biblical theology is as I have argued, then this vision is *eschatological:* Like Abraham on the way to Moriah, we continue to seek that integrated understanding of God, of ourselves, and of the world that is the goal of all

Christian knowing, believing (with Paul in 1 Cor. 13) that such an under-standing is there to be grasped, but that as yet all our knowing is provi-sional, subject to debate, and ripe for revision. We will not be enthralled by the postmodern fascination with incoherence, but neither will we blind ourselves to the ambiguity of human experience and the hiddenness of God. We will wrestle with these, and with the Scriptures, looking forward to the Day when "we will know, even as also we are known."

# CHAPTER 9

# *Canonical Context and Canonical Conversations*

## ROBERT W. WALL

This chapter exploits the interest in the final literary (or "canonical") form and ecclesial (or "canonical") function of Scripture (or "biblical canon") in current discussions of biblical interpretation.[1] The so-called "canonical approach" to biblical studies centers the interpreter upon Scripture's privileged role in Christian formation rather than proposing a novel interpretive strategy. Accordingly, the biblical text, picked up and read time and again by the faith community, is thought to function in two integral ways in forming their common life — first, as a *rule* whose teaching norms the believer's theological understanding; and second, as a *sacrament* whose use mediates God's salvation-creating grace.[2] Even as the Word made flesh was "full of grace and truth" (John 1:14), so now in his absence, the word made text mediates the grace and truth of the Son to those who seek him in faith. From this vantage point, biblical interpretation is more a theological discipline than a technical skill.

Those who approach biblical texts as canonical for Christian forma-

---

1. This discussion of the canonical approach to NT interpretation draws heavily from my earlier study, "Reading the New Testament in Canonical Context," in *Hearing the New Testament: Strategies for Interpretation,* ed. Joel B. Green (Grand Rapids: Eerdmans; Carlisle: Paternoster, 1995), pp. 370-93.

2. Cf. Robert W. Wall, "Toward a Wesleyan Hermeneutic of Scripture," *WTJ* 30 (1995): 58-60.

tion are not only joined together by this orienting presumption, which then provides the chief touchstone for interpretation, but they share as well a negative appraisal of the modern historical-critical enterprise (although to different degrees and with different concerns). The methodological interests of historical criticism, which seem preoccupied by those contingencies that shaped particular biblical writings at various points of origin in the ancient world, tend to subvert Scripture's intended use as a means of grace and rule of faith by which believers are initiated into their new life with Christ in the realm of his Spirit. For all their exegetical utility, the tools of historical criticism misplace Scripture's theological reference point with a historical one, freezing its normative meaning in ancient worlds that do not bear upon today's church.

The variety of interests sponsored by the canonical approach to biblical interpretation as discussed in this chapter are organized around this orienting conception and criticism; thus, rather than approaching Scripture as an anthology of ancient literary art, a record of historical events, or a depository of universal wisdom, I will contend that the interpreter should approach a biblical text at its ecclesial address and in light of its canonical roles for Christian formation. The real payoff for biblical interpretation, then, is that the faith community orients itself toward its Scriptures with the presumption that biblical teaching will bring believers to maturity in theological understanding and in their love for God and neighbor.

## 1. The Authority of Scripture: Canonical Roles for Christian Formation

Of primary concern for the interpreter is the Bible's performance as Scripture within the community of faith. The Bible has authority to mediate God's grace to and delineate the theological boundaries of the one holy catholic and apostolic church; that is, the terms of Scripture's authority (e.g., divine inspiration, revelatory word, apostolic witness, christological confession) are understood in functional and formative rather than in epistemic and dogmatic terms.[3] Clearly, the Bible's authority within the church is imperiled whenever it fails to perform its intended roles, whether

---

3. See the convincing new study of this point by William J. Abraham, *Canon and Criterion in Christian Theology: From the Fathers to Feminism* (Oxford: Clarendon, 1998).

through unruly interpretation or simple lack of use. Believers tend not to use Scripture if they perceive that its teaching either lacks relevance for their contemporary situation or is simply incomprehensible to them. When such a situation persists, the functional illiteracy of the church will inevitably lead to a serious distortion of Christian faith, as believers turn to other, noncanonical authorities, typically secular, to rule their faith and guide their witness to Christ in the world.

The act of sound interpretation, when provoked by this theological crisis, intends to demonstrate the Bible's authority for a particular congregation of readers by first clarifying what the text actually says (text-centered exegesis) and then recovering from the text that particular meaning which addresses their current theological confusion or moral dilemma in productive ways — that is, in ways that end theological confusion and resolve moral dilemma in a truly Christian manner. Of course, the legitimacy of any biblical interpretation as truly Christian is not determined by its practical importance for a single readership but by general agreement with the church's Rule of Faith, whose subject matter has been disclosed through the incarnate Word of God, Jesus Christ, witnessed to by his apostles, and preserved by the Holy Spirit in the canonical heritage of the one holy catholic and apostolic church. While the precise relationship between God's truth and grace, which are now mediated through the biblical canon, and God's truth and grace, which are incarnate in the glorified Son, remains contested, my point for biblical interpretation is this: *The limits of a properly interpreted text are not determined by an interpreter's critical orthodoxy but by whether an interpretation's content and consequence agree with the church's Rule of Faith* (see chap. 5).

The actual performance of Scripture within diverse faith communities, where its interpretation must address diverse challenges to a robust devotion to God, requires a text sufficiently elastic to mediate the truth and grace of God across time and in place. That the canonical text gathers to itself a community of interpretations, all theologically orthodox and socially relevant for the Christian formation of diverse congregations of readers, is easily illustrated by its history of reception *(Wirkungsgeschichte)*. According to this history, the biblical text functions canonically whenever faithful and competent interpreters pick it up again and yet again to seek after its divinely inspired meaning either to "comfort the afflicted" or "afflict the comfortable." Multiple readings sought from the same biblical text are each discovered as a word on target in forming multiple congregations of God's people whose worship and witness presage a new creation as a result.

In this sense the canonical process settled on more than an agreed list of inspired writings (if this ever was the case) that might continue to function as a sanctioned sacrament of the church or as a textual norm for what is truly Christian. This same process also evinced a species of hermeneutics that ever seeks to adapt the plain teaching of a biblical text to its current audience, especially when its life with God is undermined by a theological crisis analogous to that to which the biblical text responds. In fact, the final list of canonical writings was completed by selecting from among those that were picked up again and again and reread over and over by subsequent generations of believers, who continually heard through them the empowering word of God. The trust the church now grants these sacred writings is deeply rooted in this canonical process, not as a knee-jerk response to a precedent set by the primitive church but in confidence that these same precious writings would continue to mediate a word from God to subsequent generations of believers whose faith in God is tested and resolved in ways analogous to Scripture's witness. In canonical context, original meanings are ever contemporized by the strong interpreter, for whom Scripture functions canonically in the formation of a faithful people.

The intended meaning of a biblical text, then, is not the property of its author but of the church to whom Scripture belongs. The hegemony of modern criticism in the scholarly guilds of biblical interpretation tends to hold Scripture captive to an academic rather than a religious end. While such an end may well be legitimate for the secular academy, these same interests are then transferred to the citadels of theological education with the unfortunate result of reproducing a clergy no longer interested in the formative intent of Scripture. A pedagogy of Scripture that serves purely historical-critical interests subverts Scripture's role, which intends to point believers to God rather than to the ancient world of its authors and first readers/auditors as the locus of normative meaning. In fact, it is only a slight exaggeration to say that the gaps in our historical understanding about the world behind the biblical text, which are then filled by competent historical criticism, typically contribute little to Scripture's performance as the word of God. What the interpreter must know about a text's intended audience, the circumstances that occasioned its writing, and the writer's response to it are details mostly found in the text itself and are readily available to the careful exegete. My point is this: *If the aim of biblical interpretation is theological understanding and not historical reconstruction, the test of sound interpretation is whether it makes the biblical text come alive with meaning that empowers a life for God.*

The preceding discussion of Scripture's functional authority is given added depth by the presumed simultaneity of Scripture's theological meaning — that is, every sacred part of this sacred whole, OT and NT, may be rendered coherent by the same theological beliefs and moral values of Christian faith. Of course, I am not suggesting that every biblical writing envisages the very same theology or moral vision; rather, every biblical writing contributes to — in part but not in whole — and makes sense of a common theological and moral understanding that is distinctively Christian. If the aim of biblical interpretation is Christian formation, then it is constrained by the core convictions of a Christian orthodoxy rather than by the methodological rules of a critical orthodoxy. Following the theological hermeneutics of Scripture itself, the faithful interpreter approaches a biblical text as the via media of God's truth and saving grace — as the canonical context wherein a word from God for a congregation of believers is sought and found. Thus, the normative meaning of a text sought by biblical interpretation is not that fixed in the author's mind for all time; nor is it found in the constantly shifting locations of various interpreters. Rather, Scripture is canonical precisely because believers recognize its power to convey *God's* intended meaning and transforming grace to all its faithful readers. If the meaning of Scripture is divinely intended and mediated by the inspired text itself, then it is the task of every faithful interpreter to seek after it. The act of reinterpreting Scripture as the vehicle of God's truth and grace, however provisional and seemingly tentative, is the courageous act of finding God's intended meaning for a community who in faith seek after a more mature life with Christ in the realm of his Spirit. The intertextual character of Scripture — the constant repetition of one text alluding to or citing an earlier text — reflects the simultaneity of its subject matter. Rather than signifying common meanings, the simultaneity of the biblical canon conveys a sense that the hermeneutics of its authors did not place a wedge between what their Scripture meant and what it now means; this critical construction is simply foreign to the hermeneutics of the biblical literature itself. The (OT) text a biblical author receives as canonical and the (NT) intertext he writes that then becomes canonical are equally valued texts in the dynamic process that seeks to hear and then submit to the word of the Lord God Almighty — a word that Christians believe is incarnate in God's Son, Jesus of Nazareth, and is made ever new by God's Spirit.

## 2. Literal-Sense Exegesis of Scripture

A theological reading of the Bible integrates two discrete tasks, biblical exegesis and theological interpretation. The penultimate task is text-centered exegesis, which aims at a coherent exposition of the plain or literal sense of the biblical text studied.[4] This is so not because the interpreter posits the word of God in the text (rather than in its inspired author, the historical Jesus, or some other critical construction), but because of the interpreter's practical interest in Scripture's canonical roles for Christian formation. If Scripture's lack of clarity is a major cause of its dysfunction within the church, then exegesis must make clear what the text of Scripture actually says to enable its performance as sacrament and rule. An interest in what a

---

4. By "literal sense" I am referring to the sense an exegeted text plainly makes, given the words used and their grammatical relations, its rhetorical role within a particular composition, and the composition's role within the wider biblical canon; that is, the literal sense of a biblical text is a literary-critical and not a historical-critical construction. As such, my use of "literal-sense exegesis" as a hermeneutical rubric is neither naive nor courageous. It seeks rather to exploit two important discussions of theological hermeneutics, one medieval and another modern, the first Jewish and the second Christian. The first source for defining "literal-sense exegesis" is the medieval rabbinate, whose commentaries on Scripture typically distinguished between *peshat* ("straightforward") and *derash* ("investigation") as two integral exegetical modes. If the aim of biblical exegesis is *peshat,* the interpreter engages in a closely reasoned and careful description of what the text actually says. In this first mode, the interpreter responds to the epistemic crisis of a text's lack of clarity for its canonical audience. If the aim is *derash,* the interpreter engages in an imaginative interpretation of why the plain teaching of the text has religious relevance for its canonical audience, often involving "reading in" a meaning not found in a text's "literal sense." This second task, integral with the first, responds to a different crisis in Scripture's authority, which is the audience's perception of its irrelevance for contemporary living. The first is not inherently superior to the second; both are necessary ways of seeking after God's word for Scripture's contemporary audience; cf. David Weiss Halivni, *Peshat and Derash: Plain and Applied Meaning in Rabbinic Exegesis* (Oxford: Oxford University Press, 1991). Raymond Brown has reintroduced the idea of Scripture's *sensus plenior* into the scholarly debate over biblical hermeneutics ("The History and Development of the Theory of a *Sensus Plenior,*" *CBQ* 15 [1953]: 141-62; Brown, *The Sensus Plenior of Sacred Scripture* [New York: Paulist, 1960]). According to Brown's more modern definition, the *sensus plenior,* or "plenary sense," of a biblical text agrees with the theological aspect of the entire biblical canon. Although Brown's understanding of the plenary sense of Scripture is a historical-critical construction, determined by authorial (rather than ecclesial) intent, my spin on "literal sense" includes this piece of Brown's understanding: Any interpretation of any biblical text must agree with the whole of Scripture's witness to God.

biblical text says rather than in what it meant at its point of origin, whether in the mind of its author/editor(s), its first readers/auditors, or by any of its sub- or pretexts — however important these critical constructions might finally be in determining a text's full meaning — presumes the importance of the biblical text *qua* canonical text. The exegetical aim to describe with critical attention what the biblical text actually says merely recognizes how utterly central the church's canonical heritage is for Christian formation. What is at stake in biblical interpretation is the believer's transformed life with Christ.

This is not to say, then, that the primary purpose of exegesis is apologetic — to privilege one line of interpretation as "canonical" for all believers for all time. There is an important sense in which the exegetical task must be fully collaborative, shared by an inclusive community of interpreters, whose different social locations and methodological interests help to expose a text's full meaning. It is within and for this interpretive community that practitioners of canonical criticism champion the hermeneutical importance of what the biblical text literally says, as it is constricted by the interpreter's common sense and critical attention to a composition's rhetorical design, linguistic content, canonical setting, theological conception, and the like. The postmodern quest of a text's literal sense does not mark a return to premodern biblicism, as some critics have complained; rather than proposing a more elegant biblicism, literal-sense exegesis seeks to recover the broad range of theological conceptions found within Scripture, which has protected the interpretive community against hermeneutical supersession. Actually, literal-sense exegesis initially pursues meaning with ideological blinders on and without regard for the integral wholeness of Scripture, seeking only to restore to full volume the voice of every biblical writer. The final destination is the recovery of the whole sense of Scripture, which can be vocalized only as a chorus of its various parts. To presume the simultaneity between every part of the whole, without also adequately discerning the literal sense of each in turn, undermines the integral nature of Scripture and even distorts its full witness to God. If the penultimate aim of critical exegesis is successfully to expose the theological pluriformity of Scripture, then its ultimate purpose is "to put the text back together in a way that makes it available in the present and in its (biblical) entirety — not merely in the past and in the form of historically contextualized fragments."[5] In this sense, then, exe-

---

5. Jon D. Levenson, *The Hebrew Bible, the Old Testament, and Historical Criticism* (Louisville: Westminster/John Knox, 1993), p. 79.

gesis of the literal or plain sense of Scripture is foundational for scriptural interpretation, but has value only in relationship to a more holistic end.[6]

Even though literal-sense exegesis itself works with a stable text in search of a standard, working description, the exegetical history of every biblical text is actually quite fluid. This limitation is deepened by recognition of the inherent elasticity of words or multiple functions of their grammatical relations. Further changes in the perception of a text's meaning may result from new evidence and different exegetical strategies and from interpreters shaped by diverse social and theological locations. In fact, the sort of neutrality toward biblical texts that critical exegesis envisages actually requires such changes to be made. Our experience with texts tells us that the ideal of a standardized meaning cannot be absolutized, whether as the assured conclusion of the scholarly guild or as some meaning ordained by (and known only to) God. Thus, the fluid nature of exegesis resists the old dichotomy between past and present meanings, and between authorial and textual intentions.

As a practical discipline, literal-sense exegesis intends only to bring greater clarity to the subject matter of Scripture, which in turn supplies the raw material for theological reflection that is formative of Christian faith. The straightforward description of the variety of biblical writings, considered holistically, helps to delimit the range and determine the substance of the church's current understanding of what it means to believe and behave as it must. Yet, whenever biblical theology is executed, it remains (with few notable exceptions) exclusively an exegetical enterprise, as though a careful description of the Bible's theology is sufficient to perform its canonical roles. It is in response to this misconception that I claim exegesis is the means but not the end of the hermeneutical enterprise. The literal sense of Scripture must come to have contemporary meaning for its current readers before it can function as their Scripture.

## 3. Theological Reflection on Scripture

The interpreter's ultimate task reflects upon what relevance the canonical text might have for its current audience. The task of theological reflection upon what Scripture says turns again on the orienting concern of the ca-

6. Esp. Brevard S. Childs, *Biblical Theology of the Old and New Testaments* (Minneapolis: Fortress, 1992), pp. 719-27.

nonical approach. If the subject matter of Scripture aims at God, so must its interpretation. Biblical interpretation, properly "ruled," is formative both of Christian theological understanding and of a life with Christ in the realm of his Spirit. If Scripture's lack of perceived relevance is a major cause of its lack of use by the church in matters of Christian formation, then theological reflection seeks to make meaningful what the text actually says about our relationship with God and neighbor.

Toward this end, a taxonomy of theological reflection on Scripture must include as primary the translation of exegesis into practical terms adaptable to the church's work of Christian formation. Exegetical conclusions are "ruled" by the church's Rule of Faith — in the theological terms and narrative logic of a Christian grammar of fundamental beliefs (see chap. 5). No interpretation of Scripture can stand as a truly Christian interpretation unless it coheres to this Rule. No interpretation of Scripture can contribute to the church's theological formation unless it coheres to this Rule. No interpretation of Scripture can mediate the transforming grace of God unless it coheres to this Rule; no sacrament of the church is foolishly or falsely distributed. My point is simply this: The principal aim of theological reflection is not to norm once and for all what all true Christians believe and how they must live, but it is formative of Christian faith — to construct a canonical context within which the Spirit of the risen Christ might be allowed fuller rein to constitute or correct Christian understanding and living. Thus, the ultimate purpose of the biblical interpreter's translation of what literal-sense exegesis has supplied her is to describe how a particular biblical text, read as Scripture, informs more precisely what manner of life and faith her particular congregation of believers holds to be truly Christian. I suspect this theological work is "critical" in the best sense in that it should have the practical result of leading them into a more mature life with Christ.

This is so as well because theological reflection on Scripture targets the social contexts of the faith community where the word of God, mediated through Scripture, is ultimately heard and embodied. Biblical interpretation, as I understand it, is fully contextual from beginning to end; not only must the exegetical task be executed within canonical context, but then subsequent theological reflection upon the text aims at an imaginative (i.e., analogical) adaptation of biblical text to social context so that the faith community might know who it is as God's people and how it is to act as God's people within the new situation. While literal-sense exegesis aims to restrict the subject matter of a studied text to a standard description (at least in theory), the interpretive task seeks to adapt what the text says to the contemporary life of a people of God whose faith and life are being challenged anew. Of course, the problem to which the act of interpretation responds is the recognition that biblical writings are all occasional literature, written by particular authors for particular audiences in response to crises of a particular time and place. No biblical writing was composed for the biblical canon nor for the universal readership it now enjoys.

In fact, the interpretive presumption of my account of canonical criticism is that current readers will not draw out the very same meaning from a composition that might have been intended by its author or understood by its first readers. Times and places change the significance of texts for new readerships. Rather than de-canonizing certain Scripture as "irrelevant" for contemporary readers, an interpretive strategy that engages a text as canonical must seek after a meaning that is meaningful for its current readers. In this sense, the crisis of biblical authority is the propriety of prior interpretations of Scripture — including those of the biblical writer's — for a "new" situation. This is ultimately a theological crisis, since the subject matter of biblical revelation fails to convey God's Word to a particular people with clarity and conviction, either because they cannot understand what Scripture says or because they cannot understand its immediate relevance for life and faith.[7] In this case, then, imagination is required by the interpreter to exploit more easily the inherent multivalency of biblical teaching in order to find new meanings for new worlds. Thus, the interpreter presumes that the literal sense of a biblical text, carefully exegeted, embodies a community of analogical meanings, while at the same time recognizing that not all of these meanings hold equal significance either for a particular interpreter or for the interpreter's faith community. One's interpretations of Scripture seek to clarify and contemporize the Bible's subject matter for those who struggle to remain faithful at a particular moment in time and place. In this regard, then, the act of interpretation imagines an analogue from a range of possible meanings that renders the text's subject matter meaningfully for a people who desire to remain faithful to God within an inhospitable world.

---

7. For this point, see Michael Fishbane, *The Garments of Torah* (Bloomington: Indiana University Press, 1989), pp. 16-18.

## 4. Reading the Bible as Canonical

Under the light of these conceptualizations of the tasks and distinctives of a canonical approach to theological hermeneutics, the framework for an interpretive model can now be constructed as a sequence of three discrete although integral parts, (1) canonical context, (2) canonical content, and (3) canonical conversations. What follows is a brief description of each as it relates to a ruled reading of Scripture.

### 4.1. Canonical Context

The whole of Scripture, OT and NT, when received and read as a textual deposit of the church's canonical heritage, aims at Christian formation rather than historical reconstruction. This presumes the interpreter's interest in Scripture's final literary form — in the text *qua* canonical text — and leads the interpreter to an initial set of hermeneutical clues derived from consideration of both the placement and titles of NT writings, which are properties of their canonization.

For example, quite apart from authorial intentions, the literary design of the NT canon suggests that its discrete units (gospel, acts, letter, apocalypse) have particular roles to perform within the whole. This consideration of the structure of the NT orients the interpreter to the subject matter found within each of those canonical units in terms of their theological function within Scripture. Often the title provided each unit by the canonizing community brings to clearer focus what particular contribution each unit makes in forming a truly Christian faith. In this regard, the sequence of these four units within the NT envisages an intentional rhetorical pattern — or "canon-logic," to use Outler's apt phrase[8] — that more effectively orients the readership to the NT's pluriform witness to God and to God's Christ. By the logic of the final literary form of the NT canon, each unit is assigned a specific role to perform within the whole, which in turn offers another explanation for the rich diversity of theology, literature, and language that casts Scripture's subject matter.

Thus, the literary conventions of the canonical process, such as the

---

8. Albert C. Outler, "The 'Logic' of Canon-Making and the Tasks of Canon-Criticism," in *Texts and Testaments: Critical Essays on the Bible and Early Church Fathers,* ed. W. Eugene March (San Antonio: Trinity University Press, 1980), pp. 263-76.

final arrangement of canonical writings and their titles, purpose to facilitate their use as Scripture. For example, the fourfold Gospel is placed first in the NT to underscore the importance of the story of Jesus' earthly ministry as the subtext for all the writings that follow in the NT. Among the four Gospels, Matthew (not Mark, in spite of its probable historical priority) comes first since its portrait of Jesus best clarifies his (and therefore the entire NT's) relationship with the OT: "I did not come to abolish the law and prophets, but to fulfill them" (Matt. 5:17). Consider also the title given to *The Acts of the Apostles,* which is another property of the canonical process. Surely this title does not reflect the intentions of the author, who claims to have authored a literary "narrative" (*diēgēsis;* Luke 1:1-4) rather than a literary "acts," and whose central character is the Spirit of God rather than the apostolic successors to Jesus. The church titles this composition to facilitate its performance as Scripture by reorienting biblical readers to the story *The Acts of the Apostles* narrates as the NT's introduction to the apostolic letters that follow. What biblical reader can now deny the authority of Paul, whose powerful "acts" prove his importance not only to God's plan of salvation, but also then the importance of his NT letters for Christian formation?

Along with the theological placement of writings and collections within the biblical canon, new titles were provided individual compositions, sometimes including the naming of anonymous authors. These properties of the canonizing stage shed additional light on how these compositions and collections, written centuries earlier for congregations, regarding religious crises long since settled, may continue to bear witness to God and God's Christ for a nameless and future readership. The importance of any one biblical voice for theological understanding or ethical praxis is focused or qualified by its relationship to the other voices that constitute the whole canonical chorus. Extending this metaphor, one may even suppose that these various voices, before heard only individually or in smaller groups, became more impressive, invigorating, and even "canonical" for faith only when combined with other voices to sing their contrapuntal harmonies as the full chorus.

A final literary characteristic of the final form of Scripture is that it is constituted of OT and NT as integral and inspired parts of a canonical whole. The nature of their relationship is envisaged by the NT handling of OT texts. The free and fluid interplay between biblical texts, one repeating another by echo or citation, is an inherent feature of its revelatory power. My interest in the intertextuality of biblical literature for the present discussion is to underscore its importance in constructing a hermeneutical model that enjoins OT with NT as an interdependent (or intertextual) medium for the word of the Lord. The current reductionism of interpreting the OT or NT in isolation from the other, thereby regarding the NT's relationship to the "Hebrew Bible" as insignificant, is subverted by the NT's appeal to and exegesis of the OT. Sharply put, the Scriptures of the OT writers are "neither superseded nor nullified but transformed into a witness of the gospel";[9] certainly on a canonical level of authority, this point funds the orienting concerns (rather than the exegetical methods per se) of a hermeneutical model for our ongoing consideration of the relationship between OT and NT within the church's Christian Bible.

What follows are several observations, sharply stated, of this relationship between OT and NT as integral parts of a canonical whole. Again, the interpretive point is this: The exegesis of an NT text as an intertext requires the interpreter to listen for echoes sounded or allusions made of the writer's own Scripture (OT). Only by doing so is the reader able to gain the fullest possible sense of what the text actually says. (1) The OT is the via media of God's word that is now "brought near" to God's people through its christological interpretation, and its current authority for God's people is constantly demonstrated by the confession of faith, "Jesus is Lord," it evokes from them (Rom. 10:8-9). The theological authority of the OT presumes its trustworthy witness to the God who is now incarnate in Jesus; as such, and only as such, can the OT function as Christian Scripture. In fact, the theological subject matter and perspicuity of OT and NT cohere around this single christological confession that brings to maturity the interpreter's perception of Scripture's own intertextuality. (2) This same Jesus refuses to de-canonize the OT (Matt. 5:17-18); rather, we have received the OT from and with him as the normative context in which his people deepen their faith in him as Lord.[10] (3) Paul's difficult claim that Christ is the *telos* (or "aim") of Torah (Rom. 10:4; Gal. 3:24) may provide another biblical analogue for relating NT (= "Christ") and OT (= "Torah") together. In this statement both Christ and Torah function as Pauline metaphors for particular patterns of salvation, the one worked out in the history of Israel and the other on the cross. Clearly for Paul, the Christ event

9. Richard Hays, *Echoes of Scripture in the Letters of Paul* (New Haven: Yale University Press, 1989), p. 157.

10. Cf. Francis Watson, *Text and Truth: Redefining Biblical Theology* (Edinburgh: T. & T. Clark; Grand Rapids: Eerdmans, 1997), pp. 181-85.

is the climax of God's redemptive purpose for Israel, which is promised in Torah; and it is this Christ event that insinuates itself upon Torah to bear authoritative witness to that divine intent. That is, the redemptive function of Torah in Pauline thought is no longer as medium of the community's devotion to God; Christ is. The role of Torah in this new dispensation is rather to reveal the hard beginnings of God's redemption of creation which now has its climax in Christ. In an analogous way, the NT is the *telos* of the OT within the Christian Bible. (4) That is, in a narrative sense, neither the OT nor the NT is complete without the other, and together they form an irreducible and self-sufficient whole; we expect no "third testament" beyond these two. Thus, what is "new" about the NT's testimony to the Messiah's *kairos* (or "time") and kerygma can be adequately discerned by the biblical interpreter only in relationship to what has become "old" about the OT as a result. From this perspective, the Christ event is the climax of a variegated history whose beginning is narrated by the OT. (5) Indeed, the Christian Bible, which narrates the beginnings of God's reconciliation of all things (OT) that climaxes with Jesus' messianic mission (NT), heralds the consummation of this history with the coming triumph of God on earth as now in heaven, to which all Scripture bears proleptic witness. (6) In a kerygmatic sense, the theological subtext and deeper theologic of NT proclamation is the OT narrative of God's response to a fallen creation and to an elect people, Israel, whom God has called out of this broken and sinful world as a light to all the nations. Every redemptive *typos* claimed by the OT prophets is embodied by Jesus, and every promise made by God through them is fulfilled through him. In this sense, then, the OT narrative of God continues on in the NT; every event of God's saving activity in Israel's history, as narrated and interpreted by the OT, is logically related to every event of God's saving activity in Christ, as narrated and interpreted by the NT. (7) While nowhere about Jesus, the OT must be understood entirely in relationship to this gospel typology about him. That is, the "truth and grace" now disclosed in the messianic event, to which the NT bears normative witness, establishes a theological and historical continuity with the truth and grace disclosed in the Israel event, to which the OT bears normative witness. (8) The intertextuality of OT and NT, then, is this: The OT supplies the NT with its normative theological and historical markers, while the NT witness to the risen Messiah supplies the subject matter for a Christian hermeneutic by which the OT is rendered as Christian Scripture. The "old" meaning of the OT is now relativized and made "new" by this christological midrash.

## 4.2. Canonical Content

A biblical text, once placed within its distinctive canonical context, acquires a potential for enhanced meaning that should help to guide the exegetical task. A canonical approach to exegesis is first of all concerned with a careful and critically constructed description of what the biblical text plainly says — with what its grammar allows; with the role the text performs according to its wider rhetorical design, according to the writer's literary artistry and thematic/theological tendencies; and with the distinctive contribution each witness makes to the overall canonical project (see above under "Literal-Sense Exegesis of Scripture"). In many ways, this part of the canonical critical enterprise is the most traditional; yet, again, the canonical approach to theological hermeneutics does not sponsor any new exegetical strategy; rather, it sponsors a particular orientation toward the biblical text whose principal interest is its literal sense — of biblical text *qua* canonical text.

## 4.3. Canonical Conversations

The intended role of the biblical canon is to adapt its ancient teaching to contemporary life; this is also the primary objective of biblical interpretation. Under this final rubric, the results of the first two tasks are now gathered together as the subject matter of two formative and integral "conversations" about the community's life of faith. The first conversation is *intercanonical* (i.e., conversations between different biblical traditions/writers) and the second is *interecclesial* (i.e., conversations between the Bible and different faith traditions); the first "norms" and guides the second.

Although a number of metaphors work well to express the Bible's theological plurality coherently and constructively, my preference for the interpreter's practical task is *conversation*. Naturally, there are different kinds of conversations between people. A canonical approach to the NT's pluriform subject matter envisages a conversation that is more complementary than adversarial. In one sense the intercanonical conversation is very much like an intramural debate over the precise meaning of things generally agreed to be true and substantial. The purpose or outcome of debate is not to resolve firmly fixed disagreements between members of the same community or panel as though a normative synthesis were possible; rather more often, it is the sort of debate that clarifies the contested content of their common ground. Likewise, the biblical canon stabilizes and bears continuing witness to the historic disagreements between the traditions of the church's first apostles, which were often creative and instructive (cf. Acts 15:1-21; Gal. 2:1-15). Not only do these controversies acquire a permanent value within Scripture, but Scripture in turn commends these same controversies to its current readers, who are invited to engage in a similar act of what Karl Popper calls "mutual criticism"[11] in order to provide more balance to parochial interests or supply instruction to clarify the theological confession of a particular faith tradition.

In fact, the point and counterpoint of this sort of conversation sometimes work better than those that seek agreement, in that they more readily expose the potential weakness of any point made *to the exclusion* of its counterpoint. In this sense I presume that a more objective and functional meaning emerges that is neither the conception of any one biblical writer — a "canon *within* the canon" — nor the presumption of any one expositor — a "canon *outside* of the canon." Rather, the canonical interpreter seeks to relate the different ideas of particular biblical writers and canonical units together in contrapuntal yet complementary ways, to expose the self-correcting (or "prophetic") and mutually-informing (or "priestly") whole of NT theology. In this way the diversity of biblical theologies within the NT fashions a canon of "mutual criticism," resulting in a more objective interpretation of scriptural teaching. A NT theology thus envisaged underscores what is at stake in relating together the individual parts, whose total significance is now extended beyond their compiled meaning; the NT's diverse theologies, reconsidered holistically as complementary witnesses within the whole, actually "thicken" the meaning of each part in turn.

Take, for example, the relationship between the two collections of NT letters, Pauline and Catholic. Each bears trustworthy witness to God, but in part, not in whole. At the very least, the sum of all their various theologies constitutes Scripture's whole epistolary witness to God. Yet, different communions privilege different witnesses, each following a "canon within the canon" in turn. For example, the Pauline collection has served Protestant believers as the singular context for their theological reflection

11. I learned of Popper's helpful categories for determining textual objectivity as good reason for both receiving and preserving literary texts from Mark Brett, *Biblical Criticism in Crisis? The Impact of the Canonical Approach on Old Testament Studies* (Cambridge: Cambridge University Press, 1991), pp. 124-27.

and moral guidance. This preferential option for the Pauline witness has led some to a Pauline reductionism, which either reinterprets the Catholic in Pauline terms or neglects the Catholic entirely. For example, the Letter of James, which Luther at first de-canonized because it communicated a contrary gospel to the one he found in Galatians and Romans, is often still read through a Pauline filter as a way to preserve its authority. Theological coherence is maintained, then, but at a cost: James is read as a Pauline book, and so its distinctive message is distorted or denied.

The witness of the full canon of letters, however, is that diverse theologies are gathered together to form a community of meaning inclusive of Pauline and Catholic. There is a sense in which this epistolary whole is actually better focused not in agreement but in disagreement. The text's "objective" witness to the truth is better forged by the mutual criticism of its contributors. Thus, the whole is greater than the sum of its parts, more robust than merely adding the contributions of James to what Paul has already brought to the table. The full effect is more like the vibrant sound produced by a complement of different and sometimes dissonant voices, intoned in this case by both Pauline and Catholic collections. The critical point is that the relationship between these two collections, complementary and reflexive, is absolutely strategic in their interpretation; one cannot be read in isolation from the other for fear of diminishing their canonical purpose. More specifically, the theological substance of the second collection of letters actually extends and enhances the theological setting for reading the first. These epistolary writings, whose names and sequence recall the faith of the "pillars" of the Jewish mission (Gal. 2:7-9), provide an authorized apparatus of various checks and balances that prevent the distortion of and finally "thicken" the church's understanding of the Pauline and so of the full gospel. In doing so, the Catholic voices are neither those of a ventriloquist nor of adversaries, but are those of colleagues whose authoritative witness to God in conversation with Paul deepens our understanding of what counts for faith.

The midrash-like character of this species of biblical interpretation compels the contemporizing of texts, so that "new" meanings are not the result of textual synthesis but arise from contextual significance. Thus, by reconstituting these intercanonical disagreements into a hermeneutical apparatus of checks and balances, the interpreter may actually imagine a comparable dialogue that aids the church's awareness of how each part of the NT canon is important in delimiting and shaping a truly biblical religion. In fashioning a second conversation under the light of the first, therefore, the checks and balances are reimagined as interecclesial conversations that continue to guide the whole church in its various ecumenical conversations. How the intercanonical conversations are arranged and then adapted to a particular faith tradition is largely intuitive and depends a great deal upon the interpreter's talent and location, both social and religious. Informed readings of biblical texts and ecclesial contexts can be more easily linked together, particular communions with particular NT writers, in order to define the normative checks and balances of a complementary conversation that maintains and legitimizes traditional distinctive, on the one hand, with the prospect of correcting a tendency toward triumphal sectarianism on the other.

# CHAPTER 10

# Tradition, Authority, and a Christian
# Approach to the Bible as Scripture

## TREVOR HART

A project that declares its intention deliberately to bring the concerns of theology and the interpretation of the Bible into a single frame draws attention usefully to the ways in which these concerns have, in "professional" contexts at least, become separated from one another. This has not happened accidentally, but as part of a hermeneutical strategy to purify the "scientific" study of the biblical text from pollution by dogmatic and personal influences. The academy has, in other words, adopted its own rigorous version of the Reformation principle of *sola Scriptura:* only the text itself, it is held (attended to now in its proper historical and social setting and with the attendant skills, tools, and prejudices of the historical-critical method), should be allowed to shape our interpretations of it. All other considerations or influences must be set aside, at least in the first instance. In particular, the interests of Christian faith and theology must be set aside for the purposes of this exercise lest they skew the outcome in inappropriate ways. The naïveté of the premise (which in practice results only in the substitution of one commitment-laden approach to the text for another) is largely responsible for the relative fruitlessness for faith of much of what this approach has produced. It has also spawned suspicion and alienation between the guilds of biblical and theological scholars (which is only now starting to thaw) and the methodological crisis that appears to beset contemporary biblical scholarship.

183

What I wish to draw attention to here is the parallel between the avowed objectivism of some historical-critical approaches to the text and the assumption treasured in parts of the Christian community that an approach to this same text (albeit now for the purposes of faith and the nurturing of Christian identity) is possible and desirable which proceeds without the influence of extratextual voices, either ecclesial or secular. I am thinking of claims that "the Bible alone" can and should be authoritative for the shaping of Christian faith and practice, at least in the first instance. Concern that the Bible should function as the church's primary authority for the formation of Christian identity at every level is, I shall suggest, basic to a properly Christian treatment of it as Scripture. This commitment, however, does not so much resolve the matter of how the text can and should be approached (whether in itself or in relation to other influences and sources of understanding) as raise it. Naive appeals to "what the Bible says" fail to take seriously the impact of the historical and social location of every act of interpretation. Far from safeguarding or respecting the authority of Scripture, such appeals actually threaten finally to erode it, and to replace it with the authority of particular interpretations. Since these interpretations are often rival and conflicting ones, this mistake can quickly lead to a factional Christianity and a divided church. To protect ourselves from it, we need not to retreat into crude attempts to isolate our interpretations from all influences outside the text itself, but rather to recognize the way in which our interpretations are and will always be shaped by other factors, taking full account of these, and thereby being better equipped to identify and deal with those influences that are pathological rather than healthy and beneficial.

The point this essay will explore is that theological concerns (in the guise of "tradition")[1] are always present and always important in any approach to the text of the Bible as Scripture. Theology, that is to say, is something we bring with us to the text as well as something the raw materials for which we quarry from it. It is not, to be sure, the only thing we bring with us. Many voices shape our interpreting, but theological tradition is important among these. There is nothing to be gained and every-

---

1. By "tradition" I have in mind not just the narrow selection of creedal and confessional statements that formally define and divide particular groups within the church, but rather the wider living body of beliefs and practices of which such statements are abstract and partial crystallizations. See further on this, Trevor Hart, *Faith Thinking: The Dynamics of Christian Theology* (London: SPCK, 1995; Downers Grove, Ill.: InterVarsity, 1996), chap. 9

thing to be lost by pretending otherwise — that is, to allege either that this influence is not there or that we are immune to it. Indeed, it will be my claim that such immunity is not only impossible but undesirable. The ways in which what we bring with us to the reading of Scripture enable us to make sense of it are vital to that reflex by which the text itself subsequently speaks to us in our particular set of circumstances. It is not an inert text, trapped in the specificity of its own historical time and space, but a living voice that addresses the community of faith ever and again and new every morning. Thus, our place within a living tradition of readers and interpreters of Scripture is vital to Scripture's place as the Word of God in our midst, and our attempts to interpret it as such.

In what follows we shall consider some aspects of this relation between the biblical text, our approach to it as readers located within a tradition as well as a wider context of human understanding, and the authority the text possesses as the church's Scripture. We begin by considering the suggestion that the church's approach to the biblical text is and must be one in which certain rules of reading are carefully observed.

## 1. Rules for Reading?

The notion that the primary concern of the theologian (or of Christian doctrine) is in some sense with the generation and subsequent policing of rules for Christian thinking and speaking about God, and hence the shape or "grammar" of a distinctively Christian way of being in the world, has enjoyed renewed prominence in the last decade or so;[2] but its roots are ancient ones. A vital part of this regulative task has always been a regulation of the ways in which Scripture is read within the church.

Given the ways in which, historically, the church's identity has been closely bound up with readings of the biblical text, it should not surprise us that such readings have been carefully regulated. As one recent discussion observes, in such circumstances "systematic anti-determinacy in interpretation will result in paralysis and instability in practice."[3] In other

---

2. So, e.g., in George Lindbeck, *The Nature of Doctrine* (Philadelphia: Fortress, 1984), and writings responding to it.

3. Stephen E. Fowl, *Engaging Scripture: A Model for Theological Interpretation* (Oxford: Blackwell, 1998), p. 56.

words, a radical plurality of (potentially diverse and conflicting) readings all granted equal validity or "authority" could never sustain and act as a resource for a community's life and practice in the way that the Bible has in fact done through the church's history. Hence, there have always been rules for the ways in which Scripture might properly be approached and read within the church. For most of Christian history, of course, this has not been a consensus born of such purely pragmatic considerations, but has reflected a basic conviction that issues of right and wrong, truth and falsehood are at stake in the task of reading itself, and reading *this* text above all. The question has generally not been, Can just any interpretation be entertained as "Christian"? but, Which of the following interpretations is appropriate or true? This is not to deny that there have been differing interpretations of particular portions of Scripture, or differing emphases of belief and practice arising as a result. Nor, indeed, is it to overlook the fact that the "rules" themselves have varied from time to time and place to place, with consequent identifiable variations between different forms of Christian community. But in general terms, and at certain key junctures, difference has always been constrained, contained within carefully defined limits beyond which lies exclusion from the category "Christian reading" as such, and hence (in some cases) exclusion from the category "Christian community."

On the whole we are not sanguine these days to regulation of any sort. We prefer to be allowed and to allow others to do their own chosen thing to the greatest possible extent. We live in a period, therefore, when the very idea of rules for reading is likely to attract disapprobation. The reader, we are frequently told, has long since been "liberated" from the oppressive, ideologically generated claim that there are correct and incorrect ways of reading texts.[4] Religious life is generally regarded as a context where such "freedom" is sacrosanct. Here the perfectly proper concerns of those who, at the Reformation, sought to free individual Christian readers of the Bible from the hegemony of ecclesial interpreters overlap curiously with contemporary advocacy of the autonomy of both the text and the reader alike. Yet the wedding of interests is at best partial and more apparent than actual. My suggestion here is that some set of constraints has always existed (not least among sixteenth-century advocates of the Refor-

4. See on this Kevin Vanhoozer's helpful discussion in "The Reader in New Testament Interpretation," in *Hearing the New Testament: Strategies for Interpretation*, ed. Joel B. Green (Grand Rapids: Eerdmans, 1995), pp. 310-11.

mation itself)[5] and *must exist* in order for Scripture to function as such within the church, and for the church to be the community whose life and identity are decisively shaped by a reading of this text. Let others do as they may with the text, therefore, but a Christian reading of the Bible as Scripture must be one conducted within certain identifiable constraints.

A historical survey of the idea of a *regula fidei* (Rule of Faith) or its functional equivalents would certainly reveal a wide variety of types, shapes, sizes, and contents.[6] The usual suspect for having introduced this basic idea into theology is Irenaeus of Lyons, who, writing *Against Heresies*, alights quickly on the realization that there is rather more to the production of a "biblical" engagement with theological or practical questions than at first meets the eye. The problem with many of those whose views he expounds and criticizes (the "heretics") is not that they do not possess or deploy the text of the Bible, even quite extensively, but precisely that, in his words, they "falsify the oracles of God, and prove themselves evil interpreters of the good word of revelation" (1.1). In other words, they read the Bible in inappropriate ways, taking portions of it and "twisting" its sense in order to bolster opinions derived ultimately from elsewhere than the Bible itself (1.9.4). In response Irenaeus urges his readers to consider the various passages of Scripture in their proper context, and thereby to substitute their "natural" sense for the "unnatural" substitute offered by improper readings. This is a point that was picked up again at the Reformation, especially in response to some of the more far-fetched appeals to the fourfold sense in medieval exegesis.[7] Here, then, we might say, is a formal "rule" for

---

5. See, e.g., the account of Bucer's approach to Scripture in Henning Graf Reventlow, *The Authority of the Bible and the Rise of the Modern World* (Philadelphia: Fortress, 1985), chap. 4.

6. On this theme see, e.g., the helpful study by Paul M. Blowers, "The *Regula Fidei* and the Narrative Character of Early Christian Faith," *Pro Ecclesia* 6 (1997): 199-228.

7. So, e.g., Huldrych Zwingli writes (in a treatise from 1522 originally delivered as a sermon to nuns in the convent at Oetenbach, and intended to encourage them to read the Bible for themselves rather than relying on the renderings of their Dominican mentors): "Oh you rascals — you are not instructed or versed in the Gospel, and you pick out verses from it without regard to their own context, and wrest them according to your own desire. It is like breaking off a flower from its roots and trying to plant it in a garden. But that is not the way: you must plant it with the roots and soil in which it is embedded. And similarly we must leave the Word of God its own proper nature if its sense is to be the same to all of us. And those who err in this way we can easily vanquish by leading them back to the source, though they never come willingly" (*Of the Clarity*

reading: always look first at a passage in its proper context and pursue its natural sense. But Irenaeus also knows that in disputes over what the text *means* rather than simply what it *says,* it is frequently not possible to resolve things by return to the text alone. So he also appeals to what he dubs the "rule of truth" which Christians "received" (owned or submitted to?) at their baptism. From what he says, this appears to be a brief and informal narrative account drawn from Scripture, recounting God's actions toward humankind from creation to the consummation of all things, and clearly centered in the life, death, and resurrection of Jesus. This thumbnail sketch, he insists, is the "faith" transmitted from the apostles themselves, and may usefully be used as a yardstick or a framework for evaluating the "Christianness" (not his term) of readings of Scripture. Anything that detracts from it, even though it be thoroughly steeped in the words of the text, must be rejected (or at least suspected and investigated) as an unchristian reading. Here, then, we have a mixture of substantial and formal rules for reading. Certain procedures must be prioritized over others, and certain interpretations may not ordinarily be expected to be tolerated.

Another example from the patristic period is the dispute between the Arians and the Nicene theologians in the early fourth century. Whatever we make of the Nicene *homoousios,* we must recognize that its intended role was to lay down certain rules for reading the text of Scripture, and thereby to secure what was deemed to be a proper rather than an improper (sub-Christian) reading of the text.[8] The issue at Nicaea, that is to say, was a dispute about the interpretation of the text of Scripture, a dispute that extended beyond the particulars of the case to general considerations. Arius's appeal to the NT was every bit as thorough and detailed as that offered by his opponents. It was so thorough, in fact, that it proved impossible to refute Arius on the basis of biblical texts alone. Any biblical text supplied in order to do so proved capable of an Arian reading. Thus, in order

---

*and Certainty or Power of the Word of God,* in *Zwingli and Bullinger,* The Library of Christian Classics, vol. 24, trans. and ed. Geoffrey W. Bromiley [Philadelphia: Westminster, 1953], p. 87). I am grateful to one of my research students, Scott Amos, for supplying this reference. On the fourfold sense and the Reformation see, e.g., Anthony C. Thiselton, *New Horizons in Hermeneutics: The Theory and Practice of Transforming Biblical Reading* (Grand Rapids: Zondervan, 1992), pp. 179-80.

8. See on this David S. Yeago, "The New Testament and the Nicene Dogma: A Contribution to the Recovery of Theological Exegesis," in *The Theological Interpretation of Scripture: Classic and Contemporary Readings,* ed. Stephen E. Fowl (Oxford: Blackwell, 1997), pp. 87-100.

to secure what was held to be the proper Christian reading, the Nicene theologians were driven to employ extrabiblical language and conceptuality in order to clarify the meaning of the text. *Homoousios* refutes the Arian reading of "Son of God," "Logos," and so on in a way that no purely biblical vocabulary could, because it was precisely the meaning of the available biblical vocabulary itself that was at issue. In addition to this substantive point of clarification, Athanasius's dispute with the Arians also tackles formal points, such as the ways in which metaphors such as "Father" and "Son" should and should not be handled when applied to God. Precisely because the terms are used metaphorically (or analogically), he argues, we cannot treat them as if everything that is generally true of human sons and fathers is true of the God to whom these terms properly apply. The task of engaging in theology *(theologein)* (as opposed to "mythologizing" [*mythologein*] or the "epinoetic" confusion of the creaturely with God of which Athanasius accuses the Arians)[9] is, through allowing the reality to define our understanding of the relevant terms rather than vice versa, to discern the contours of similarity and difference that make metaphor what it is. Again, then, we are offered both substantive (particular) and formal (general) rules for an approach to the text of the Bible as Scripture within Christian theology. Approaches or interpretations that breach these rules may not be considered properly Christian readings.

Many similar examples could be supplied from the history of theology. The general point is that, although the specifications have varied quite considerably over time and space, the church has always found it necessary to offer rules for reading Scripture, both general rules and rules for reading particular passages. It is one of the primary and basic functions of Christian theology to forge and subsequently to clarify and to regulate the rules for a Christian reading of Scripture. Thus, an important task of Christian

9. On the distinction between doing theology and "mythologizing," compare Athanasius's criticism of pagan philosophies and religion in *Contra Gentes* 19. See Robert W. Thomson, ed., *Athanasius: "Contra Gentes" and "De Incarnatione"* (Oxford: Clarendon, 1971), pp. 54-55. For the use of *epinoia* in the related sense of human devising or construction, see, e.g., *Contra Arianos* 2.38 (Migne, *Patrologia Graeca*, 26:228.A). Cf. John Henry Newman, ed., *Three Discourses of Athanasius against Arianism* (London: Longmans, Green & Co., 1903), p. 298. On the basic point see also the discussion in *Contra Arianos* 1.6 (Newman, pp. 181-82; Migne, *Patrologia Graeca*, 26:56A-57B). For discussion of these matters in Athanasius's thought, see esp. Thomas F. Torrance, *Theology in Reconstruction* (London: SCM, 1965), chap. 2; Torrance, *Theology in Reconciliation: Essays towards Evangelical and Catholic Unity in East and West* (London: Geoffrey Chapman, 1975), chap. 5.

theology as such is to offer what are in some sense "authoritative" interpretations of the text, judging and unfolding what the text means when, e.g., it speaks of God as Father, Son, and Holy Spirit, or of Jesus as the Christ, or of the death of Jesus as having been "for us." Such clarification will entail, among other things, locating particular portions of the text within its wider patterns (see below on treating Scripture as a whole), discovering contemporary analogues through which the voice of the text may helpfully be translated and duly heard (a process that goes far beyond the actual "translation" of words as such), and bringing the text into creative interaction with the ever changing state of wider human understanding.

Questions about such matters cannot be answered in the abstract, since the answers to them will depend in part on the particular concerns with which the text is approached. Furthermore, the answers given in one social or cultural context will not, in and of themselves, be likely to serve other contexts especially well, and must be reforged as the question of meaning is asked ever afresh in the church's constant return to the text of Scripture. There is a diachronic and a synchronic dimension to this sense in which the text of Scripture will always "mean" something slightly different, depending where, when, and for what purpose we interrogate or seek to hear it. This is not to suggest that particular communities may do with or make of the text what they like, so that in theory radically different or contradictory answers could easily be entertained. It is simply to acknowledge the truism that saying "the same thing" in another time and place is not really saying the same thing at all, and that the event of meaning is shaped by what the interpreter brings to the text as well as what she encounters there. There is a contribution to be identified on both sides which implies that "meaning" is essentially a dynamic and not a static entity. Handling the implications of this realization for issues of identity and continuity ("tradition" in its widest sense) is vitally important. It is precisely this task of managing the shipment of semantic freight from context to context, or perhaps the relationships between distinct but related layers or spheres of meaning, that the theologian is called to, and for the purposes of which rules of reading are developed and subsequently applied.

The senses in which these theological interpretations are held to be authoritative will, of course, vary considerably. In the case of the trinitarian and christological doctrines articulated in ancient catholic creeds, for example, the level of authority is high and formally recognized. But in all sorts of less formal ways, "doctrine" in the wider sense functions similarly to guide, and hence to authorize, certain sorts of readings of the biblical text and, tacitly or explicitly, to prohibit or constrain others. In both cases, the formal and the more informal, we may identify a dialectical movement between theology and Scripture which is vital both to the latter's functioning as Word of God and to the momentum through which alone the living tradition of Christian faith is extended through time and space. As the figure illustrates, there is a progressive hermeneutical spiral in which this oscillation moves understanding forward through a constant return to the text of Scripture itself — T1 furnishing a framework for the subsequent reading of Scripture and, in its turn, being modified (T2, T3, etc.) through the reflexive impact of this and subsequent fresh readings of the text upon it. What is not (and could not easily be) shown in this simple figure, but must be taken into consideration, is the fact that "Scripture" may refer to the same precise passage or some other portion of the overall text, the complex of other factors that feed into the interpretive process, and the consequent fact that a "naked" reading of Scripture (S) is in practice a convenient fiction since even an initial approach to the text is already shaped by all manner of things which we bring to it.[10]

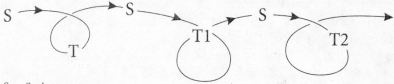

S = Scripture
T = Tradition (theology, liturgy, and other ways in which the text is interpreted and embodied in the life of the church)

To admit this is not to detract in any way from the Bible's role as the primary source and norm for Christian faith and the fashioning of Christian identity. Nor is it to go back behind the Reformation principle of *sola Scriptura* and to elevate human tradition (in the guise of rules for reading) above the text. Those who insisted upon giving the Bible primacy over tradition in the sixteenth century were not so naive as some who have bandied their political slogans around since. They knew perfectly well that the

10. For a helpful discussion of this complex set of relations, see Richard Bauckham, "Tradition in Relation to Scripture and Reason," in *Scripture, Tradition, and Reason: A Study in the Criteria of Christian Doctrine: Essays in Honour of Richard P. C. Hanson*, ed. Richard Bauckham and Benjamin Drewery (Edinburgh: T. & T. Clark, 1988), pp. 117-45.

Bible was not a cultic object, but a text that must be interpreted by human readers if it was to function authoritatively within the church, and that could actually be interpreted in a variety of ways. Anyone who reads any of the great Reformers will soon stumble across a variety of significant rules for reading Scripture: the importance of attending to its "literal" or "natural" sense, strategies for typological readings, ways properly to interpret the relationship between law and grace, and so on. The point is that these same rules, like those we have considered, are not derived a priori but emerge from a long and careful engagement with the text of the Bible itself within the church. The fact that we bring them with us to the text as aids to a proper reading of it should not lead us to overlook the fact that they were themselves worked out in the light of prior engagements with that text, representing, as it were, the accumulated wisdom of generations of reading of this text as Scripture. In the task of reading Scripture, every generation within the church must undergo an apprenticeship, and this means learning to read the text at the feet of those masters of reading who have preceded us, learning from both their successes and their failures over the centuries. The *regula fidei*, the set of rules for reading adopted in any community, will commend themselves to us as the best guidance toward a likely fruitful engagement with the text that those who have engaged with it fruitfully before us have to offer. If the fear be that "bringing to the text" is a likely formula for making of it a wax nose, then I would suggest that in fact some version of the *regula fidei* is precisely a defense against this, for what it does is to keep us focused on ways in which the text has been read by Christian readers over the generations. It is anything but a license to make of the text what we will.

The burden of this section, then, has been to insist that a Christian reading of Scripture has always been and must be a regulated reading. Reading the Bible as Scripture involves more than just adopting a particular attitude toward the "authority" of the text. We read deliberately within an identifiable tradition of reading, and in accordance, therefore, with rules or guidelines which that tradition has laid down or lays down. This is not to deny that other ways of reading the text are possible. Nor, at this stage, is it to say anything about the truth or falsity of properly Christian readings (although questions about this will not be kept at bay for long, nor should they be). It is simply to observe that there are limits to what may count as a properly Christian reading. This, perhaps, is the first "rule for reading" — namely, that reading shall be in accordance with the rules.

## 2. The Presumption of Presence

That Scripture is authoritative for the church is not a point for which I wish (or feel that I have) to argue. I simply observe that it is so, and has always been so. There are, of course, those who wish to abandon the notion of scriptural authority at the theoretical level, and probably plenty of Christians for whom Scripture does not function authoritatively in any very identifiable way. But formally it has always been held and continues to be held by every major Christian tradition that Scripture is to be treated as "authoritative" in some sense. This "in some sense" is no doubt important, as David Kelsey's seminal study demonstrated in relation to theology more than twenty years ago.[11] But Kelsey himself showed precisely that, such important differences notwithstanding, the basic claim that "Scripture is authoritative for the church" functions effectively as a tautology, its two key nouns being in effect mutually defining: "Scripture" is that text which functions authoritatively within the church, and "church" is that community which treats Scripture as authoritative for its life and faith, and allows it to shape its own distinctive identity. If, though, a text (*qua* text rather than cultic object) is to function authoritatively within a community, then, we might suppose, it is vital that the "meaning" of that text be discerned and more or less agreed upon. A text that means nothing or everything, or whose meaning is a source of dispute rather than consensus, is unlikely to function authoritatively in any sense and to be a source of crisis rather than a stabilizing force in the attempt to locate and to nurture Christian identity.

Formerly this was a relatively unproblematic assumption. The question was, What does this text mean? and there were tools to be acquired and skills to be learned by anyone who would deign to attempt to answer this question. After a long apprenticeship in the academy, armed with a barrage of historical, lexical, and other equipment, the novice scholar attempted to dig meaning out of the text for himself or herself. The increased complexity of contemporary hermeneutics lies chiefly in its having introduced a new set of questions for consideration. Now we are advised that the question, What does the text mean? is insufficient, perhaps even entirely inappropriate. From a circumstance in which meaning was generally held to be a property attaching to texts (or texts in relation to their au-

---

11. David H. Kelsey, *The Uses of Scripture in Recent Theology* (London: SCM; Philadelphia: Fortress, 1975).

thors), and thus a relatively objective and singular entity which might be laid hold of by those possessed of the requisite skills, we have moved to a very different culture. Now the existence of meaning as in any sense an objective commodity is frequently called into question. Meaning is defined by some as what the reader creates, or brings with her to the text, or the effect the text produces in the reader, or what the reader chooses to do with the text. This "deregulation" of meaning might be thought highly threatening to the church as a community whose identity is rooted in a reading of an authoritative text. Are we not likely to collapse all too quickly into "paralysis and instability in practice"? There are certainly versions of this phenomenon that appear to be wholly incompatible with a Christian approach to the reading of Scripture. The answer does not lie, though, in retrenchment within the old objectivist models of biblicism in either its ultraconservative or its historical-critical versions. We have much to learn from the question, How does a text mean?, and some of the answers given to it in recent discussions, and what at first sight may seem to present a crisis, may actually offer the basis for a renewed way of thinking about the Bible's role as Scripture. My specific claim here is that when it comes to the question of the "meaning" of Scripture, both those approaches that claim too much and those that claim too little concerning our capacity to appropriate this meaning result in an effective taming of the text that is utterly inappropriate for a Christian reading of it as Scripture.[12] Our attempts to interpret the text must presume presence, but of an elusive kind.

Determinate readings (those which suppose that a single fixed and authoritative meaning is there to be had by readers with the requisite tools and skills) make the presumption of "presence" in their engagement with the text.[13] In this, I would suggest, they are quite correct, but they do not discern the elusiveness of that presence. Insisting that the "true" meaning of the text is established and laid bare in their commentary upon it, they succeed only in confusing the two. In doing this they effectively render themselves immune to any alternative readings of it. They "have" the text. They are no longer open, therefore, to fresh considerations of it, or to hear it speaking in any

---

12. For a development of the case see Hart, chaps. 6-7. For a wider discussion of the hermeneutical issues, see Fowl, *Engaging Scripture;* Thiselton, *New Horizons in Hermeneutics;* Kevin J. Vanhoozer, *Is There a Meaning in This Text? The Bible, the Reader, and the Morality of Literary Knowledge* (Grand Rapids: Zondervan, 1998); and in this volume, Max Turner's contribution (above, chap. 3).

13. For the categories "determinate," "indeterminate," and "underdetermined," see Fowl, *Engaging Scripture.*

other voice than the one they have trapped, tamed, and packaged for observation. Thus they allow their own readings to have a finality bestowed upon them, a sufficiency that lifts them above the level of the text itself and out of reach of its criticism. Far from establishing the text's "authority," therefore, this is a strategy that effectively subverts it and enthrones our "objective" readings in its place. Indeterminate readings (those that refuse any notion of authorized readings and exalt the interests of the reader over those of the text) mistake the elusiveness of presence for absence. Thus they set about the task of creating meaning to fill the void. For such approaches there is nothing whatever in or attaching to the text which might constrain our reading. Such constraints as bear upon us come from the community to which we belong, or from our own particular perspective as readers. Unable to transcend this particularity, we are incapable of hearing any strange or uncomfortable voice speaking through the text. We are protected from doing so. The meanings we retrieve are those our context authorizes. In other words, the text means what we will allow it to mean — no more, and no less. Here too, then, there is an effective relocation of authority from the text to the reader. The possibility of the text challenging us or speaking with a strange voice is undercut.

There is little doubt that the presence of meaning in relation to texts can be very elusive. We should neither exaggerate nor underestimate the extent to which this is the case; and we should recognize that while it is always true, it is true to a different extent in different cases and with regard to different aspects of the same texts. There is a curious mix of universality and radical particularity about any event of communication. Relatively straightforward evocations of the familiar that transcend time and place are fused with the enigmatic and baffling traces of radical particularity, both cultural and personal. But the "wager on transcendence," as George Steiner calls it, is one we must make if we would venture forth from our own particular standpoints and make meaningful contact with the other. And, despite the risks and the fragility of our attempts to do so, Steiner observes, vulgar fact contradicts the claim that it cannot be done and should not be attempted. We are all engaged in constant acts of communication, speaking and hearing across personal, social, cultural, and historical boundaries many times every day of our lives. That we are not always as successful as we hoped does not invalidate either the desire or the attempt both to transmit and to receive in events of meaning.

Steiner points to the unstable balance between the objective and the personal, the determinate and the indeterminate, as the locus of the genius of language, which provides both sufficient stability for genuine communication to occur and sufficient instability for language itself actually to be used to refer us to a world of experience that is highly complex, ever changing, and open-ended. Words and "meanings" are solid enough to be traced and handled, but malleable enough to be molded and shaped creatively to meet new circumstances and new realities. Along similar lines it might be suggested that God was wise to commit himself to language as a medium within which his self-communication to humans might in large measure occur. On the one hand, the abiding objective form of the text, taken together with the context within which it was fashioned, constitutes some form of "given" to which our reading has a moral obligation. Insofar as our interpretations approximate to the speech act intended by the writer in deploying this text, there will be an identifiable continuity between them, even though they will all differ by virtue of what we bring with us to the task. The text stands over against and over us, and calls us first to hear it speak. In this role it may judge us, as well as encourage and confirm our insights and understanding. On the other hand, the inherent instability of texts bestows upon the task of reading a freshness and a vividness, and again a responsibility to submit our readings ever afresh to the constraints and guidelines laid down by a text the resources of which to provoke ever new resonances of association and response are nonetheless as endless as the differently attuned perspectives with which we come to it. We do not need to "play" with the text in order to persuade it to render meaning for our particular circumstance. If we listen to it, and consider carefully what it says, it will address us in our particularity, and possibly surprise us in doing so by allowing us to transcend that particularity.

A properly Christian approach to Scripture, then, I suggest, will be one that seeks to submit to the text, presuming on the presence of communicative intent mediated through the text, seeking to be constrained in its initial approaches and subsequent responses by a discipline of hearing what the text is saying, so far as this is possible, and recognizing the partial and provisional nature of all its readings, thereby being open and committed to a continuing process of disciplined listening and hearing.

## 3. Attending to Scripture as a Whole

Another feature of a distinctively Christian approach to the text of Scripture is that it will seek to hear the voice of the text as a whole. That does not, and clearly cannot, mean that it attends to the whole text each time it approaches it, but rather that its approach will always treat the text as "a whole" rather than as a loose collection of discrete documents or textual particles. Behind this lies the conviction that Scripture treated as a literary whole tells a story in which God's distinctive identity is made known. Again, this does not mean forcing a wide variety of different genres onto an interpretative bed of which Procrustes would have been proud. Not all the texts are "narrative" in the technical sense. But treated as "a whole," Scripture, in all its diversity of types, offers a narrative world the reader is invited to indwell, and from within which she is now expected to view things. In the familiar parlance of Wittgenstein, Christians are required to take the world "as" the world that Scripture portrays, to indulge in an imaginative shift that transforms the way the world looks and the ways in which, as Christians, we live in it. Without the space here to develop this claim, I would suggest that this is precisely what Christian faith, Christian identity are all about. The world of the biblical writers "becomes" our world in some identifiable sense. Or, put differently, we discover that it was our world all along.

One implication of this is that for the purposes of a Christian reading of the text, while a historical-critical approach to it is invaluable for many things, the fascinating task of scraping away the surface of the text in order to discover what lies behind it ("Just give me the facts, ma'am") is not one likely to generate significant results. Instead, the professional scholar can provide enormous insight that grants us the possibility of hearing more clearly the natural voice of the text or, rather, the "texts" in their final form. The attempt to hear this voice will be an important step in our effort to treat Scripture as "a whole," a process that certainly must not mean failure to attend to particular books in their final form. This, presumably, is the logic behind the traditional practice of writing commentaries that focus on particular "books" of the Bible, rather than on bits of books, or on the Bible treated as an undifferentiated unity. It follows naturally enough from the logic attaching to discrete texts as crafted pieces of verbal communication. We want to know what the writer was attempting to share with us through this carefully constructed form. To erase the picture he paints in the pursuit of something hidden behind it, or to allow its distinctiveness to be obscured by a careless treatment, is to commit acts of textual vandalism. So an important part of a canonical reading will be a careful effort to understand the individual books, to hear their distinctive theological voice.

197

A reading of Scripture as a whole will, of course, involve going further than this. It will involve asking how our understanding of this distinctive voice has now to be modified or deepened by its location within a wider set of textual relationships. This will not mean overriding or ignoring the natural sense of the text, but it will certainly entail seeking to hear this voice speaking alongside others and, within the logic of the relationship between the first and second Testaments, allowing some voices to assume particular roles with respect to others. Returning to the metaphor of narrative, if we assume that Scripture as a whole tells a story, then we may for some purposes relate the chapters or stages in this story to one another in ways analogous to those that we find in the structure of any other story. Early chapters set the vital context for making sense of what comes later. Without them (were we, for example, to stumble across the final 30 pages of a 150-page novel unfortunately detached from the book as a whole), although we might be able to make some sort of sense of later stages in the story, we should have to do so by supplying our own matrix for interpretation, and the result would not be the same story at all. Similarly, possession of the first part of a story in the absence of its proper narrative denouement would spoil the story as such, because these closing sections are intended to resolve the narrative tensions, tie together loose ends, and cast new light on all that has gone before.

Applying this to Scripture as "a whole," then, we may say that the books of the first Testament are vital in their distinctive voice (and must be heard ever afresh in that voice) because they furnish what T. F. Torrance refers to as the conceptual tools and the hermeneutical matrix for making sense of the revelation of God in Jesus Christ (the denouement in the story that Scripture tells).

> That is why the Church is built upon the foundation not only of the apostles but of the prophets. . . . Let us not forget that the Old Testament constituted the Holy Scripture for Jesus and was the only Holy Scripture known to the authors of the New Testament. This implies that only as we are able to appropriate and understand the Old Testament in its mediation of permanent structures of thought, conceptual tools, . . . shall we be in a position really to understand Jesus even though we must allow him to fill them with new content and reshape them in mediating his own self-revelation to us through them.[14]

14. Thomas F. Torrance, *The Mediation of Christ,* 2nd ed. (Edinburgh: T. & T. Clark, 1992), p. 18.

So, if the story is to be told and heard, then the early chapters cannot be dispensed with without total distortion, a fact the church has learned whenever the attempt has been made to abstract the figure of Jesus from this vital context. Christians are precisely those who confess the Messiah of the Jews to be also the Lord of the church, and they can never sever the bond with Israel and its Scriptures without suffering loss of their own identity. But these same Scriptures are, nonetheless, transformed in our reading of them as part now of a different "whole" — namely, Christian Scripture.

Should we choose not to construe Scripture under the likeness of story in this way, then, of course, quite different sets of textual relationships might be proposed within a canonical reading. We might, for example, choose to allow every text to speak in isolation (reading "canon" as meaning simply "these particular texts and no others" rather than "these texts as a whole"). This is the essential logic behind the "proof texting" beloved of some "biblical" approaches to theology in which the smallest atoms of the text are torn away from their textual, let alone their canonical, contexts and reassembled within some other framework of interpretation, often in order to demonstrate a point that is anything but natural to them. This approach also tends to raise or lower every such "text" to the same level of theological significance, which, again, is an odd way to treat any text. It is the complexity of a text as a whole (and various identifiable "wholes" within it — in the case of the Bible, letters, parables, historical narratives, etc.) that should determine the weight to be afforded to individual atoms. This does not mean, of course, that individual sentences or phrases from Scripture may not function or be used in isolation, but simply that the implications and possible dangers of such use must always be fully considered.

Another possible approach would be to configure the whole differently, allowing some other portion of it to function as the natural focal point in relation to which other parts must finally be understood. But the practice of Christians treating Scripture not just as a whole but as a particular sort of whole (a narrative world as I have called it) is no arbitrary imposition of a certain textual pattern. It is finally an expression of the conviction that, while the task of the Christian reader is to attend to these texts rather than excavating them for some more ultimate basis for faith, nonetheless the texts themselves do refer us appropriately to the reality and structure of God's dealings with humankind and the world as the God known to Israel as the Lord; that these dealings, extended through time,

199

come to a head in the story of Jesus Christ, his ministry, death, and resurrection, and the outpouring of God's Holy Spirit in power at Pentecost. The construal of Scripture as "story," that is to say, reflects the intrinsically vectorial (eschatological) structure of Christian faith and identity itself, a faith rooted in hope in the God of Israel who became the human Jesus Christ, indwells his church, and is yet to come to fulfill his promise of a new creation in which he will be all in all.

A reading of Scripture as a whole (and as a narrative whole), then, might be described as a reading with both the Father and the Son clearly in view, rather than allowing either to be swallowed up by the other. The claim that the God revealed in Scripture is the Father of Jesus Christ is not only a claim that arises out of our reading of the text as a whole, it is also one that should provide us with a basic rule for reading it.

Before moving to my final point in this essay, let me make one further observation about the implications of reading Scripture as a literary whole. I have focused here on the relationships pertaining between textual voices in the first and second Testaments. But similar issues also arise within the Testaments, and here the metaphor of narrative structure does not really help. It is a commonplace of modern biblical studies to observe that different books within (let us say) the NT present, and may even contain within themselves, diverse theological perspectives. On the whole, more has been made of this diversity than it warrants. But we cannot ignore such diversity, and it is important that the move to a canonical reading does not entail blending the various voices into a mulch of identical texture. Nor, as I have already suggested, should the engagement of systematic theology with the text entail taking it to a hermeneutical breaker's yard where its smallest manageable component parts ("proof texts") are eventually resold for the purposes of constructing or authorizing neat but artificial theological "systems." That both of these practices have been common enough in the past is no reason for perpetuating them. Both a canonical reading and a "systematic" engagement with the text must take care to allow distinct theological perspectives to be heard, and in relating them to one another must not do so in ways that belittle or erode their particularity even (especially?) when it presents a problem of apparent conflict. Both "canon" and "theology" may prove to be more complex and dialectical realities than they have sometimes been supposed, and the dialectic may be of a Kierkegaardian (i.e., inherently irresolvable) rather than a Hegelian sort. Were there space here to explore Bakhtin's model of "dialogism" in texts (a model approximated to in certain respects by

Brueggemann's recent *Theology of the Old Testament*),[15] we might usefully do so. The task of a responsible "theological" reading of any book, therefore, will be both to allow the distinctive voice of the text to be heard and to inquire how this same distinctive voice might relate to other canonical voices and systematic theological concerns.

## 4. Reading in the Spirit

I have spoken in this essay both of Scripture as an authoritative text for the church and of the need to "presume presence" in our approach to the text if it is indeed to function thus. The presence I have in mind is that which, I suggest, characterizes any and every act of human communication or bid for self-transcendence. But in a Christian reading of Scripture, there is another dimension of presence to be reckoned with — namely, the supposition that this text does not only speak about God, but that in and through the medium of this text God has spoken and speaks. It is here that we must finally discern the root of the claim that Scripture is authoritative for the structuring of Christian identity. Sociological tautologies may be apposite (no doubt most Christians do afford authority to Scripture in the first instance because they quickly learn that this is something that Christians do) and even necessary, but they are certainly not sufficient to bear the weight of the claim that Scripture is authoritative. We have to reckon not only with a human but also with a divine presence encountering us through these texts. Such a claim has at least the testimony of centuries of Christian history in its favor and is an important part, I suggest, of a properly Christian approach to the reading of the text. If we are not expectant that God has spoken and will speak in and through the complexities of our reading, then we are engaged in a reading of some other (perhaps entirely legitimate) sort.

The claim that God speaks does not in itself entail a return to the idea that authority is invested in some nebulous "property" of the texts themselves. This is a peculiar claim easily gainsaid by the fact that many people who read these texts are not encountered "authoritatively" in the process. It is too easy simply to suppose that their readings are intellectually or hermeneutically deficient as such. They may be, but that may have

15. Walter Brueggemann, *Theology of the Old Testament: Testimony, Dispute, Advocacy* (Minneapolis: Fortress, 1997).

little to do with the fact that, when they read, God does not "speak" through the text. I would prefer to construe the authority of the text, or the "presence" upon which it reposes, not as a property of the texts themselves (although their various properties are certainly not irrelevant) but rather as a "property" or aspect of the event in which text and reader together are drawn into a relatedness to the living God whereby God "speaks" or is known in and through the reading.

In terms of God's identity as known to Christians, the most natural name for God at this point is not Father or Son, but Spirit. Reading the text of Scripture, in other words, should be a reading that occurs "in the Spirit." Of course, this is not a condition human readers themselves are in any position to supply or determine. There are considerations of divine freedom and election to be reckoned with. But so far as we are able, it is incumbent upon us to prepare ourselves for a reading of this sort. I do not have space here to engage directly with the now-regular suggestion that a Christian reading of Scripture will be contingent on the cultivation of certain "virtues" as well as skills of other sorts.[16] Some of the concerns that appear to lie behind this claim overlap with what I am suggesting here, but with the (perhaps significant) difference that the emphasis tends naturally to fall on human preparations for reading, whereas I would wish to stress instead the capacities of the God who chooses to enter into fellowship with us and transforms our character in and through the processes of reading. These are not incompatible perspectives, but they are differences of emphasis that could ultimately lead in significantly different directions.

What, then, is being said when the phrase "reading in the Spirit" is deployed? And how does it relate to more traditional categories such as the "inspiration" of Scripture or the "internal testimony of the Holy Spirit"? It is certainly closely related to each of these, but is also distinct from them as such. Inspiration has often been a category intended to say something about the mode of origin of the texts and their consequent character. Although I think a Christian approach to Scripture must assume the intricate involvement of God in furnishing the textual resource of the Bible and, through it, the "permanent structures" and "conceptual tools" for thinking and speaking of him of which Torrance speaks, and the "narrative world" into which, I have argued, Christians are drawn in the relation of faith, I do not think that a properly Christian reading need adopt any particular model for the origin of these texts. Most of those that have been en-

16. See, e.g., Fowl, *Engaging Scripture.*

tertained are problematic in one way or another. Thus I would prefer simply to commit Christians to the "en-spiriting" of the text in the sense of the Spirit's involvement in the entire process of its production and its interpretation within the household of faith, spanning the gaps between world and text, and text and interpretation, enabling and directing both the "speaker" and the hearer in the endless and ever-new acts of communication that Christian reading of Scripture has involved, and doing so in ways that fashion the community's identity, understanding, and practice ever anew. This cannot mean that all interpretations or readings are underwritten by the Spirit, but the question of discernment involved here is one lying beyond the scope of this paper.

The notion of the "internal testimony of the Holy Spirit" has sometimes been deployed as if to suggest that the Spirit is the one extra hermeneutical tool required for a "correct" interpretation of the biblical text, a tool with which no module in biblical studies can equip the student. My model of "reading in the Spirit" construes things differently. The Spirit is not an aid to getting at the meaning of Scripture. The Spirit is God in his relatedness to us in the event of meaning through which he addresses us. He is the "presence" who finally renders the text "authoritative" for faith. The church turns to the text seeking an event in which, as the text is interpreted, it will speak authoritatively for the community. This event happens. That it does so is something to which the community bears witness, but which lies beyond its own control. God speaks. As he speaks we are drawn into the world of the text; the story it tells overlaps with our own story and becomes part of it. But this happens not simply through the "illumination" of our minds to perceive an encoded message in the text (although what God "says" will have to be related in some identifiable way to what the text "says"),[17] but rather because we are now encountering, in fellowship with, the God who is the primary character in that same story. We understand the text in profound ways otherwise hidden from us because we now understand this God whose story it is and of whom the text speaks. In the presence of this God, who is the same yesterday, today, and forever, the gaps between differing cultures and times fade somewhat in their significance. "In the Spirit" we read, and this breaks the text open because it was in this same Spirit that the text was produced and to which the text itself refers us.

17. See on this the detailed discussion of Nicholas Wolterstorff, *Divine Discourse: Philosophical Reflections on the Claim That God Speaks* (Cambridge: Cambridge University Press, 1995), chap. 12.

Reading the Bible as Scripture, then, is never a mere matter of handling texts and the relationships between texts. It is above all a matter of being in the presence and open to the handling of the One who, in some sense, is the final "author" of its message, because he is the one whose story it tells, and it is as we know him, as we dwell in his presence, and as he dwells in us that we see and hear what he is saying and showing to us through it. At this point general hermeneutics falls short, and we must confess the Christian reading of the Bible as Scripture to be *sui generis*.

# CHAPTER 11

# *The Letter to the Galatians:*
# *Exegesis and Theology*

## N. T. WRIGHT

The dense and dramatic argument of Galatians excites and baffles by turns. Sometimes perceived as a flamboyant younger sister of the more settled and reflective letter to Rome, this epistle has provoked endless controversy at all levels, from details of exegesis to flights of systematic theology. Nobody reading it can be in any doubt that it all mattered very much indeed to Paul. But what it was that mattered, and why, and why it should matter to anyone two thousand years later — these are far harder questions to answer. Nor can this chapter do more than restate the questions and hint at possible answers. Our aim here is not to solve the problems in question but to discuss and illustrate the task.

Our aim is to discuss, particularly, what might happen when we allow questions of exegesis and theology to stare each other in the face. It is of course generally recognized that anyone grappling with the exegesis of Galatians must do business with "theological" questions. One must, that is to say, know something of the grammar of theological concepts, how God-language works (particularly, how it worked in the first century), how justification might relate to law and faith, and so on. One must, in particular, be familiar with how Paul uses similar ideas in other letters, in this case especially Romans. It is not that one should allow Paul's meaning in one place to determine ahead of time what he might have said elsewhere, but that even if development, or a change of mind,

205

has occurred, we are still dealing with the same person talking about more or less the same things. Equally, no systematic or practical theology that would claim to be Christian can ignore the central and foundational texts of the NT. Particularly, anyone offering a theological account of, say, justification would feel bound at least to make a visit to Galatians and to fit it somehow into the developing scheme. And anyone wanting to offer a serious Christian account of central topics on contemporary applied theology — liberation, for instance, or postmodernity — ought, if such theology is to be fully Christian, to ground their reflections in the NT.

However, a good deal of historical and exegetical scholarship on this letter, as on others, has in fact proceeded in recent decades with only minimal attention to theological discussion — an omission sometimes justified on the grounds of maintaining historical neutrality, though sometimes in fact masking the historian's unawareness of the deeper issues involved. Likewise, many systematic theologians, in this and other fields, have become impatient with waiting for the mountain of historical footnotes to give birth to the mouse of theological insight, and have proceeded on the basis of an understanding of the text that simply reflects, it may not be too unkind to say, either the commentary that was in vogue when the theologian was a student or the pressing contemporary issues that condition a particular reading of the text.[1]

I intend in this essay to approach the problem from both ends, and to examine the bridge that might be thrown between these two now traditional positions. This task is not to be thought of as one element in the wider project of bridging Lessing's Ugly Ditch. Such a project presupposes that which ought to be challenged — namely, the existence of such a ditch in the first place. To be sure, a ditch between the historical and the theological task does indeed exist within Western consciousness, and the rise of historical scholarship owes something to it, since in that context the ditch has acted as a moat, protecting the historian from the prying eye and the heavy hand of the theological censor. But the question always arises as to who is being protected from whom. The ditch is equally useful to those who want to maintain a traditional faith within a pure ahistorical vacuum. But the idea that there is a great gulf fixed between historical exegesis and Christian theology — this Enlightenment presup-

1. Cf. the remarks of Karl Barth in the preface to the second edition of his famous commentary on Romans (Oxford: Oxford University Press, 1933), pp. 2-15.

position is precisely what ought to be challenged, not least when commenting on a biblical text.

One way of hinting at answers to the wider problems is to read a particular text without bracketing off any of these questions — or, to put the matter another way, one might propose putting to the text the questions that have accrued, and those that are newly emerging, out of the long history of the church's engagement with its own faith (and, one should say, with its God) — and giving the text a chance to answer them, or at least to insist on their rewording. With this in mind, I offer here (1) a brief account of the major exegetical issues that meet us in Galatians; (2) a suggestion of which major theological questions might profitably be put to the letter, and what answers might arise; and (3) some proposals about how these two tasks might be brought into fruitful interaction with one another through the work of a commentary and the further work (not least preaching) that a commentary is supposed to evoke.

## 1. Exegetical Issues

The basic task of exegesis is to address, as a whole and in parts, the historical questions: What was the author saying to the readers; and why? These questions ultimately demand an answer at the broadest level in the form of a hypothesis to be tested against the verse-by-verse details. One may, perhaps, allow the author some imprecision, particularly in such a heated composition, but if even a small number of details do not fit the hypothesis, it will be called into question. Exegetes of course have ways of making things fit. A puzzling verse can be labeled as a pre-Pauline fragment or an interpolation, or perhaps a mere "topos" in which a well-worn phrase, whose history-of-religions ancestry can be shown with an impressive footnote, should not be pressed for precise or powerful meaning. (As though Paul, of all people, would be content to write a letter that was merely a set of conventional noises whose meaning could thus be reduced to a set of evocative grunts!) Failing that, one can suggest that a puzzling verse simply reflects a moment where either Paul or his amanuensis lost the train of thought. But I take it as a general rule, consonant with the wider rules for hypotheses and their verification, that the more moves like this one makes, the more one's hypothesis stands condemned for lack of appropriate simplicity. One must assume that there is a train of thought, "that the text has a central concern and a remarkable inner logic that may no longer be entirely comprehensible to us."[2] One must get in the data, and one must do so without undue complexity, without using that brute force which swaggers around the byways of a text arm-in-arm with ignorance.

At the level of large-scale exegesis, this problem meets us when we ask the questions normally thought of under the heading "Introduction." What was going on in Galatia that made Paul write the letter? Which "Galatia" (north or south) are we talking about anyway? When did Paul write the letter? What relation, if any, did the episode have to the so-called "apostolic conference" of Acts 15? Who were Paul's opponents, the shadowy "agitators" who flit to and fro through the undergrowth of the epistle?

One well-worn path through these thickets has been made by those who insist that the agitators are legalists: proto-Pelagians who are trying to persuade the Galatians to seek justification by performing good moral deeds. Among the many problems this view faces is the question, Why then does Paul spend so long, in chapter 5 in particular, warning the Galatians against what looks like antinomianism? It will scarcely do to say (though many have) that he has suddenly focused on a quite different problem, with perhaps a quite different set of opponents or agitators. A different basic analysis seems called for — one that will hold the two emphases of the letter (if that is what they are) in a single larger context, and that will perhaps question whether what appear to our post-Enlightenment and post-Reformation eyes as two separate, almost incompatible, emphases, would have appeared like that to either Paul or his readers. And any such analysis must face the question from the theologian, and from those (such as preachers) who look to theologians' work for help: Of what use are these "introductory" questions for theology? Since two hundred years of research has failed to solve them, is there not something to be said for bracketing them and going straight into reading the text?

A similarly large-scale question to be addressed is, Why does Paul spend so long recounting his early visits to Jerusalem and his meeting with the apostles there? Almost one-quarter of the letter (1:10–2:21, 36 verses out of 149) is devoted to this subject, and there may be further echoes of the subject elsewhere (e.g., 4:25). Many readers have, of course, bypassed this question, regarding material prior to 2:11 as "introduction" and seeing what follows as the beginning of a systematic theological exposition of the doctrine of justification. But Paul at least reckoned it necessary to preface

2. Ernst Käsemann, *Commentary on Romans* (Grand Rapids: Eerdmans; London: SCM, 1980), p. viii.

the body of the letter with *this* introduction rather than something else; and, since his introductions are normally good indicators of the main thrust of the letter, we should at least make the attempt to investigate the possible integration of the first two chapters with what follows.

A question that relates to this but has recently taken on a life of its own (particularly since the appearance twenty-five years ago of the commentary by H.-D. Betz) is, To what rhetorical genre does the letter belong?[3] Is it deliberative, apologetic, or what?[4] It has, I believe, been good for Pauline exegetes to be reminded that Paul wrote from within the wider world of Greco-Roman late antiquity, where there were well-known literary forms and genres that would, in themselves, give off clues as to what the writer thought he (or, less likely, she) was doing. But it is important not to let the literary tail wag the epistolary dog. Paul was an innovator, living in two or more worlds at once, and allowing them — in his own person, his vocation, his style of operation, and his writing — to knock sparks off each other (or, as it might be, to dovetail together in new ways). Consideration of literary genre must always remain in dialogue with the question of what the text actually says. Neither can claim the high ground and dictate to the other. The same is true of the various forms of structural, or structuralist, analysis.

Similar points need to be made about the current burgeoning of social-scientific reading of Paul's letters.[5] To be sure, Paul and his readers lived within a social context in which all sorts of pressures and presuppositions operated that are quite unlike those in modern Western society. A good many things that have traditionally been read as abstract ideas or beliefs did in fact come with heavy agendas attached in the areas of social grouping, organization, and culture, and we ignore this at our peril. Equally, recognizing the existence and nonnegotiable importance of the social-scientific dimension of Paul's letters does not mean denying that these same letters set out a train of thought that cannot, or at least cannot

---

3. Hans-Dieter Betz, *Galatians: A Commentary on Paul's Letter to the Churches in Galatia*, Hermeneia (Philadelphia: Fortress, 1979).

4. On this see now Ben Witherington III, *Grace in Galatia: A Commentary on St. Paul's Letter to the Galatians* (Edinburgh: T. & T. Clark; Grand Rapids: Eerdmans, 1998), pp. 25-36; he argues strongly against Betz that Galatians is an example of deliberative rhetoric, designed to convince its audience to take a particular line on an issue currently facing them.

5. See the (to my mind overstated) claims of Philip F. Esler, *Galatians* (London: Routledge, 1998).

a priori, be reduced to terms of cryptic social agendas. Just because every word and phrase carries a social context and dimension does not mean that Paul is not setting out a train of thought, a sequence of ideas. We must beware, here as elsewhere, of false antitheses.

These are exactly the sorts of questions, once more, that will tend to make the theologian impatient. Of what relevance, people sometimes say and often think, are these questions for the major and urgent issues that crowd in upon the church and its proclamation to the world? The answer is that each of them demonstrably affects how we read the key texts for which the theologian or preacher is eager. The question of justification by faith itself is intimately bound up with them. Ernst Käsemann's caustic remark, that those eager for "results" should keep their hands off exegesis, comes uncomfortably to mind.[6]

The influence of social context upon exegesis and theology is most obviously the case with the passage where many will feel that the letter finally "gets going" — namely, 2:11-21. The brief and dense statement about justification in 2:15-21 is part of Paul's description of what happened between Peter and himself at Antioch; we cannot assume, as many have done, that because we think we know ahead of time what Paul meant by "justification," we can deduce that precisely this was the subject of the quarrel (imagining, for instance, that Peter was arguing for a semi-Pelagian position on the question of how people go to heaven after death). Paul's description of the altercation pushes us in quite another direction. The question at issue was not, How can individual sinners find salvation? but rather, Are Christian Jews bound, by the Jewish kosher laws, to eat separately from Christian Gentiles, or are they bound by the gospel to eat at the same table with them? We may and must assume, indeed, that reflection on these questions would not only be influenced, in the minds of Peter and the others, by "pure" intellectual and theological arguments; Paul was asking them to break the habits not only of a lifetime but of a tightly integrated social grouping that had survived, precisely by maintaining these habits, for hundreds of years. The detailed exegetical debates that have swirled around these verses have, as often as not, been caused by a sense that the traditional reading does not quite work, does not quite fit the words that Paul actually used. Attention to the wider context on the one hand, and to theological issues of how the basic concepts function in general and in Paul in particular, may provide fresh ways forward. And if that is so, a care-

6. Käsemann, p. viii.

ful reading of this passage in Galatians might well send shock waves through the reading of other Pauline texts, such as Romans 3–4 and Philippians 3.

The long argument of 3:1–5:1, which forms the solid center of the letter, offers almost endless puzzles for the exegete, down to the meaning of individual words and particles and the question of implicit punctuation (the early manuscripts, of course, have for the most part neither punctuation nor breaks between words). And it is here that the larger issues of understanding Galatians, the questions that form the bridge between exegesis, history, and theology, begin to come to light. Where does Paul suppose that he stands in relationship to the covenant that Israel's God made with Abraham? And to that with Moses? And to the Torah, the Jewish law, which, though giving substance to the historical Mosaic covenant, seems to have taken on a life of its own? What, in short, does Paul wish to say about what he himself, surprisingly perhaps, calls "Judaism" (1:13)? Does he see it as a historical sequence of covenants and promises that have now reached their fulfillment in Jesus? Or does he see it as a system to the whole of which the true God is now saying "no" in order to break in, through the gospel, and do a new thing? A further important question, not usually considered sufficiently: Does Paul's actual handling of the Jewish Scriptures, in terms of quotation, allusion, and echo, reflect the view he holds, or do the two stand in tension?[7]

These questions can, of course, only be resolved by detailed examination of the text, verse by verse and line by line. But it is important to notice here the way in which, classically within the discipline of Pauline scholarship, two questions, in principle separable, have in fact been fused together in uncomfortable coexistence. (1) What is Paul's *theological* relationship to Judaism? (2) What is Paul's *historical* relationship to Judaism? The two have often been allowed to spill over into each other. Thus, if Paul is perceived to have criticized "Judaism" (e.g., for its belief in justification by works of the law), it is assumed that he cannot have derived his basic ideas from Judaism — and that therefore the historical origin of his theology is to be found not in Judaism at all, but either in the Christ event as a totally new and essentially non-Jewish irruption into the world or in the pagan systems of religion, cult, and moral philosophy. Conversely, if Paul is

---

7. On these questions see, among recent literature, Bruce W. Longenecker, *The Triumph of Abraham's God: The Transformation of Identity in Galatians* (Edinburgh: T. & T. Clark, 1998).

perceived to stand in a positive relation to Judaism at the historical level — i.e., if one supposes that Paul's basic thought structure and beliefs remained Jewish after his conversion — it is often assumed that therefore he can have had no real critique of "Judaism." Both of these questions, of course, need integration with wider issues, not least Paul's actual practice in its social setting.

Anyone who wishes thus to skate to and fro between history of religions and theological analysis should be warned that the ice here is dangerously thin. Among the key characteristics of Paul's Judaism were precisely critique from within on the one hand and confrontation with paganism on the other. The fact that Paul criticized some aspects of his native Judaism and that he announced a gospel to the Gentiles does not mean that he broke with Judaism in order to do so. On the contrary; by his own account (to hint for a moment at the solution that I prefer), he claimed to be speaking as a true Jew, criticizing — as did many who made similar claims — those who embraced other construals of Judaism, on the basis that Israel's God had now acted climactically and decisively in Jesus, the Messiah. For the same reason, he was now announcing to all the world that the one true God was addressing, claiming, and redeeming it by the Jewish Messiah, the Lord of the world.

This discussion should be sufficient to show the way in which the exegetical and theological issues that arise from Galatians 3 and 4 are bound so closely together that it is impossible to separate them. But we should also note the way in which such deliberations have also invoked, from various angles, the wider contexts both of theology and of contemporary meaning. In the church's preaching, the assumption that Paul was straightforwardly distancing himself from "Judaism" has had, notoriously, disastrous effects at social, cultural, political, and theological levels. Equally, if it is supposed for a moment that Paul simply saw himself as a good Jew who merely knew the name of the Messiah, but otherwise had nothing to add to his Jewish heritage, all chance of understanding him is lost. The only way of dealing with Galatians 3 and 4 is for all these issues to be on the table at the same time.

The exegetical problem(s) of Galatians 5 and 6 grow out of, and contribute further to, these questions, but add extra ones of their own. Lulled perhaps by a belief that Paul follows the Enlightenment's division of theory and practice, of theology and ethics, many have simply supposed that the "theology" of the letter is now finished and that all that remains are some guidelines as to how to behave. But to approach the chapters thus is to be further puzzled. Paul does not say quite what (from this perspective) we would expect. His key statements are not of the form "this, then, is how to behave," but instead things like "if you are led by the Spirit, you are not under the Law" (5:18) and "those who belong to Christ have crucified the flesh" (5:24). The detailed instructions of 6:1-10 (which, if they have a connecting theme, are still not so tightly sewn together as the previous argument) continue to refer not to a general need for the Galatians to behave in a proper fashion, but rather to a particular social situation within which certain styles of behavior are particularly appropriate. And the letter closes with a strong statement of the basic point that, arguably, Paul has been making all through: Neither circumcision nor uncircumcision matters, since what matters is new creation. What, then, does Paul's "ethics," if we should call it that, have to do with the fundamental thrust of the letter as a whole? This exegetical problem is of course of huge interest to theologians, but it will not be solved by broad generalizations that sit loose to the detail of the text, or to its historical and social origins.

## 2. Contributions to Systematic Theology

After this brief review of the exegetical problems of the letter, it is now time to approach the matter from the other end. What theological issues might we hope to see advanced by the study of this text, and what problems face us as we press such questions? We shall maintain, for the purpose of this article, a traditional distinction between "systematic" and "practical" theology, although in today's practice such things are increasingly merged together. In both cases all we can do is to note some possible questions out of the many that could arise, and to suggest some possible answers. The object of the exercise here is to be exemplary rather than in any way exhaustive.

We have already mentioned justification, and the interrelation of theology and ethics (with its subset, the interrelation between justification by faith and life in the Spirit). These are not the major questions that systematic theologians have struggled with throughout the history of the church; indeed, Paul himself is capable of writing letters in which one or both play little or no role. But we cannot imagine Paul writing a letter in which Jesus Christ played no part, or in which the purpose and nature of the one true God were not under consideration; and these are of course the central subject matter of traditional Christian systematic theology.

What, first, does Paul have to say in Galatians that will address the traditional questions about God? Such questions concern, for instance, the identity and description of God, or a god; how knowledge of this god is to be had (whether innate in humans, specially revealed, or whatever); the relationship of this god to the world; the power and operation of the god, not least his or her activity within the world; what one can say about evil in the world, and what (if anything) this god might be doing about it; the nature of human being and existence; the question of appropriate human behavior. Allowing Paul to address these questions from his own angles, we can at once make the following observations, which, though quite obvious, are not always highlighted.

First, the god of whom Paul speaks is without question the one God of Israel, the God of Abraham, Isaac, and Jacob. This God is the creator of the world, and pagan idols are shams, or demons in disguise. Even if Paul sometimes seems to be saying that the God of Israel has behaved in an unforeseen, perhaps an unpredictable, maybe even an unprincipled, fashion, it is still the God of Israel he is talking about. We should expect Paul therefore to be on the map of first-century Jewish thought about God — and this is indeed the case, though not always in the ways one might imagine. When we glance across at the other Pauline letters, and out into the rest of the NT, we find at this point a remarkable unanimity. Despite two millennia of Jewish protest to the contrary, the NT writers, with Paul leading the way chronologically, firmly believe themselves to be writing about, worshiping, and following the will of the one God of Israel, and rejecting paganism.

Second, in line with this, Paul believes that this God has a purpose for the created world. More specifically, he believes that "the present evil age" will give way, in God's good time, to "the age to come," in which Israel and the world will be redeemed from the power of the false gods. This apocalyptic belief was widespread in Paul's Jewish world, certainly in sectarian Judaism but also in groups that would not have thought of themselves in that way. This belief is not, or at least not necessarily, "dualistic"; indeed, insofar as it envisages the present world being set to rights rather than being abandoned, it emphasizes the goodness and God-givenness of creation, while allowing fully, perhaps too fully sometimes, for creation's having been invaded, taken over, distorted, and deceived by forces of evil and destruction. Paul's understanding of God in Galatians includes the belief that the true God has broken into the world, in the person of Jesus and the power of the Spirit of Jesus, to usher in the long-awaited new age and so to redeem Israel and the world (cf. esp. 1:4). Here too Paul is in fundamental agreement with the other NT writers.

Third, this God is revealed and known in the Jewish Scriptures, in actions within history through which the scriptural promises are fulfilled, and climactically in the coming of the Messiah. The apocalyptic intervention of God in Israel and the world, sweeping aside all that stands in the way of the dawning new day, is paradoxically for Paul the completion, the fulfillment, and the climax of all that God had done and said to and for Abraham, Isaac, and Jacob.[8] The dense and difficult discussions of the Jewish law in Galatians owe their very existence to the fact that Paul is unwilling to declare, as many theologians since his day have done, that the Jewish law was shabby or second-rate, or even demonic and dangerous. He is determined to insist, despite the problems he is storing up for later readers, *both* that God gave the law and accomplished his purposes through it *and* that the Galatians must not submit to it, *since it was given a specific role for a certain period of time that has now come to an end.* Eschatology, not religious critique, is what counts. To dissolve the resultant paradox one way or another is a sure way of misunderstanding Paul.

It is sometimes said that Galatians has a negative view of the law, and Romans a positive one; it would be truer to say that in both letters Paul wrestles mightily with this paradox, to address very different situations and contexts. It would be truer, thus, to find a deep compatibility within the two that, when discovered, will reach out further to embrace such other statements as 2 Corinthians 3 and Philippians 3. This eschatological reading of Paul's understanding of the Scriptures in general and the law in particular is the necessary corrective to any idea that Paul is speaking in the abstract, either about "law" in general or about the Jewish law in a timeless way. His thought is controlled throughout by the sense of God's purpose within and beyond history, and of where he and his readers belong within that story.

All of this leads, of course, to the second area of major importance for systematic theology to which Galatians might be supposed to make some contribution. What does Paul say about Jesus? Merely collecting the relevant isolated verses does not address the question. We need to discover

---

8. The sense in which, according to Paul, Jesus also brings to fulfillment the Mosaic covenant is exceedingly complex, and is, more or less, the subject of N. T. Wright, *The Climax of the Covenant: Christ and the Law in Pauline Theology* (Edinburgh: T. & T. Clark; Minneapolis: Fortress, 1991), chaps. 7-13.

what role Jesus plays within Paul's ongoing *arguments*. As I have urged elsewhere, the basic answer for Paul is that Jesus is the Messiah of Israel, in whom the promises made to the patriarchs have finally come true.[9] In particular, his death has solved the problem of evil that lay heavily upon the world in general and, because of the warnings and curses of the covenant, upon Israel in particular. Though Paul mentions the death of Jesus dozens of times in his writings, he never says exactly the same thing twice (though the phrase "died for us" or something similar is a regular refrain); he allows the specific needs of each argument to determine what particular meaning he will draw out in each case. Underlying each of these, however, is Paul's deeper meaning of messiahship, visible in (for instance) Galatians 2:17-21: The Messiah represents his people, so that what is true of him becomes true of them. His death becomes their death, and they find their new life within his. Underlying this, and I believe foundational for Paul's thinking about what we call "atonement" theology, is the belief that what God does for Israel is done not for Israel only, but for the whole world. Israel's Messiah is the world's Lord; the crucified, saving Messiah who brings Jews out of their real exile is the crucified Lord who by the same means rescues pagans from their bondage to nongods. This, I suggest, is the clue to that "incorporative" Christology that is so frequently discussed, and of which 3:23-29 provides such a good, though complex, example.

Hidden within the category of messiahship, in Paul's construction of it, is a deeper belief about Jesus which, so far as we know, was not held by any non-Christian Jews in relation to any of the would-be Messiahs who make their brief appearances in the tragic story of first-century Judaism. Drawing on the occasional but important biblical statements about the Messiah being the adopted son of Israel's God (e.g., Pss. 2:7; 89:27; 2 Sam. 7:14), Paul describes Jesus as the unique son of God, sent from God to effect the divine purpose — i.e., the purpose that in Scripture Israel's God reserves to himself — of redeeming his people and thereby saving the whole world from destructive demonic powers. Thus, almost casually within this letter, written within at most twenty-five years of Jesus' crucifixion, we come upon what with hindsight we may see as the first steps toward trinitarian language (4:1-11). The God whom Christians worship is the Jewish God, the God of Abraham, of the exodus (exodus language, and the retelling of the exodus story, permeate this context), and of Wisdom (the figure of "wisdom" is of course in some Jewish texts — e.g., Wis.

9. Wright, *The Climax of the Covenant,* chaps. 2-3.

10:15-21 — a way of talking about the God of the exodus); but this God is now to be known as the God who sends the Son, and who then sends the Spirit of his Son. And it is to this God alone that the Galatians must give full allegiance; otherwise they will slide back to a state similar to what they were in before. You must either have the triune God, Paul is saying, or you must have a form of paganism.

This early form of proto-trinitarian theology thus appears *as a variant within Jewish monotheism,* not a form of crypto-paganism. Exactly like classic Jewish monotheism, it stands opposed both to paganism and to dualism. Just as Israel's God made himself known as such in the exodus, fulfilling the promises to Abraham and calling Israel his son, so this same God has now revealed himself fully and finally in the new exodus of Jesus' death and resurrection, fulfilling the promises to Abraham in their widest sense, challenging and defeating the pagan powers that had kept humanity as a whole under lock and key. To go back to allowing one's self-understanding, corporately or individually, to be determined by ethnic boundary markers rather than by the new life given in the Messiah is therefore to embrace again a form of paganism, however paradoxical this may seem when what one thought one was doing was taking on the yoke of the Jewish Torah. A good case can be made for seeing this critique underlying many of Paul's other statements about the Torah, not least in Romans.

Talking about God and Jesus in relation to Galatians has thus inevitably embroiled us in talking about the plight of Israel and the world. Paul, in this letter and everywhere else, takes it as axiomatic that all human beings are under the power and rule of sin, and that the Jewish Torah, so far from releasing people from this state, merely exacerbates it. It is quite wrong to say, as has often been done in recent scholarship, that Paul's thinking about Jesus preceded his thinking about the plight from which people needed rescuing. To be sure, the revelation of the risen Jesus on the road to Damascus gave new shape and direction to his thinking, on this and on everything else; but the pre-Damascus Paul was well aware that there was a "problem" to be addressed. This was not, perhaps, the problem of an unquiet conscience wished on him by theologians from Augustine to Luther and beyond, but it was, certainly, the problem of the pagan world under the power of evil, and the problem that so much of the Jewish world seemed hell-bent on compromising with paganism. For himself as a zealous Pharisee, there was the very specific problem that, even if he and some others were "blameless concerning the law" (Phil. 3:6), Israel's God had so far not acted within their history to send the Messiah, to fight the decisive battle against evil, to reveal his "righteousness" — that is, his faithfulness to the covenant promises with Israel, to redeem his people, to judge the wicked world, and to set up the long-awaited kingdom of justice and peace. That was the problem the pre-Christian Paul possessed. His conversion deepened it, pointing at himself the accusing finger that he would formerly have pointed at almost everyone else; but it did not create a problem out of nothing.

The solution Paul embraced, which emerges clearly though briefly in Galatians, to be elaborated in different situations in the other letters, can be summed up in two closely related words: "Christ," "Spirit." In Jesus the Messiah Israel's God has dealt with sin and established the new world, the "age to come," calling the Gentiles to belong to his renewed people. Paul's theology of the cross, which receives repeated emphasis in Galatians, stresses both the solidarity of Jesus with his people and the unique weight of sin and its effects which were borne by Jesus himself. Though, as we saw, Paul never articulates a single "theology of atonement," his many rich statements of Jesus' death, in this letter and throughout his works, together form a many-sided doctrine that must be seen as central to his whole thinking.

One of the many ways Paul can refer to this whole achievement of Jesus is in terms of Jesus' "faithfulness" to the covenant; this, I think, is the correct interpretation of the much-controverted *pistis Christou* problem.[10] As with so many issues, linguistic study by itself will not solve the problem of whether, when Paul says *pistis Christou*, he means "faith *in* the Messiah" or "the faith(fullness) *of* the Messiah." Both ideas play a role in his thought. In Galatians 2:16, after all, he does say "we believed in the Messiah, Jesus," and in Romans 5:15-19 the "obedience" of Jesus the Messiah is the key category that sums up all that Paul said about Jesus' death in 3:21-26 (Phil. 2:5-8 confirms that this is the correct interpretation). Romans is, indeed, the key to understanding the concept; in Romans 3:1-8 the problem that faces God, as well as the whole human race, is that Israel has been "faithless" to the commission to be the light of the world (cf. 2:17-24). How then is God to reveal his own covenant faithfulness? Paul's answer is that God's faithfulness is revealed in and through the faithfulness of Jesus the Mes-

---

10. See the commentaries on Gal. 2:16; 3:22, etc., and discussions in most recent monographs on Galatians. For the debate, see Richard B. Hays, "*Pistis* and Pauline Christology: What Is at Stake?" *SBLSP* 30 (1991): 714-29; James D. G. Dunn, "Once More, *Pistis Christou*," *SBLSP* 30 (1991): 730-44.

siah, the representative Israelite. Confusion arises not only because this is not the train of thought readers of Romans in much church tradition have been expecting — it is too Jewish by half for that — but also because Paul also says, sometimes in the same breath, as in Romans 3:22 and Galatians 2:16; 3:22, that the beneficiaries of this covenant faithfulness of the Messiah are precisely those who in their turn "believe" or "are faithful."

By the Spirit of God, the Spirit of Jesus, this God has called and is calling Jews and Gentiles alike to belong to the one family of Abraham, and equipping them to believe the gospel (such faith being the one identifying badge of membership within this family) and to live in love one to another and in witness to God's love to the world around. Like the texts from Qumran, Paul's letters articulate an inaugurated eschatology in which the new age has already begun but is yet to be completed. "We by the spirit and by faith wait for the hope of righteousness" (5:5). The Spirit is the power of the new age breaking into the present, but future hope remains vital for the complete picture. This, though briefly stated in Galatians, points toward wider statements of the same theology elsewhere in Paul (e.g., 1 Cor. 15) and indeed, though sometimes differently stated, in the rest of the NT. For Paul, of course, as most Christian theology has always insisted, the Spirit is the same Spirit through whom God spoke and acted in the history of Israel; the key difference in the new thing that has come about through Jesus is that the Spirit is now poured out on all God's people, Jew and Gentile alike.

God, Jesus, Spirit, plight, and solution: the final question the systematic theologian might want to put to Galatians would be about theology and ethics. Here again the letter restates the question, and answers it in its own way. Earlier readings of Galatians, particularly in the Reformation tradition, had so emphasized the wrongness of "justification by works," understanding that phrase in a Pelagian or Arminian sense, as to make it difficult to articulate any sense of moral obligation or moral effort within the Christian. There are signs that Paul faced similar problems (e.g., Rom. 3:7-8; 6:1, 15), but this does not seem to be why, in the final two chapters of Galatians, he provides such a lengthy discourse on Christian behavior (the term "ethics" is itself loaded, belonging already to the too-sharp distinction between theory and practice of which I spoke earlier). Though he undoubtedly wants his converts to avoid what he calls "the works of the flesh" and to exhibit what he calls "the fruit of the Spirit," the actual argument in which those phrases and the things they denote occurs is more subtle than simply exhortation. It has various overtones and echoes of that classic passage on the law, Romans 7, and may, like that passage, be deliberately doing several things at the same time (see, e.g., Gal. 5:17: "spirit and flesh fight against each other, so that what you wish you cannot do"). It is an argument about the law, and about how, though the law is God's law, it cannot give the thing to which it points, and about how, nevertheless, those who discover that to which it points are in line with what the law intended, even though they may be neither possessors nor, in its boundary-marking sense, keepers of it.

He is saying, in effect, "If you insist on embracing the Jewish law, and particularly on getting circumcised, you are declaring that you belong in the realm of the 'flesh'; but if you go and live in that realm, you must look at the company you will be keeping, and the sort of life into which you will be drawn." (The only sort of "fleshly" behavior he thinks the Galatians are actually exhibiting is factional fighting, as 5:15, 26 suggests; these angry divisions in their community, he is saying in effect, are a sign that they are in fact living according to the flesh, confirming the analysis he is offering of their desire to get circumcised.) The pagans who live in that fashion are heading for destruction, but those who live and walk by the Spirit, whose first fruit is love, find that although they are not behaving this way in order to conform to the Jewish law, so that they may thereby be defined as ethnically the people of God, they are not condemned by the law. "Against such there is no law" (5:23). With this we are back once more at 2:17. Just because we have come out from under the rule of the Torah through baptism and faith, through dying and rising with Christ, this does not mean that the Torah (by which Paul presumably means the God who gave the Torah) is displeased with us. That Paul is working with this same train of thought is indicated in 5:24: those who belong to the Messiah have crucified the flesh with its passions and desires (compare 2:19-20; Rom 7:4-6).

"Ethics," then, understood as Paul's arguments about Christian behavior, function within Galatians not as an appendix to "theology," nor simply (as in Luther) as a *tertius usus legis*,[11] nor as an awkward concession after an antilegalistic "justification by faith," but rather as part of the inner working of the gospel itself. Through the gospel events of Jesus' messianic death and resurrection, the God of Israel delivers Israel and the world from the rule of evil and the "powers" who perpetrate it. Through the Spirit-

---

11. The "third use of the law" was a way of rehabilitating the OT law as a moral guide once one had firmly rejected it as a way to justification. (The "second" use was in relation to civil government, etc.)

inspired proclamation of the good news of Jesus as Messiah and Lord, this same God calls into being the redeemed family he had promised to Abraham, whose distinguishing mark, over against those of Judaism, is "the faithfulness of Jesus" — i.e., Jesus' own faithfulness, reflected now in the faith/faithfulness (would Paul have distinguished these two?) of Christians. Precisely because this family is the Christ-and-Spirit people, they are set free from the destructive powers and solidarities (including social solidarities) of evil, and are under the obligation of freedom, namely, to sustain this life by Spirit-given love for one another. That they are free to do so is given in the fact that they have been crucified with the Messiah (5:24; 6:14; 2:20). This is Paul's answer in Galatians to the question of "ethics," and it conforms well to his other similar treatments elsewhere.

## 3. Galatians, the Church, and the World

What then has Galatians to say to the large debates that concern Christian theologians today, living often at the interface of church and world? Again, we can present some sample questions only, with some tendentious possible answers.

The question that hangs over all contemporary intellectual discourse in the Western world concerns the very foundations of all knowing and being. The great project of the last two or three hundred years, sometimes known as "modernity," has given way in many quarters to "postmodernity." Modernism claimed to know things objectively, at least in principle; postmodernism applies a ruthlessly suspicious understanding to all such claims, showing in case after case that, as Nietzsche argued a century ago, claims to knowledge are in fact claims to power. The correlate of this was that modernism claimed that there was a real world independent of the knower. Postmodernism collapses this claim; all we are left with are the prejudices of the would-be knower.

Likewise, modernism told a great story of progress, enlightenment, and development, and insisted that this story — in which, of course, the Western world of the eighteenth century and subsequently was the hero — be imposed on the rest of the world, in a secular version of the Christian missionary enterprise that was burgeoning at exactly that time. Postmodernity declares that all such large stories — "metanarratives" is the word usually employed to denote the stories that stand behind or above the smaller stories people tell and live — are destructive and enslav-

221

ing, and must be deconstructed. All we are left with are the various smaller stories by which individual communities order their lives, and even they are constantly under suspicion.

What about the individual himself or herself? Modernity vaunted the great individual, the lonely and lofty "I" — the master of my fate, the captain of my soul. Postmodernity has deconstructed this figure, too. Each of us, we are now reminded, is a shifting mass of impulses and feelings, without a stable center that can be held up and inspected. Impressions to the contrary are just so much posturing. These are the main elements of postmodernity, which filter through into popular consciousness in thousands of ways even among those who know nothing of the technical terms of the discussion.

How can a Christian theologian, with Galatians open before her or him, address these questions? Galatians is, after all, concerned with truth (2:5, 14; 4:16; 5:7); with claims and counterclaims to knowledge, including knowledge of God (e.g., 4:8-9); with a great story that began with Abraham, climaxed in Jesus the Messiah, and is moving outward to embrace the world (3:6–4:11; etc.). The most fundamental answer, I believe, is that in Galatians Paul is concerned precisely with the breaking of the bonds of slavery and the setting free of captives. He retells the exodus narrative, in 4:1-7 in particular, showing how in Jesus the Messiah and by the Spirit those who were enslaved to nongods have been liberated (4:8; cf. 1:4). The story he tells certainly is a grand overarching narrative, beginning with Israel and reaching out to embrace the world, but it is a story that leaves no human being, organization, or ethnic group in a position of power over others. It is the Jewish story, but it is not the typical Jew who says, "I am crucified with Christ; nevertheless I live; yet not I, but Christ lives in me." This is the story precisely of how those who were kept as second-class citizens are now welcomed in on equal terms. This is a metanarrative like no other.

The same text (2:19-21) is Paul's answer to those who would see the individual deconstructed into various shifting forces and impulses. Paul goes further. The individual, especially individuals who pride themselves on their status, must die in order to live. And the new life they are given is not their own, is nothing to be proud of, is nothing to give them status over others; it is the life of the crucified and risen Messiah. This is an individuality like no other.

And the result of the gospel is that those who are liberated from slavery have come "to know God" (4:9) — or rather, as Paul quickly modifies it, to be known by God (cf. 1 Cor. 8:1-6). Just as the Israelites were granted a fresh revelation of the true God in the exodus, so the events of the new exodus have truly revealed this same God in a new way. But the whole idea of "knowledge," and with it of truth itself, is hereby set on a new footing. No longer is it the brittle and arrogant knowledge of the post-Enlightenment world, making the hard sciences its primary paradigm and "relationships" simply a matter of "feeling." Nor is it the soft and fuzzy knowledge of the postmodern world, where "feeling" and "impression" are all that there is. The primary knowledge, declares Paul, is the knowledge of God — God's knowledge of you, and yours of God in grateful answer. This is a relationship, one that produces the deepest feelings ever known, but it is true knowledge nonetheless — both in that it is knowledge of the truth and in that it constitutes the truest mode of knowing. All other knowing is first relativized and then, when and as appropriate, reaffirmed in new ways from that point. This is a knowing like no other, because it is knowledge of a reality like no other.

This account is, of course, so brief as to be no more than a signpost. But it makes the point that the issues Paul is addressing in Galatians can provide us with starting points to address the major issues of our own day. The opponents, after all, whoever they were, were seeking to establish a way of being, a grand story, a form of knowing, a type of identity, upon the converts. The pressure to get circumcised was precisely an insistence on establishing one kind of ethnic or para-ethnic identity over against others. Paul deconstructs these claims, showing that they themselves are dehumanizing, based on "the flesh." In particular, he shows — a point that must be reemphasized both in the clash between modernity and postmodernity and in the dawning of a new millennium — that the single moment by which history was changed forever was the moment when Jesus the Messiah died and rose again. Modernity, postmodernity, and various sorts of millennial speculation all offer their own counter-eschatology, but to take Galatians seriously is to insist that the real turnaround, the real moment of liberation, occurred not with some great cultural shift in the Western world of the last few centuries, but when Jesus of Nazareth rose from the dead, having "given himself for our sins" (1:4).

Of course, it is fatally easy for Christians to embrace Paul's gospel as a new way of being in control of the world, a new power game, a new way of establishing one's identity as a matter of pride. To what extent this has happened and does happen in different churches and their claims is a question that cannot be ignored. But the key thing about Paul's gospel is not power, but love: the Son of God "loved me and gave himself for me" (2:20); "faith working through love" is the sign of true life (5:6); love is the first fruit of the divine Spirit, a love that leads to mutual service (5:22, 13). Paul offers no encouragement to those who want to go back to modernity. He agrees with the postmodern critique of all human pride; but when all is said and done, God is creating in Christ a new world built on love and characterized by love. Postmodernity preaches a stern and judging law against all human pride, but those who walk by the Spirit "are not under the law" (5:18).

One of the great crises in the contemporary world, which brings to a head the sense of uncertainty within the formerly all-too-certain Western world, is the situation of global security on the one hand and long-running tribal or geographical conflict on the other. A century ago many in the West believed that war was a necessary part of human development, leading through conflict at the societal level to the survival of the fittest, on a loose analogy with Darwin's theory of evolution. Two world wars and hundreds of smaller ones later, few believe this anymore; and the "Cold War" that hung over the world for nearly half a century reflected this growing uncertainty. But the modernist paradigm still remained in place, and when the West effectively won the Cold War, a victory symbolized by the destruction of the Berlin Wall, there was a widespread assumption that this would mean the worldwide triumph of so-called "Western" values. What has happened, of course, is very different. The Balkans, the Middle East, many African countries, and many other parts of the world are a grim reminder that hatred and violence based on tribe, race, and geography have not disappeared overnight, and remain deep-rooted. The world is full of evidence for Paul's warning: "If you bite and devour one another, take care that you are not destroyed by each other" (5:15).

It will not do simply to say that into this world must be spoken the gospel of Jesus Christ, the gospel Paul articulates and defends in Galatians. This is of course true, but what will it say to the Serb and the Croat, to the Tutsi and the Hutu, to the Palestinian and the Israeli? Will it simply say, If only you would all believe in Jesus, none of this would be necessary? (If it did, it might find further problems: the Serb and the Croat, the Catholic and Protestant in Northern Ireland, all in theory believe in Jesus; and to modify the statement to say "if only you would believe in Jesus *the same way I do*" would stand revealed as a new sort of tribalism.) The most powerful statement it can make must be made symbolically, through the coming together in a single worshiping family, eating at the same table, of all those who belong to Jesus the Messiah, despite their apparently irreconcilable racial, tribal, or other tensions. That is the powerful message of Galatians 2:15-21. That is a first step.

But second, the gospel as articulated in Galatians points to the hard double-task described brilliantly in a recent book by Miroslav Volf.[12] Himself a Croatian, reflecting on the conflict in his native land, Volf wrestles mightily with the gospel imperative toward forgiveness, reconciliation, and inclusion, on the one hand, and the absolute need to name and expose evil, and to deal with it, on the other. One cannot have the embrace of reconciliation without also having the exclusion of evil. The older liberal agendas that insisted only on the former, and the tribal agendas that name as "evil" all that the other tribe does or seeks to do, must be challenged by a larger vision, a harder agenda. And those who read Galatians must, I suggest, be in the forefront of those presenting this agenda and vision to governments and policy makers, often at a loss as they are to know where to turn for guidance now that the old rules of modernity have let them down. The church must not only symbolize in its own life God's victory over all the powers of evil, the powers that keep peoples locked in their own separate stories, fighting all others. The church must present the world and its rulers with ways of "excluding" that will lead to "embrace" — just as Paul, confronting Peter and the others at Antioch, and the opponents in Galatia, named as clearly as he could the antigospel forces to which he saw them succumbing, with the aim that all those who named the name of Jesus should be able to share in the one family meal.

The particular conflict in our world to which Galatians must be addressed is, of course, that which disfigures to this day the land of Jesus' birth. The story is so complex, presenting analysts with a huge tangled ball of wool to unravel before a coherent solution can even be thought of, that it is presumptuous, almost dangerous, even to raise the question in a context like this.[13] Yet there are two points on which Galatians would insist, and which could have a profound effect on the way people regard the situation and act, individually and corporately, in relation to it.

The first is the insistence, once again, that all Jesus' followers belong together in worship and table fellowship. In the Middle East, at the moment, it is sadly true that most indigenous Christianity seems to be dying out. The old monasteries, many of which have maintained unbroken their traditions of worship for fifteen hundred years or more, are almost empty,

---

12. Miroslav Volf, *Exclusion and Embrace: A Theological Exploration of Identity, Otherness, and Reconciliation* (Nashville: Abingdon, 1996).

13. For a somewhat fuller statement on the Palestinian/Israeli question, see the epilogue to my *The Way of the Lord* (Grand Rapids: Eerdmans, 1999).

and many have been demolished by hostile authorities.[14] The small Palestinian Christian communities, which trace their roots back to the first century and have lived in the land ever since, find themselves caught between the self-righteous "settlers" on the one hand — Paul would, I think, have called them "unsettlers" — and the increasingly strident Islamic militants on the other. Many have simply left, and do not expect to return. The tiny Israeli Christian communities live, theoretically, in daily risk of losing their citizenship for renouncing their Judaism. There are reports of many meeting in secret. But there are few, very few, places where Israeli and Palestinian Christians can meet and worship together and share in trusting fellowship. And the immigrant Christians — the Protestant, Catholic, and Orthodox, with their multiple subdivisions — are no better, but instead play similar territorial and other battles with one another. How can one even glance at Galatians and shrug one's shoulders at this situation? Jesus is not Lord where churches divide along ethnic, tribal, or geographical lines. That was "the truth of the gospel" for which Paul contended in the first century, and it remains the truth of the gospel today.

The second point is that, despite the extravagant claims of some, there is no biblical warrant whatsoever for the suggestion that the reestablishment of the state of Israel in the 1940s constituted the fulfillment of biblical prophecy and that, as such, it should be supported by right-thinking Christians. Galatians is one of the biblical books that most strongly gives the lie to this. Paul is at pains throughout to distance himself from any geographical or territorial claim; these things are done away with in Christ. "The present Jerusalem is in bondage with her children; but the Jerusalem that is above is free, and she is the mother of us all" (4:25-26). Nor is this a mere assertion. Paul's whole argument is that "the Israel of God" (6:16) consists of all those, Jew and Gentile alike, who believe in Jesus the Messiah.[15] "If you belong to the Messiah, you are Abraham's seed, heirs according to the promise." How then can the "inheritance" of the "heirs" be translated back into terms of a few square miles of sacred land, kept for the descendants of Abraham "according to the flesh"?[16]

14. For a moving account of the whole situation, with some deeply telling comments on the Palestinian problem in particular, see William Dalrymple, *From the Holy Mountain: A Journey in the Shadow of Byzantium* (London: HarperCollins, 1997).

15. See the similarly strong statements in, e.g., Rom. 2:27-29.

16. Were we to bring Romans into the argument as well, there would be more points to make. See Wright, *The Climax of the Covenant,* chap. 13; for a more popular-level statement, see my *For All God's Worth* (Grand Rapids: Eerdmans, 1996), chap. 13.

The greatest question, of course, which hangs over all Christian thinking and speaking in our day, and which poses an equal challenge to systematic and practical theology, is: How can we speak truly and appropriately of God within a world that has forgotten most of what it thought it knew about God and has distorted much of the rest? And what weight, what "authority," can such speaking command?

We may remind ourselves of the problem. Most people rooted in contemporary Western culture assume, unless they have been specifically shaken out of this way of thinking, that the word "God" refers, more or less univocally, to a being who is detached from the world, living at some great ontological remove (most know that Christians and others do not believe in God as a being literally "up in the sky," but most assume a similar detachment in some other mode of being). They then tend to assume that when Christians talk about God becoming human in Jesus, about God addressing individuals or the world, or about God active within the world, this must be a matter of God's "intervening" from a distance. They assume, moreover, that all religions are basically trying to be about the same thing; this idea is frequently supposed to be a very recent innovation or discovery, but was of course the common coin of the eighteenth-century Enlightenment and indeed has roots much further back in some aspects of classical paganism.

And they assume that this general thing — which may as well be called "religion" for want of a better term, though that word is so over- and ill-used that one wonders if a moratorium would not be a good idea — has basically failed. It has collapsed, so it is thought by those who think about these things, under the critique of Marx, who said that talking about God was what those in power did to keep the rest quiet; of Darwin, who said that we were all descended from the apes anyway, and that the world could be understood successfully without a creating or sustaining God, since it works on the basis of competition; of Freud, who said that God-language was projection of a latent father image; and of Nietzsche, who despised Christianity for being wet and wimpish while also exposing its truth claims as power games. Of course, as C. S. Lewis used to say, if people really *thought* about these things, it might become clear that the attacks, though sometimes interesting and important, are not ultimately valid. But most people in western Europe, and many in North America, do not think very hard about such issues. They assume, not least because the media tell them so, that "God" and "religion" are somehow out of date. Within the postmodern world it is feelings that count, not arguments; and there is a general feeling, widespread in much (though not all) Western culture, that all that sort of thing has had its day — certainly in any form that the culture has known for the last several hundred years.

Of course, this is not the only side of the story. New Age movements have brought "religion" of a sort back into fashion; and the oldest form of Christianity in Britain at least, that of the Celts, who evangelized much of Britain before the Romans arrived and effectively took over, has had a revival as well. Celtic Christianity was earthier, less authoritarian, more in tune with the created order than the Roman variety, and this has made its appeal powerful. But at a time when hardly anybody thinks about the niceties of theology (they are prepared to think about nuclear physics, about economics, about anything the media bombard them with, but not usually about theology), it is difficult for many to sort out the difference between the God-language of the New Age movement and the God-language of mainstream Christianity.

The God of whom Paul speaks in Galatians, of whom I have already written at the start of the previous section, is not a private God, to be worshiped by initiates but kept secret from the outside world. This God must be spoken of in the public arena. This God claims the allegiance of all, because this God is both creator and lover of all. This God is the reality of which the idols of the world are the parodies (4:8-11). But how can one speak of this God without being instantly misunderstood? If one uses the word "God," people will suppose one is speaking of the detached, deist God of popular supposition. If one even pronounces the name and title "Jesus Christ," one will at once send half one's hearers off down the wrong street. Among those to whom the phrase is not simply a meaningless swearword, many will simply hear it as another signal of that "religion" which is assumed to be out of date and irrelevant.

Paul, we know from Acts, faced similar problems, and he got around them by telling the story of Jesus, perhaps with visual aids to show what he was talking about ("You before whose eyes Jesus the Messiah was publicly portrayed as crucified" [3:1]; did Paul draw one of the first-ever "crucifixes" as an aid to evangelism?).[17] The story itself, climaxing with Jesus' death and resurrection, and his enthronement as Lord of the world, carries its own power (Rom. 1:17; 1 Cor. 1:18–2:5). The story must be told faithfully, accurately, and Jewishly (it only makes the sense it does in its Jewish

---

17. This is what the word in question means; despite most commentators, we should not be too ready to read the word metaphorically.

context).[18] However, even this needs a hearing. Paul seems to have obtained his not least because of his original appearance in Galatia, which aroused their sympathy and showed them that he was already living by a different way when compared to other teachers and wandering philosophers they might have met.[19] Paul was *embodying* the message he was announcing. The story of Jesus was being recapitulated through his own actual life — which was why, Paul would quickly have said, the power of the Spirit of Jesus was at work when he told them of the Jewish Messiah, the Lord of the world. If there is a lesson for Christians today in all this, it is the one that is both obvious and also still sorely needed. Those who name the name of Jesus must be seen to be living the life that results from worshiping the true God. Their own genuine humanity, resulting from worshiping the God in whose image they are made, must be recognizable. The fruits of the Spirit, when we meet them, are impressive, particularly in our cynical age. If we are to get a hearing to tell the story of Jesus, this is the only way to start.

But there is more. The church must be active at the places where the world is in pain. The church must be in the forefront of work in the world to alleviate hunger and poverty, to remit major and unpayable international debt, to make peace and prevent war. The church must be on the front line in the fight against crime and the fight for proper punishment and rehabilitation of those convicted of crime, as well as for the rights of the victims of crime. Christians must be active not only in advocacy of the moral standards in which all are treated as full human beings, not as toys or as trash, but also to stand alongside and help those who, having been treated like that themselves, treat others the same way because that is the only way they know. In these and many, many other ways, those who would tell the story of Jesus must first live it, bearing a measure of the world's pain as they do so.

In the process, though the words of the story remain important and ultimately nonnegotiable, the actions themselves will speak. They will provide, as it were, the grammar book and the dictionary that will enable people to understand that when we speak of God today we are not using the

18. On the narrative substructure of Paul's theology in Galatians, see above all Richard B. Hays, *The Faith of Jesus Christ: An Investigation of the Narrative Substructure of Galatians 3:1–4:11*, SBLDS 56 (Chico, Calif.: Scholars, 1983).

19. Without prejudice to the meaning of 4:13-15 (was Paul unwell, or did he bear the marks of recent persecution?); see esp. 6:17 ("I bear the marks of Jesus on my body").

word in the normally accepted sense; that when we speak of Jesus we speak of a real human being in whom the living God was and is personally present, in whom the love of God was fully acted out. If the story is told with those lexical aids to back it up, it will be understood. People may not like it, but the message will be plain. And to those who respond, the challenge will come to continue with this God: "Then, when you did not know God, you were enslaved to beings that by nature are not gods. But now that you know God, or rather have come to be known by God, how can you turn back?" (4:8-9).

## 4. Galatians: Exegesis and Theology

We have now arrived back at the point where the detailed historical exegesis of Galatians and the wider theological reflections may, in some measure and very briefly, be joined together. My overall contention, as will by now be obvious, is that they belong closely with each other, need each other, and are mutually illuminating. It will take an entire commentary to demonstrate this point, but four major features may at least be outlined in conclusion.

First let me raise a point of method. Galatians offers itself to the reader as a text emerging from, referring constantly to, and intending to have serious effect upon a highly complex and many-sided social situation. At no point can we abstract Paul's ideas from this setting; and this, within an incarnational religion such as Christianity, has almost always been and is undoubtedly a strength, not a weakness. To suppose that one must boil off doctrinal abstractions from the particularities of the letters in order to gain material that can be usable in different situations is at best a half-truth; it always runs the risk of implying that the "ideas" are the reality, and that the community in which they are embodied and embedded (Paul's community on the one hand, ours on the other) is a secondary matter. Those who, like the present writer, work as theologians within actual ecclesial communities for which they have pastoral, organizational, and teaching responsibilities know otherwise. It is in taking seriously Paul's struggles with authority, with other apostles, with agitators in a congregation, with division and reconciliation within a community, that we discover what the "doctrines" he seems to hold actually mean. This in no way reduces theology to sociology. Nor does it suggest that theological argument is shadowboxing, pretending to reason something out when what is going on is in fact disguised power play. It is a way of doing justice to Paul's intention not least, but not only, in the first two chapters of Galatians: to enable his readers to understand what the gospel is, what his own relation to it is, and where they, his converts, belong on this map.

This intention, second, is expressed in Paul's major concern throughout the letter but particularly in its central two chapters, 3 and 4. Here he tells the story of Israel, the people of God, as the story of Abraham and exodus. God made promises to Abraham, promises that (as in Gen. 15, to which, here and in Rom. 4, Paul refers repeatedly) envisaged God's future rescue of his people from Egypt. God has now fulfilled those promises, Paul says, in Jesus Christ. His aim throughout is to persuade his hearers to understand themselves within this narrative structure, which I have elsewhere characterized as "covenantal." He wants them, that is, to think of themselves as the children of Abraham, the heirs of the entire Jewish narrative.[20] A good example is 1 Corinthians 10:1-13, written of course to an ex-pagan congregation; the foundation of the argument is Paul's reference to the wilderness generation as "our fathers."

His deep-rooted negation of the Jewish Torah as the mode or badge of membership in this family is, of course, the central problem he faces, and hence the central problem of the letter; this rejection of the *Mosaic* covenant has influenced many contemporary writers to deny that Paul held any "covenantal" theology at all.[21] This, I am persuaded, is a radical mistake. Paul utterly discarded the ethnic and Torah-based shape of Judaism in which he had been so deeply involved before his conversion, and to this extent his theology is radical, apocalyptic, innovative, dialectic, and so forth. But all this is held within his conviction that the God whom he now knows in Jesus Christ and the Spirit is the God of Abraham, whose purposes have now taken a decisive turn in which the character of the community as defined by Torah is left behind (not, it should be noted, criticized as theologically repugnant). He tells the story of Abraham, Israel, Moses, Jesus, and himself — Paul himself becomes a character in the narrative, since he is the unique apostle to the Gentiles, a point that is foundational for Galatians — in order to help his readers understand where they in turn belong within the same narrative.

20. Wright, *The Climax of the Covenant*, passim.
21. Cf., e.g., J. Louis Martyn, *Galatians: A New Translation with Introduction and Commentary*, AB 33a (New York: Doubleday, 1997).

Because the letter indicates this as a very basic aim of Paul all through, I am persuaded that he has not simply introduced Abraham, and allusions to other biblical passages and stories, in order to meet points raised by his opponents. Indeed, even if his opponents had never mentioned Abraham, perhaps especially if they had not, Paul would have wanted to tell this story to address and controvert the point the agitators were urging, that Gentiles who wanted to join the people of Israel had to be circumcised. His way of telling the story of Abraham makes it abundantly clear that the promises God made to the patriarch cannot be fulfilled through Torah. According to Galatians 3:10-14, God promised Abraham a worldwide family, but the Torah presents Israel, the promise bearers, with a curse. God deals with the curse in the death of Jesus, so that the promise may flow through to the world, renewing the covenant with Israel as well. According to 3:15-22, God promised Abraham a *single* worldwide family, but the Torah would forever keep Jews and Gentiles in separate compartments (exactly the problem of 2:11-21 and, we may assume, of the Galatian congregations). God has done in Christ and by the Spirit what the Torah could not do (3:21-22; 4:1-7; cf. Rom. 8:3-4), so that there now exists the single promised multiethnic monotheistic family, God's "sons" and heirs.[22] According to Galatians 4:21-31, insofar as Abraham has two families, they can be characterized as the slave family and the free; and it is the multiethnic people defined by faith, the people formed through Christ and the Spirit, who are the Isaac children, the free people of God. Paul has other ways of telling the story of Abraham and his family as well (e.g., Rom. 9:6–10:4), but it is this narrative, however articulated, that provides the theological grounding for the formation and maintenance of the community he believes himself called to address.

Third, we can now see that the regular theological dichotomies that have been used in debates about Paul for the last hundred years are in fact inadequate to the task. Schweitzer and Wrede insisted on "being in Christ" as a more central category than "justification by faith." Sanders, similarly, prioritized "participationist" categories in Paul over "juristic" ones. More recently, Martyn and others have urged "apocalyptic" readings of Paul against "covenantal" ones. Granted that these broad-brush categories are imprecise, there is clearly a strong feeling among Western readers of Paul that one is faced again and again with different kinds of emphases, which may not always be strictly compatible. This works out in Romans, for in-

22. Cf. Wright, *The Climax of the Covenant,* chap. 8.

stance, in terms of the playing off of one of its clear sections (chaps. 1–4, 5–8, 9–11, 12–16) against the others.

I believe, and I hope that detailed exegesis will support this hypothesis, that in each case these dichotomies have failed to grasp the more fundamental structures of Paul's socially contextualized and literarily structured theological thought. Once we grasp the covenantal narrative that Paul sets out in Galatians as the world he invites his readers to inhabit, we discover that these elements — which appear disparate when seen from a post-Reformation, post-Enlightenment, or postromantic viewpoint — belong together within the much richer tapestry he is weaving. The story of the new exodus in Christ, and the homeward journey of God's people led by the Spirit, provides the setting for incorporative and participationist language to have its full meaning and weight simultaneously with the juristic meaning of justification. Because of sin, and the distortion of Torah by the people to whom it was given, the fulfillment of the covenant cannot but come about as an apocalyptic event, declaring God's judgment on what has gone before and God's new creation of what is now beginning. But when the dust settles and God's renewed people look around them, they discover that this apocalyptic event is indeed the fulfillment of God's promises to Abraham. This is how God is faithful to the covenant. It will take all of the letter to the Romans to set this out in full detail and most of the rest of the NT to explore the point from a variety of other angles, but the major components of the argument are already complete in Galatians.

What, fourthly and finally, about justification by faith? This is the subject that most expositors of Galatians have found to be central to the argument of the letter itself. But what is it actually about? There is no space here for a full exposition of the doctrine. Rather, I wish to pose the question thus: What particular emphases does Galatians, read historically and exegetically, provide in this central matter?

The first point we have already noted. Paul's initial introduction of the topic is embedded within, and seems to be the sharp edge of, the question that was at issue between himself and Peter in Antioch and, we may assume, bears some close relation to the dispute between himself and the "agitators" in Galatia. This was not the general, abstract theological issue of, shall we say, how to go to heaven when one dies. It was not part of a theory of soteriology, understood in this way. It was the question of whether Christian Jews ought or ought not eat with Christian Gentiles. In other words, it addressed the question of the *identity* and *demarcation* of the people of God, now redefined in Jesus Christ — a question that is both sociological, in the sense that it has to do with a community and its behavior, which can itself be understood by the proper application of sociological methods, and theological, in the sense that this community believes itself to be the people of a God who has drawn up quite clear conditions precisely for its communal life.

Paul's answer to the question is complex and dense, but its heart is simple. Because he, and all Jewish Christians, have "died to the law" through sharing the messianic death of Jesus, their identity now is not defined by or in terms of the Jewish law, but rather in terms of the risen life of the Messiah. The boundary marker of this messianic community is therefore not the set of observances that mark out Jews from Gentiles, but rather Jesus the Messiah, the faithful one, himself; and the way in which one is known as a member of this messianic community is thus neither more nor less than (Christian) faith.

Although this account (Gal. 2:15-21) is not itself about soteriology per se, it carries, of course, huge soteriological implications. If one has already died and risen with the Messiah, and if one has been grasped by the grace of God and enabled to come to faith and (by implication, brought into daylight in) baptism (3:26-28), then one is marked out thereby precisely as a member of the renewed, eschatological community of Israel, one for whom the act of God in the Messiah has dealt finally with one's sinful past, one who is assured of God's salvation on the Last Day. But the point of justification by faith, in this context, is not to stress this soteriological aspect, but to insist that all those who share this Christian faith are members of the same single family of God in Christ *and therefore belong at the same table.* This is the definite, positive, and of course deeply polemical thrust of the first-ever exposition of the Christian doctrine of justification by faith.

I have already provided a summary account of Galatians 3 and 4, seen as a narrative, or part of a larger implicit narrative, about the promises of God to Abraham and the way in which these are fulfilled in Jesus the Messiah. It remains here simply to note the way in which justification emerges within this structure of thought, which itself is grounded in Paul's sense of the community he is addressing.

His emphasis throughout is that the true people whom God promised to Abraham are defined by their faith. He is not here concerned with how one enters the family, but with how, once one has entered, the family is then defined, assured of its status as God's people. The arguments in chapter 3 about the curse of the law, and how it is exhausted in the death of

Jesus, and about the apparent tension between the promise and the law, are not primarily abstract statements about the atonement on the one hand and about the existential or spiritual superiority or preferability of trusting promises rather than keeping moral codes on the other. No doubt they contribute to discussions at these more abstract levels, but such matters were not what Paul was basically talking about. And in the great climactic passage at the end of chapter 3 and the start of chapter 4, the question of justification is set within the narrative about slavery and sonship — that is, the exodus story, in which the key interlocking categories for the present status of Christians are incorporation into Christ and the indwelling of the Spirit. These are not "about" something other than justification. Rather, justification by faith itself, in the letter to Galatia, is all about the definition of the community of the people of the true God.

This is, of course, a puzzling conclusion for those who have learned the word "justification" as a technical term for the way in which someone becomes a Christian. But it is noticeable that when Paul discusses that question (e.g., 1 Thess. 1), he does not use the language of justification. He talks about the way in which, through the gospel proclamation of the crucified and risen Jesus as Messiah and Lord of the world, God's Spirit is at work to bring people to faith, a faith specifically in the God now known in this Jesus. *This process, though, is not what Paul means by "justification."* Justification, to offer a fuller statement, is the recognition and declaration by God that those who are thus called and believing are in fact his people, the single family promised to Abraham, that as the new covenant people their sins are forgiven, and that since they have already died and been raised with the Messiah they are assured of final bodily resurrection at the last. This, of course, is the argument of (among other passages) Romans 5–8, and in a measure also Philippians 3. In Galatians it is hinted at but never spelled out, for the good reason that Paul's eye is on one thing principally — namely, the unity of the single Jew-plus-Gentile family in Christ and the consequent impossibility of that family being in any way defined by the Jewish Torah.

Fully to grasp this, I realize only too well, will demand of those who wish to be in tune with Paul, on the one hand, and to continue to preach the gospel and thereby to evoke and sustain Christian faith, on the other, that they think through afresh the language they use, the passages upon which they draw to make their point, and the detailed theology they are presupposing. But I am quite convinced that this essentially "new-look" reading of justification in Galatians does not undermine the traditional theology and spirituality that former generations, and other ways of reading Paul, have for so long built upon this text. Indeed, when the bricks of the house are taken down, cleaned, and reassembled in the right order, there is every hope that the building will be more serviceable and weatherproof than before.

There are of course many other issues that cry out to be discussed. I have said very little, for example, about the Spirit in Galatians, and the relation of what Paul says on this topic to other NT evidence. But I hope to have shown that the task of bringing together exegesis and theology is valid and fruitful, if demanding, and that a commentary series that attempts such a task has every chance of providing fresh stimulation and insight to a new generation for whom neither dry historical exegesis nor flights of theological fancy will do by themselves. Galatians is a wonderful example of a text that needs history and theology to be working at full stretch and in full harmony. But there is every reason to suppose that the rest of the NT will respond excellently to the same treatment.

# AFTERWORD

# *Rethinking History (and Theology)*

## JOEL B. GREEN

I learned today that my daughter's junior high science teacher follows the prescribed curriculum in the classroom but actually believes that no other humans existed alongside Adam, Eve, and their sons, so that Seth was married off to a female from a community of Neanderthals; that God created the earth with a prehistoric fossil record intact, so that dinosaurs never actually roamed the earth; and that in all other matters as well the Bible must be taken literally. I do not know how the Genesis record, when taken literally, can allow for Neanderthals and human-Neanderthal interbreeding but disallow the stuff of *Jurassic Park,* nor what it would mean to read biblical poetry or parable literally (that is, literalistically). However, my daughter's rehearsal of this information highlighted for me yet again that our contemporary crises concerning the Bible are many and varied.

It is now common to hear voices decrying the crisis of authority in the church, which invariably relates to the status and role of Scripture in Christian communities, or the crisis of relevance, or the crisis of biblical illiteracy. To these must clearly be added crises of interpretation, and these are related to what Robert Wall refers to in chapter 5 as a crisis of theological illiteracy. Undoubtedly, the two are related, our dilemmas with Scripture and theology. In this brief afterword, I want to suggest that both derive from a crisis of history — though perhaps not in the expected sense of the term "history."

On the face of it, the dilemma we face with respect to biblical interpretation is historical, in the sense that our history is not the history of the biblical writers, and their world is not ours. Some six decades ago Rudolf Bultmann put this in an especially memorable way: "It is impossible to use electric light and the wireless and to avail ourselves of modern medical and surgical discoveries, and at the same time to believe in the New Testament world of spirits and miracles."[1] Of course, this statement, when read at the turn of the twenty-first century, illustrates the problem. "What is a wireless?" my daughter might ask; and what passed for "modern medicine" for Bultmann in the 1940s will seem quite primitive by contemporary comparison. In fact, though he did little to account for it, "*the* scientific worldview" of which Bultmann wrote had in his own lifetime already given way to the influence of Einstein and a plethora of scientific worldviews. This, however, is not the problem.

The "crisis of history" to which I refer lies elsewhere, in the modernist fascination with the historical and, especially, with our problematic notions of what constitutes the historical (that is, the particular brand of historicism that has occupied our thinking for two centuries). This historicism locates meaning primarily, if not solely, "back there" — and especially "back there" in the facts that could be guaranteed by the assured results of modern scholarship. More recently, this crisis has taken on a new form, but it is the same crisis. As it became increasingly evident that modern scholarship was less and less sure of its results and could guarantee less and less, the response for many was to rotate the discussion by 180°, to forms of study for which there are thankfully no facts, only perspectives. According to this way of thinking, texts are sundered not only from the sociohistorical contexts within which they were generated, not only from those texts alongside which they reside within the canon of Scripture, not only from the traditions of interpretation that have grown up around them over these two millennia, but also from whatever interpretive constraints might have been suggested by the texts themselves. In the first instance, under the old historicism, textual meaning could be tied with certainty to historical reconstruction. In the second, this confidence was rejected completely in favor of endless meanings; indeed, the search for certainty was not only abandoned but rebuffed. The first saw a commitment to forms of biblical interpretation that kept at arm's length the communicative claims of scriptural texts, working with the presumption that those claims are of antiquarian interest but not existentially compelling. The response to this modernist project has been equally debilitating to con-

---

1. ET: Rudolf Bultmann et al., *Kerygma and Myth: A Theological Debate,* ed. Hans Werner Bartsch (New York: Harper & Row, 1961), p. 5.

structive or prescriptive theology and ethics, since the interpretive enterprise is alleged to offer no canons against which to measure a "right" reading from a "wrong" one, or a "good" reading from a "bad" one.

The dilemma we face is historical and is grounded in modernity's firm embrace of a historicism that postmodernity has just as firmly rejected.[2] The resolution is not to be found in the false choices thus offered, voting yea or nay for a modernist historicism oriented around scientific objectivity and facts. The way forward is in learning to think (and live) with history, to borrow a phrase from historian Carl Schorske. "Thinking *with* history implies the employment of the materials of the past and the configurations in which we organize and comprehend them to orient ourselves in the living present." We thus grapple with the substance of historical inquiry as we form our own identity in relation to the past, whether by difference or resemblance or both. And we situate ourselves within the stream of history, self-reflexively, of which we are then a part. This of course flies in the face of the biases many of us in the West have nurtured since childhood, biases toward constructing ourselves and our projects neither in continuity with nor simply "against" the past but, indeed, detached from it.[3]

What would it mean for spanning NT studies and systematic theology were we to adopt such a perspective?

1. We would recognize that the relationship of Scripture and church is not a casual one nor one of convenience, but is integral to the meaning of both. When these biblical texts are embraced as Scripture, they no longer (simply) tell the story of ancient Israel or of Christian witness in the apostolic age; rather, they tell our story. The people of whom Scripture speaks — they are our people, our mothers and fathers, brothers and sisters. That community is our community. Thinking with history means that we locate ourselves in that biblical narrative whose fountainhead is creation and whose destination is new creation.

2. In fact, since at this point postmodernity is simply realizing the modernist dream of sundering itself from a past that belongs to other people, it is arguable whether our age is aptly characterized as *post*modern at all.

3. Carl E. Schorske, *Thinking with History: Explorations in the Passage to Modernism* (Princeton: Princeton University Press, 1998), pp. 3-16 (3). I say "many of us" since there are important exceptions, perhaps most significantly the rise of African American biblical scholarship which seeks deliberately to set itself in continuity with the history of the African and African American past — see, e.g., Cain Hope Felder, *Troubling Biblical Waters: Race, Class, and Family* (Maryknoll, N.Y.: Orbis, 1989); Felder, ed., *Stony the Road We Trod: African American Biblical Interpretation* (Minneapolis: Fortress, 1991).

2. We would recognize that any NT text to which we might turn has its own history. This "history" is more than the history behind the text, and more than the history within which this text was generated. It is also the history of this text's transmission and the history of its reception — including, though not limited to, its inclusion in the Christian canon. These all impinge on the significance of this text within those communities who regard this text as integral to their history.

3. We would recognize, then, that we do not and cannot come to these biblical texts "fresh," that we are not the first ones to read these texts and struggle with their relation to faith and practice, and that we are part of a global community of believers who over time have returned again and again to these texts for stability and challenge and encouragement. Not only the people of whom Scripture speaks, but also the people who have embraced the Bible as Scripture — they are our people, our mothers and fathers, brothers and sisters. The global community of God's people through time is our community, and our readings of these texts must be placed in relation to theirs in ways that are mutually correcting and confirming. Our identity is formed, then, not simply by these biblical texts since, in a real sense, we have no direct access to them. Scripture is mediated to us in countless ways, both formally and informally. Scripture is never really "alone."

4. We would recognize that, in a crucial sense, the ditch separating us from biblical text and biblical text from us is much less historical and far more theological than has generally been allowed. It is true, of course, that no concordance will direct the concerned reader to the Bible's treatment of (say) managed health care or the Human Genome Project or the use of Prozac, just as it is also true that the level of interest displayed in the NT regarding meat sacrifices to idols will leave many Western readers nonplussed (though not some of our sisters and brothers in the Eastern or Southern Hemisphere). This is precisely why the first questions to be addressed are theological rather than historical, however, since there is no practical obedience, no prophetic challenge, no pastoral care worthy of the adjective "biblical" or "Christian" that is not theologically consonant with the God who delivered "us" out of Egypt and who raised Jesus from the dead.

5. We would recognize — against major currents in both modernism and postmodernism — that these texts and their interpretation are implicated in a series of concentric contexts. A narrative text like the Gospel of Mark, for example, is generated at the interface of two historical moments

— the past of Jesus being represented and the present within which Mark remembers and narrates the past. It is also true, however, that our reading of Mark's narrative introduces into the interpretive equation yet another historical moment, our own. "Meaning," then, is always related to and shaped by each new discourse situation in which readers engage with these texts. To allow the text its own history (that is, its own integrity as a communicative act set within a particular sociohistorical context) is to privilege the text as arbiter of meaning, but this does not detract from the anthropological reality and Christian necessity that we come to biblical texts to address to them our questions. Of course, as Scripture, these texts may urge us to rethink those questions, or serve to form us in ways that give rise to altogether different ones!

6. We would recognize that the biographical and historiographical narratives of the NT (i.e., the Gospels and Acts), no less than the letters of Paul or Hebrews, are *theological* in nature. In the case of these narratives, history and (textual) interpretation exist always in a reciprocal relationship. Whereas "modern" biblical studies have continued to work with a commitment to the segregation of "history" and "interpretation," thinking with history would constantly remind us that verification and significance, interpretation and documentation run inescapably through every sentence of these works.[4] Historical *and* theological questions are thus, together, endemic to these narratives. There is a theology of Mark to be discerned, then, and this must be placed alongside and in conversation with other voices at the biblical-theological roundtable. Additionally, attending to the character of these narratives *as* narrative-theological enterprises fosters in us both awareness and capacity to discern and grapple with the theological issues that litter the landscapes of our lives.

Undoubtedly, more could be said by way of exploring the promise of a new historicism[5] that locates our lives and the vitality of the church uni-

---

4. See Albert Cook, *History/Writing: The Theory and Practice of History in Antiquity and in Modern Times* (Cambridge: Cambridge University Press, 1988), esp. pp. 55-72; David Lowenthal, *The Past Is a Foreign Country* (Cambridge: Cambridge University Press, 1985).

5. This choice of words may be unfortunate, as I am not hoping to endorse without reservation that development in contemporary criticism known as "new historicism" (see, e.g., H. Aram Veeser, ed., *The New Historicism* [New York and London: Routledge, 1989]). Among its "key assumptions" that are especially problematic to the agenda I have sketched are its tendencies not to take seriously the status of the texts it studies as cultural products with their own integrity and to reify Marxist analyis.

versal more fully and integrally in relation to Scripture's story and the narrative of God's redemptive purpose in the world. It remains to be said that the direction of study sketched here requires less in terms of methodological agreement and more in terms of the cultivation of particular theological interests and hermeneutical sensibilities. This is especially true insofar as we stand in these days at a new threshold of perception — where some older questions lose their brilliance while others take on a new aspect when seen from different vantage points, and where still other questions are raised as though for the very first time. Just as, in these last decades, homogeneity of exegetical method has disintegrated, so we may anticipate diversity of approach to issues concerned with the interface of biblical exegesis and the contemporary theological enterprise. On the other hand, just as we have seen that, in the end, different exegetical approaches often lead to similar and even harmonious conclusions, so we may expect sometimes dissimilar emphases in theological hermeneutics to lead to complementary insights on the relation of NT text, the church's witness, and the world in which faithfulness is finally tested and lived.

What I hope has become clear is that, whether we are struggling with the question of Genesis and dinosaurs or of the appropriateness of eating meat sacrificed to idols, we are interested in more than biblical "knowledge" or "content." The literature of the Bible conveys information, to be sure, but it also evokes response, and this perspective on the communicative intentions of these texts is fundamental to how we construe the theological interests of Scripture. In the same way, theological formation and a keen awareness of our historical identity vis-à-vis the canon and reception of Scripture must emerge as priorities in theological hermeneutics.

# Index of Authors

# Index of Authors